LANGUAGE DEVELOPMENT AND APHASIA IN CHILDREN

New Essays and a Translation of
Kindersprache und Aphasie
by Emil Fröschels

PERSPECTIVES IN
NEUROLINGUISTICS AND PSYCHOLINGUISTICS

Harry A. Whitaker, Series Editor
DEPARTMENT OF PSYCHOLOGY
THE UNIVERSITY OF ROCHESTER
ROCHESTER, NEW YORK

HAIGANOOSH WHITAKER and HARRY A. WHITAKER (Eds.).
Studies in Neurolinguistics, Volumes 1, 2, 3 and 4

NORMAN J. LASS (Ed.). Contemporary Issues in Experimental Phonetics

JASON W. BROWN. Mind, Brain, and Consciousness: The Neuropsychology of Cognition

SIDNEY J. SEGALOWITZ and FREDERIC A. GRUBER (Eds.). Language Development and Neurological Theory

SUSAN CURTISS. Genie: A Psycholinguistic Study of a Modern-Day "Wild Child"

JOHN MACNAMARA (Ed.). Language Learning and Thought

I. M. SCHLESINGER and LILA NAMIR (Eds.). Sign Language of the Deaf: Psychological, Linguistic, and Sociological Perspectives

WILLIAM C. RITCHIE (Ed.). Second Language Acquisition Research: Issues and Implications

PATRICIA SIPLE (Ed.). Understanding Language through Sign Language Research

MARTIN L. ALBERT and LORAINE K. OBLER. The Bilingual Brain: Neurophysiological and Neurolinguistic Aspects of Bilingualism

TALMY GIVÓN. On Understanding Grammar

CHARLES J. FILLMORE, DANIEL KEMPLER and WILLIAM S-Y. WANG (Eds.). Individual Differences in Language Ability and Language Behavior

JEANNINE HERRON (Ed.). Neuropsychology of Left-Handedness

FRANÇOIS BOLLER and MAUREEN DENNIS (Eds.). Auditory Comprehension: Clinical and Experimental Studies with the Token Test

R. W. RIEBER (Ed.). Language Development and Aphasia in Children: New Essays and a Translation of "Kindersprache und Aphasie" by Emil Fröschels

LANGUAGE DEVELOPMENT AND APHASIA IN CHILDREN

New Essays and a Translation of
Kindersprache und Aphasie
by Emil Fröschels

Edited by

R. W. RIEBER

John Jay College
City University of New York
and
Columbia University
College of Physicians and Surgeons
New York, New York

1980

ACADEMIC PRESS
A Subsidiary of Harcourt Brace Jovanovich, Publishers
New York   London   Toronto   Sydney   San Francisco

Cover art by Louise Rieber

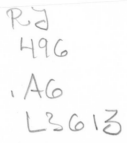
ACADEMIC PRESS, INC.
111 Fifth Avenue, New York, New York 10003

United Kingdom Edition published by
ACADEMIC PRESS, INC. (LONDON) LTD.
24/28 Oval Road, London NW1 7DX

Library of Congress Cataloging in Publication Data

Main entry under title:

Language development and aphasia in children.

(Perspectives in neurolinguistics and psycho—
linguistics)
  Includes bibliographical references and index.
  1. Aphasic children. 2. Language acquisition.
3. Children--Language. 4. Fröschels, Emil,
1884–1972 Kindersprache und Aphasie.
I. Rieber, Robert W. II. Fröschels, Emil,
Date   Kindersprache und Aphasie. English.
1980.
RJ496.A6L3613   618.9'28'552   79–26057
ISBN 0–12–588280–7

PRINTED IN THE UNITED STATES OF AMERICA

80 81 82 83   9 8 7 6 5 4 3 2 1

EMIL FRÖSCHELS
(1884–1972)

Contents
Part I—New Essays

Contents
Part II—A Translation of
Kindersprache und Aphasie

List of Contributors

Numbers in parentheses indicate the pages on which the authors' contributions begin.

JOHN BLACK (9), Department of Speech, Ohio State University, Columbus, Ohio 43210

ERIC R. BROWN (69), Departments of Educational Psychology and Clinical Neurology, New York University, New York, New York 10003

MAUREEN DENNIS (45), Department of Psychology, The Hospital for Sick Children, Toronto, Ontario, M5G 1XS, Canada

R. W. RIEBER (3), John Jay College of Criminal Justice, City University of New York, New York, New York, and Columbia University College of Physicians and Surgeons, New York, New York 10032

JOEL STARK (33), Speech and Hearing Center, Queens College and the Graduate School and University Center, City University of New York, New York, New York 10019

Preface

A few years prior to his death, H. Schuell and I had occasion to speak with Emil Fröschels and recommend to him that he undertake the translation of *Kindersprache und Aphasie* into English. Happily, he took our urging to heart, and the translation presented in this volume is the result. Sorrowful as we are that he did not live to see this work published in English, we are nonetheless grateful that his words have been made available to those unfamiliar with Fröschels' native tongue, and we feel some pride at having been instrumental in some small way to the further dissemination of his work.

The articles in this book deal with a subject that is of great interest today. The translation of Fröschels' book (in Part II of this volume) as well as the essays that precede it share a concern with problems of theory, method, and therapy and the interpretation of the phenomena with which they deal, namely language development and aphasia.

The translation as well as the essays afford us a first–hand insight into some of the ways in which scientists develop concepts and ideas. In selecting the essays, it was our purpose to use the translation as a catalytic agent for the discussion of contemporary progress in the field of language development and aphasia in children. It is our hope that this book will stimulate further research into this most important area.

Part I
New Essays

Chapter 1

EMIL FRÖSCHELS' *CHILD LANGUAGE AND APHASIA:* AN HISTORICAL REVIEW

R. W. Rieber

Born in Vienna in 1884, Emil Fröschels was educated at the University of Vienna, where he rose to international prominence in the field of speech pathology (speech, hearing, and language disorders). Prior to World War II, he became director of the University of Vienna's Clinic of Speech, Hearing, and Language Disorders.

A dynamic and purposeful individual, it was inevitable that Fröschels would contribute substantially to the well-being of his fellowmen. A student of otologist Viktor Urbantschitsch and schooled in the ideas of Berlin speech therapist Albert Liebmann, Fröschels founded and became the leading figure of the Vienna School of Logopedics. There he demanded from his students the attributes which he instilled in his own work—scientific approach, careful observation, attention to every case regardless of the chances of success, self-criticism, and discipline.

Together with pedagogue K. C. Rothe, Fröschels also created the Wiener Sonderschule für sprachgestörte Kinder (Vienna School for Speech Disturbed Children), which is now well established. Fröschels is also responsible for inaugurating international cooperation in the field of speech and voice through his founding of the International Society of Logopedics and Phoniatrics which has, between 1924 and 1980, held numerous international congresses. As of the XIIIth Congress, held in Vienna in 1965, Fröschels has added to his distinction of being Life

3

LANGUAGE DEVELOPMENT AND APHASIA IN CHILDREN

President of Honour of the society by assuming the honorary presidency of the Austrian organizing committee.

Fröschels' work in a general respect is a by-product of the work of Viennese medical scholars of the late nineteenth and early twentieth centuries. He is known to have read the works of numerous important figures of that period: Adolf Kussmaul (*Storungen der Sprache*, 1881); Wilhelm Preyer (*Die Seele des Kindes*, 1896); Rafael Coen (*Sprachanomalien*); Gutzmann; Liebmann; Wundt; Pick; and Freud.

Of particular importance to Fröschels' development is the work of Preyer. Preyer was a German professor of physiology at the University of Jena, whose work helped to establish the field of developmental psychology, particularly in the areas of language development and language pathology. His most important work, *The Mind of the Child (Die Seele des Kindes)*, is frequently cited and referred to in the work by Fröschels presented in this volume. We will develop this point later in the chapter.

It is one of our intentions in this book to illustrate how the ideas of other influential figures laid the groundwork for Fröschels' work.

We begin this historical review[1] at the end of the seventeenth century with Géraud de Cordemoy (d. 1684), a Cartesian scholar whom Chomsky (1966) designates in his *Cartesian Linguistics* as a Chomskian before Chomsky. This may well be the case; nevertheless, in reading de Cordemoy one can hardly fail to notice certain resemblances to both Locke and Hartley. Specifically, he seems to anticipate the two English philosophers by suggesting that in language development children will learn one thing rather than another according to the degree of pleasure or pain associated with the learning situation. One may also see here, in a more rudimentary form, an anticipation of the two-factor learning theory, as well as the mediation position of Osgood (1979) and others.

De Cordemoy (1668/1975) goes on to discuss the idea of communication as a dialogue, and stresses the notion that the speech act is the basis of all behavior, including individual creativity. His position on innate ideas is clear:

> But since I only look here after the principles, I am not to proceed so far to particulars. I desire only that by the way an important truth may be taken notice of, which this example of children evidently discovers to us, *viz.*, that from their birth they have their reason entire, because indeed this way of learning to speak is the effect of so great a discerning and of so perfect reason that a more wonderful one cannot possibly be conceived.

We now jump ahead nearly a century to another much more famous

---

1. Some of this history is based upon a previously published paper (Rieber, 1979).

Frenchman, Denis Diderot (1713–1784), whose *Letter on the Deaf and Dumb* appeared in 1751. It was no particular interest in the problems of deaf people that prompted Diderot to write this book, but rather a desire to better understand how ordinary individuals develop knowledge about things in the real world, through an analysis of language and its natural development, as well as a communication disorder known as deafness (Diderot, 1751/1973).

Diderot's *Letter* begins with the linguistic problem of inversions, but ranges widely over such topics as the origin and historical development of language, epistemology, rhetoric, and so on.

Through the example of an imaginary deaf person, Diderot attempts to determine the relationship between thought and language. The deaf person represents a hypothetical prelinguistic society. Here Diderot seems to anticipate modern Gestalt psychology:

> Mind is a moving scene, which we are perpetually copying. We spend a great deal of time in rendering it faithfully; but the original exists as a complete whole, for the mind does not proceed step by step, like expression. The brush takes time to represent what the artist's eye sees in an instant.

I find this statement as provocative today as it must have been at the time it was written. Neisser (1967) has suggested that the Gestalt school of psychology is the most direct ancestor of current psycholinguistics. Others who follow the Chomskian point of view suggest Wundt, because of Wundt's emphasis upon the sentence as the basic unit of analysis. Those who think in terms of verbal behavior would probably not agree with Blumenthal (1970), but name Watson as the most likely candidate. No doubt all of the nominees have played an important part, one way or another, in setting the stage for the currently accepted version of the psychology of language.

Diderot, however, did not compromise any of his convictions regarding the psycholinguistic nature of man. He consistently assumed knowledge to be completely dependent upon the senses, and more specifically, to the number of senses actually operating. In a hypothetical experiment, he imagines a society made up of five persons, each having only one of the five senses; and he comes to the conclusion that each person in this society would have a view of the world determined by his own sensory modality, and that each individual would relate to the others as being senseless. This new and more innovative psychology was quite different from the older more absolute way of approaching the problem.

During the latter part of the eighteenth century, scholars continued to struggle with this important issue. Two other men are worth mention before we go on to the next century: Erasmus Darwin (1731–1802) and John Horn Tooke (1736–1812). Darwin's two most important works in the area of language and thought are *Zoonomia* (1794–1796) and *The Temple of Nature* (1804). The first was Darwin's best-received work; the second, containing among other things his theory of evolution and theory of languages, was not well appreciated in his time. Darwin (1804) points out carefully that "Mr. Tooke observes that the first aim of Language was to communicate thoughts, and the second to do it with dispatch, and hence he divides words into those which were necessary to express our thoughts, and those which are observations of the former." As T. Verhave points out, Darwin's psychology is a variant of eighteenth-century association theory, and is in part a restatement of views stated by David Hartley in his *Observations on Man* (1749). Rieber and Fröschels (1966) discussed Darwin's theory of stuttering, also deriving from the theory of association. This is very similar to Mendelssohn's (1783) viewpoint, which in turn was apparently influenced by a paper written by Spalding, in the *Magazine Erfahrungsseelenkunde,* an introspective report of a case of transitory sensory motor aphasia (Verhave, 1974).

We now pass over 100 years more to the latter part of the nineteenth century. Here we will be concerned with the work of Wilhelm Preyer (1841–1897), a German professor of physiology at the University of Jena. Preyer, although not well known today, was quite influential during the late nineteenth century. His pioneering work helped to establish the field of developmental psychology, and he also wrote significant works on hypnosis and neurophysiology. His most important work, *The Mind of the Child* (1881), was reprinted in 1973, unfortunately without an introduction.

Originally written in German, *Die Seele des Kindes* was translated into many other languages including English. It had a direct influence upon two of the most influential psychological theorists of our time, Jean Piaget and Sigmund Freud. Freud rarely quoted other writers, but it has been possible to establish the fact that he was familiar with Preyer's works; indeed, it is my contention that Freud was under the influence of Preyer's ideas when he established as part of his theoretical system, first, the notion that *the study of abnormal development will help us better understand normal development,* and second, *the value of using stages of development as a better means of understanding the psychological growth pattern of the child.* Preyer's likely influence upon Freud was pointed out in a previous paper (Rieber, 1979).

Freud, of course, stressed the affective, psychosexual aspect of maturation, whereas Preyer gave emphasis to the cognitive and conative. Preyer devotes the second volume of his book almost exclusively to the linguistic and cognitive development of the child. A whole chapter deals with speech and language disturbances in adults, particularly aphasia. He then draws a parallel to speech and language disturbances in childhood, thus anticipating one of the major themes of Fröschels' book (1918) (also in this volume).

Interest in the problem of the relationship between language and thought was quite strong in the 1880s and 1890s. Max Müller was the major advocate of the notion that thinking was not possible without language. The polemics on this issue were about as bad as the polemics of the last decade regarding competence and performance. Müller, a professor of linguistics at Oxford, engaged in active debate, mainly through the journal *Nature*, with such prominent psychologists as Sir Francis Galton and George Romanes (Müller, 1909).

Galton vehemently denied Müller's contentions, arguing that a careful study of congenitally deaf individuals would prove him wrong. But Galton never carried out the study himself, and it was not until the twentieth century that experimental cognitive psychologists were able to demonstrate what Galton had anticipated. Galton's warning to Müller is worth quoting, for it is as pertinent now as when he wrote it in 1887: "Before a just knowledge can be attained concerning any faculty of the human race, we must inquire into its distribution among all sorts and conditions of men on a large scale, and not among those persons who belong to a highly specialized literary class [Müller, 1909]."

Romanes used an example of a disorder of communication, namely aphasia, to challenge Müller's thesis. He pointed out that, once attained, symbolic concept formation afterward continues to operate without the use of words. He continued, "This is not based on one's own personal introspection which no opponent can verify; it is a matter of objectively demonstrable fact. For when a man is suddenly afflicted with aphasia, he does not forthwith become as thoughtless as a brute. Admittedly he has lost all trace of words, but his reason may remain unimpaired [Müller, 1909]."

What we have just discussed is the groundwork for Fröschels' book. The purpose of the book is to provide a better understanding of the problems of aphasia and allied disorders of communication through a detailed scientific discussion of the language development of children. Fröschels used the modern psychological theory of his day and related this theory to the more recent developments in linguistics that were available to him. It is quite apparent that what Fröschels was writing about in 1918 parallels or reflects the current trend in developmental psychology and neurolinguistics today. The authors of the chapters that follow all demonstrate this parallel in their own ways. Black gives us a vivid personal account of how Fröschels' work influenced him as a student in the 1920s. Stark demonstrates how Fröschels' ideas are reflected in the current status of the problems of aphasia in children, whereas Dennis gives us a detailed analysis of a case history of a child that acquired aphasia. The last chapter before the translation of Fröschels' book is by Brown, which discusses the problem of dyslexia in children.

It is our hope that this work will help the reader to better understand the present state of the art in the area of language development and aphasia as well as how we arrived at where we are in this field today.

REFERENCES

Blumenthal, A. L. *Language and Psychology; Historical Aspects of Psycholinguistics.* New York: Wiley, 1970.

Chomsky, Noam. *Cartesian Linguistics.* New York: Harper & Row, 1966.

Darwin, Erasmus. *The Temple of Nature.* New York: T. & J. Swords, 1804.

de Cordemoy, Géraud. *A Philosophical Discourse Concerning Speech, Together with a Discourse Written by a Learned Friar.* Reprint Series, "Language, Man and Society," ed. R. W. Rieber. New York: AMS Press, 1975. (Originally published, 1668.)

Diderot, Denis. *Diderot's Early Philosophical Works.* Reprint Series, "Language, Man and Society," ed. R. W. Rieber. New York: AMS Press, 1973. (Originally published, 1751.)

Fröschels, Emil. *Kindersprache und Aphasie.* Berlin: Karger, 1918.

Mendelssohn, M. Psychologische Betrachtungen auf Weranlassung einer von Spalding. *Magazine Erfahrungsseelenkunde* (vol. 1). Berlin, 1783.

Müller, F. Max. *Three Introductory Lectures on the Science of Thought.* Chicago: Open Court, 1909.

Neisser, U. *Cognitive Psychology.* New York: Appleton-Century-Crofts, 1967.

Osgood, Charles E. A Dinosaur Caper: Psycholinguistics Past, Present, and Future. In *Developmental Psycholinguistics and Communication Disorders,* D. Aaronson & R. W. Rieber (Eds.), New York Academy of Sciences, Volume 263, 1979.

Preyer, W. *The Mind of the Child,* Parts I & II. Reprint Classics in Psychology. New York: Arno Press, 1973. (Originally published, 1896.)

Rieber, R. W. The Role of Language and Thought in Developmental Psycholinguistics—An Historical Review. In *Developmental Psycholinguistics and Communication Disorders,* D. Aaronson & R. W. Rieber (Eds.). New York Academy of Sciences, Volume 263, 1979.

Rieber, R. W., & Fröschels, E. An Historical Review of the European Literature in Speech Pathology. In *Speech Pathology,* R. W. Rieber & R. S. Brubaker (Eds.). Amsterdam: North-Holland, 1966.

Verhave, T. A Man of Knowledge Revisited. Preface to new edition of E. Darwin, *Zoonomia, or the Laws of Organic Life.* Reprint Series, "Language, Man and Society," ed. R. W. Rieber. New York: AMS Press, 1974.

Chapter 2

FRÖSCHELS IN PERSPECTIVE

John Black

INTRODUCTION AND SCOPE

Fröschels' *Child Language and Aphasia* is "old home week" for me. Published in 1918, in the wake of World War I, it preceded the beginning of my study of psychology by 5 years. Fröschels cites literature that was to remain paramount throughout my undergraduate and graduate study. Kohler, cited by Fröschels many times, was one of my teachers. Sperber, another source and important for studying the relationship between language and emotion, was in an office half a dozen doors down the hall from me for a number of years. He was born in the same city as Fröschels, during the same year, and the two attended the same university and shared an interest in language. C. and W. Sterns, to whose authority on child language Fröschels so often turns, provided important library reading for me as a student. Less close but still important—indeed crucial—in my education were Wundt and Kulpe. Both were key persons for Fröschels. The former was virtually the father of experimental phonetics in the United States through the contribution of his student, Scripture, and also had a strong influence on the development of speech pathology and audiology in this country through Scripture's only professional disciple, Carl E. Seashore. Kulpe came into my life late but with great strength. He had been the mentor of Padre Agostino Gemelli, with whom I had the privilege of studying and work-

9

ing as a Fulbright researcher in the early 1950s. Fröschels prompts me to recall the potency of association psychology and of emotion as a formal topic of psychology during my period as a student.

Perello's *History of the International Association of Logopedics and Phoniatrics* (1976)—an association founded by Fröschels in Vienna—has an introductory paragraph closely related to Fröschels' topic.

In 1911, purely by chance, Karl Cornelius Rothe (1880–1931), a Viennese teacher, happened to notice that several of his pupils were absent from class as a group on certain specific days. Inquiring into the reason for this, he found that they all had speech defects and went for treatment to Dr. E. Fröschels' outpatient clinic for "Stimm- und Sprachstorungen" at the Wiene Allgemeines Krankenhaus. The Clinic occupied a spacious ground floor. As there was no waiting-room, the children sat in rows waiting to be examined. By the light streaming in through a large window and reflecting on the mirror on his forehead, Dr. Fröschels, of Professor Victor Urbantschitsch's school, carefully examined the children, one by one, as he moved among them surrounded by his pupils. Before stating his own diagnosis, he would ask his assistants' opinions and comment upon them. All of this [took place] under a pennant hanging from the roof with the command, SILENCE, printed on it. First curious, then interested, Rothe introduced himself to Froeschels, remarking that such training filled a great need [p. 10].

A photograph in this *History* is enlightening. On the left, are perhaps 8–10 schoolchildren, probably 6–8 years of age. On the right around the table are Fröschels, his assistants, and 8–9 students. The photograph might have been taken either before or after World War I, for Fröschels' activities with schoolchildren were the same except when his work was interrupted by the necessities of World War I. The photograph was taken after World War I, for it shows Dr. Esti Freud. She was not in Fröschels' group until 1926.

The preceding paragraphs touch part of the environment that surrounded *Child Language and Aphasia*. With the outbreak of World War I, Fröschels' work with schoolchildren was interrupted. Deso Weiss (1969) observed on the occasion of Fröschels' 85th birthday,

The inspiring presence and ideas of Fröschels made him a leader in more than one field. The organizational form he created for the treatment of speech and voice disorders in the public school system in Vienna has remained an outstanding example of medical–pedagogical cooperation in our field. With the advent of World War I, this work was interrupted. He became involved in the treatment of speech disorders stemming from head wounds and voice alterations caused by neuroses. His department became increasingly important until in 1917 he was appointed senior physician in the Department of Head Injuries of the Central Hospital in Vienna [p. 242].

In 1918, the University of Vienna appointed Fröschels chief physician in the Department of Speech and Voice Disorders. Evidently it was while serving in these dual roles that he wrote *Child Language and Aphasia*. Subsequently, in 1924, he was appointed Professor of Logopedics, a term he had coined, at the University of Vienna (Brodnitz, 1972). While filling these offices, he achieved what Weiss (1969) deemed "his major historical accomplishment in our field. This was the fact that he reversed the then prevailing trend (in the Europe of the 1920s) of organic orientation, especially concerning the problem of stuttering [p. 240]." In the course of his work he saw analogies—and referred to them as such—between the behaviors of children with retarded speech–language development and aphasic adults.

Analogies in themselves do not provide a strong basis for proof; however, they do give a good basis for clarifying and explaining unusual behaviors. But Fröschels was not always literal. Weiss calls attention to "his poetry in the best Viennese tradition [also appearing in various anthologies]." What Fröschels considered one of his three most important accomplishments was based on an analogy, the *F*-method:

> The *F*-method is the simplest possible approach to the widespread problem of sigmatism and among the most useful ones. The patient is required to pronounce the *F* sound and after removing his lips (first passively, then actively) to pronounce the same blowing sound by forming the necessary air channel with his tongue [Weiss, 1969, p. 241].

Fröschels has not been the last to note an apparent similarity between the behavior of aphasic individuals recovering language and speech usage and the child acquiring it. Wepman wrote cautiously on this topic. His view as summarized by Eisenson (1977) follows:

> Wepman (1970) observes that in their recovery from aphasic involvements, many subjects "follow a well worn and previously travelled path thought to be not dissimilar to the stages of development of language in children. . . . Thus, if one considers only free, spontaneous use of language these stages are frequently seen and easily described." Earlier, Wepman and Jones (1964) described these recovery stages as five aphasias: global (pre-language, characterized by an absence of speech); jargon (meaningless utterance); pragmatic (increasing acquisition of comprehension and oral production of words and neologisms for the most part "unrelated to meaning or below level of comprehension"); semantic (the beginning of substantive language parallelling normal language acquisition in children in single- and two-word stages); [and] syntactic ("the use of syntax or grammar in oral expression"). In a recent paper, Wepman (1976) carries out his thesis that for some aphasic patients the regression is primarily in thinking and so becomes expressed in impaired language. We may recall that Jackson (1879) almost a century ago characterized the aphasic as "lame in thinking" [pp. 69–70].

I have labeled Fröschels' view as representing an analogy and Wepman's view as tentative. Jakobson (1968) was more positive and all-encompassing. His was an important description for two reasons. First, Jakobson is an outstanding linguist with a central European background; he is familiar with all of the literature cited by Fröschels and frequently alludes to Fröschels himself. Second, Jakobson's materials, broadly based, are frequently taken as justification for linguists to consider the matter of the language of aphasia as falling within their discipline. Jakobson wrote that:

> The speech of dysarthritics suffers only to the extent that their speech apparatus suffers, and it does not reveal any constant sequence of mutilations: "if the lips are damaged the labials are affected, etc." Similarly, there is no permanent and uniform sequence of babbling sounds in the speech of the infant. On the other hand, aphasic sound disturbances exhibit a strictly regular sequence of stages, and are therefore similar to those found in the actual linguistic progress of the child.
>
> The dissolution of the linguistic sound system in aphasics provides an exact mirror-image of the phonological development in child language. Thus, e.g., the distinction of the liquids *r* and *l* is a very late acquisition of child language, and, as Froeschels observes, it is one of the earliest and most common losses in aphasic sound disturbances. Also, in the restitution of language the "*r–l* symptom" often remains as the last distinct sign of an aphasic. Similarly, in those aphasics whose speech contained a uvular *r*, the confusions of the two liquids is characteristically almost a standard phenomenon which once again confirms the insignificance of the place of articulation as far as the liquids are concerned. The very late emergence of the sibilant *r* in Czech child language is one of the most typical and well-known phenomena of Czech speech pathology. The nasal sounds, which in French children appear only after all of the other vowels, usually disappear earliest in French aphasics. English children acquire the interdental fricatives only after the corresponding *s*-sounds and, according to Head's statements (1963), English aphasics lose the interdentals earlier than the *s*-sounds. In the intervening period both children and aphasics replace the interdentals with *s*-sounds (*zis* 'this', etc.).
>
> In aphasics, secondary vowels are lost earlier than primary vowels; affricates are given up "in a childlike fashion"; fricatives then fall together, as in children, with the corresponding stops. Forward articulated consonants are more resistant than palato-velar sounds, and the latter become dentals for the most part, for which phenomenon there are again exact correspondences in child language. Nasal palato-velar sounds generally merge with *n* (velar ŋ in English as well as French and Czech ŋ), and a parallel change occurs in fricatives and affricates, to the extent that these sounds are not yet eliminated. ʃ, ʒ, tʃ change to *s, z, ts* in Czech aphasics, which has been characterized as "infantile." And, finally, the back oral stops, as is well known, become *t* and *d*, or else the difference between *k, g* and *t, d* is preserved; but *k, g* are changed to the glottal stop, which, from the point of view of the phonemic system, subsumes only the distinctive feature of closure (or explosion) and consequently functions as an "indeterminate stop phoneme."
>
> The order in which speech sounds are restored in the aphasic during the process of recovery corresponds directly to the development of child language. Prof. B. I. Jacobowsky, Director of the University Psychiatric Clinic in Uppsala, has drawn my

attention to the rapid (approximately half an hour) course of development from speechlessness through aphasia to the complete recovery of language in the awakening process of mentally diseased patients who have been treated with insulin. Thanks to the kind cooperation of Prof. Jacobowsky, I was able to observe that there are processes, similar to an accelerated film, which are extraordinarily valuable for the study of the acquisition of speech sounds and which must be systematically observed and examined. A schizophrenic in the process of awakening at first omitted the liquids in the pronunciation of his name, "Karlson," and for a while initial *k* could not be restored and was replaced by the glottal stop. For a considerable period the rounded palatal vowels, and in particular *r*, were omitted by Swedish insulin patients; the lack of aspiration in the unvoiced stops was also striking, as was the strong palatalization of *t*.[1]

As may be inferred from the preceding paragraphs, Jakobson is interested in language universals, matters that are not restricted to particular languages. He amplifies this point.

The development of child language, the dissolution of aphasic language, and the synchrony and diachrony of the languages of the world all exhibit a sequence of common laws of solidarity. These laws attest to the step-by-step development of the linguistic system, and in particular of the phonemic system, and their universality establishes the fixed nature inherent in their order of precedence. This system is by its very nature closely related to those stratified phenomena which modern psychology uncovers in the different areas of the realm of the mind. Development proceeds "from an undifferentiated original condition to a greater and greater differentiation and separation" [Jakobson, 1968, p. 64].

The preceding view is somewhat countered by Luria (1958) who noted that in aphasic persons who exhibit a phonemic breakdown (paraphasic), the roots of words are affected while the suffixes remain intact:

Observations by Bein (1950) in recent years show that such patients lose the power to understand the roots of words, of which there are a great many in each language and for the precise understanding of which it is specially indispensable to differentiate them from many other complexes, phonetically similar but having a different meaning; on the other hand, suffixes of words, which are relatively few in a language and do not have such a multiplicity of possible phonetic connections, ordinarily remain considerably more comprehensible. Hence arises the paradoxical and apparently little-understood fact—so contrary to the widely held belief that in the pathology of these cases invariably those elements are earliest broken down which were last formed—that patients with the form of aphasia described lose the concrete meaning (attached to the root of the word) and retain abstract meanings, attached to such suffixes of abstract state, as **-ost** (*vidim-ost*) or **ie** (*sostoyvan-ie, obrazovan-ie*) in Russian, **-heit** (*Treu-heit*) or **-keit** (*Nachbarkeit*) in German, **-ance** (*vigilance*) in English or French, and so on [p. 60].

1. Jakobson's material is amply documented. The documentation is omitted from the quotation. It represents much material that is both unfamiliar to me and unavailable. This quote is taken from Jakobson (1968, pp. 60–61).

SOME ANALOGIES AND EXTRAPOLATIONS

Fröschels presents a number of cases of disordered speech or language among schoolchildren, and notes their similarities to particular types of aphasia or to particular cases of aphasic patients. Case 1 was an instance of a clutterer. This disorder is somewhat identified with the Viennese group of logopedists. Fröschels described the disorder as fast speech, "piled up," swallowed, and with gaps or omissions. Renditions of two stories a clutterer retold after hearing them read aloud can easily be imagined to fit this description. Fröschels named the analogous condition among adult aphasics as paraphasia. This is a disintegration of the articulation of words and not of the formulation of language as such.

Fröschels maintained that the clutterer views the formulation of his language as complete. He has the whole story in mind; he simply fails to articulate it. This brings up the relationship between language and speech and between language and thought. Fröschels would probably agree with Wepman (1976) who cited Piaget to the effect that language is not the source of logic but is structured by logic. Wepman continued,

> It is held to be true that without thought there would be no meaningful language; that without thought language would be merely barren repetition. A necessary corollary of this view is that man possesses the capacity for nonverbal thought which may or may not take a linguistic form of expression. When cortical impairment produces an observable linguistic deficiency, the disturbance may lie in the language structure and form of expression or it may lie in the limitation of the underlying thought processes, thereby affecting the linguistic expression [p. 131].

Fröschels' illustration of the four statements that can be made from the words (in German) *the book belongs to me* is convincing. The language is identical but the thought differs from one statement to the next. The sentence may also serve as a basis for understanding that emotion, attention, attitude, or "feeling-tone" is inextricably interwoven with (*a*) language and (*b*) speech. Fröschels is positive in writing, "[I am] by no means of the opinion that every form of aphasia can be explained by an analogy to infantile stages of speech and impediments."

Case 2 relates to a child who was apparently mute. Her hearing was seemingly normal and she responded to the word *mama*. On the twelfth day of therapy she uttered /u/. After 29 days she said /ku/ and /ko/. A feature attending the case was that the child had never babbled. Fröschels literally taught babbling, using colored pictures of objects, humans, and animals. The withdrawal of a stimulus picture often proved to be a good stimulus for eliciting a desired word. He recalled that through a similar procedure, he repeatedly succeeded in getting a missing word to be remembered by amnesic aphasics.

Obviously Fröschels placed considerable importance on a child's babbling. Different explanations have been given for its importance, all of which would seem to satisfy Fröschels. For example, De Laguna (1927) wrote:

> The little child, as we have seen, spends many hours and much energy in vocal play. It is far more agreeable to carry on this play with others, and indeed if the impulse were not encouraged by his elder companions it would soon become abortive. But the little child indulges in language-play even when he is alone. He talks to himself while he is occupied with his toys and the other affairs of childhood. When he does not talk aloud, he continues to talk to himself silently. Internal speech, fragmentary or continuous, becomes the habitual accompaniment of his active behavior and the occupation of his idle hours [p. 307].

Sperber, in "The Tyranny of Words," rephrased the same idea as he developed the role of emotion in language and speech:

> Let me remind the reader that during the first years of his life, every normal child delights in using language as a plaything. [A child] derives great pleasure from endless repetition of the same syllable; [he] rejoices in rhyme and rhythm; [he] invents nonsense words and finds it extremely funny to imitate other people's language [unpublished speech].

This is compatible with Fröschels' notion of the importance of an emotional content in vocal emission, lingual or prelingual. A more "cognitive" position than is stated and echoed in the Fröschels' monograph is described by Fry (1966).

> The learning that takes place on the motor side at this stage is therefore of a rather general nature and is absolutely basic to the acquisition of speech. The child is "getting the idea" of combining the action of the larynx with the movements of the articulators; of controlling to some extent the larynx frequency; of using the outgoing airstream to produce different kinds of articulation; and also the idea, which is quite important, of producing the same sound again by repeating the movements.
>
> The second important development at this time is the establishment of the auditory feedback loop. As sound-producing movements are repeated and repeated, a strong link is forged between tactual and kinesthetic impressions, and the auditory sensations that the child receives from his own utterances. The pleasure gained from babbling, which comes in the first instance from the sense of movement, is soon enhanced by the child's hearing of his own sounds [p. 189].

There is no pretext that these descriptions of babbling relate to amnesia. All three assume that the child takes to babbling normally. A limited longitudinal study in Japan showed no difference between the Japanese and American children until "the first meaningful speech" (Nakajima, 1962). It seems wholly out of place that a hearing child should be taught to babble, yet among the incongruities that grow out of youthful psychological deafness is the fact that babbling must be taught.

Cases 3, 4, and 5 are uniquely similar. Their similarity lies in their psychological deafness. All might have been relegated to schools for the deaf or feeble-minded. In all three instances, the patients behaved much in the manner of cases of sensory aphasia. Fröschels' shrewd and lengthy diagnosis showed the cases to be of a type that is rarely recognized. Psychological deafness is typically a topic of wartime and military service and is usually identified with feigned deafness, an escape procedure, malingering. Yet here were cases of psychological deafness in children. Once discovered, the problem became one of teaching the children to hear, a task not unlike the treatment of sensory aphasia. Persistent testing followed up irrational minor clues that audition was present, and Fröschels used some minor well-executed trickery such as leaving a room by one door, quietly reentering by another, then introducing surprise sounds from a surprise location.

A concept that is introduced later in the monograph might be mentioned here: the reciprocal action of attitude and inhibition. Attitude is a forthright participation in an event even though the attitude may be negative; inhibition is a damper placed upon this participation. Children learn to talk, as a rule, and then, confronted by society, learn to hold their peace and remain silent. Sperber, in "The Tyranny of Words," breaks the euphoria of his earlier lines with,

> To begin with, the parents share the baby's delight with these activities [babbling] and often encourage them. But this atmosphere of harmony disappears and is replaced by one of conflict as soon as the child reaches a stage of maturity that in the eyes of the surrounding persons make [him] a responsible person. Then, often rather suddenly, the liberty to do with language just as he pleases is taken away [unpublished speech].

Frequently, as adults, they must relearn to talk. Their inhibition might be self-imposed and may represent a barrier to incoming stimuli. In the instances of these three children, the barrier extended beyond audition—it was a sensory barrier. The teacher had to strive for attention in one modality or another, extend this to audition, create a condition of learning readiness, and teach language. The children had never experienced and did not recognize the aural stimuli.

The three cases of psychological deafness provide a background for more than the reciprocal relationship between inhibition and attitude;

they provide a springboard for assuming that there is no inhibition in normal behavior and that the auditory stimulus is sufficient to elicit a vocal response. A result is echolalia. This is closely related to inner speech—that is, talking to one's self both orally and silently—processes by which an "inner sound image" is implanted in the perceptual response repertoire to sensory stimulation. This inner sound image is the only "black box" that Fröschels created and to which he resorted.

Case 6 was an adult with a bullet wound. He had limited capacity for repeating. Throughout the monograph Fröschels identified poor re-repetition with transcortical motor aphasia. This may be the only instance in which I have found Fröschels in possible disagreement with Vignolo. Vignolo (1977) describes the transcortical motor aphasic as having good repetition. The two views are not necessarily at odds. Fröschels stresses re-repetition. He cites responses in which the first repetition was good, with the breakdown occurring on the second or third repetition. Case 7 was presented as a parallel to transcortical aphasia. This was a 10-year-old boy, somewhat hard of hearing and typically mute. When he talked, he made many phonemic substitutions and produced a particularly poor /s/; he was able to imitate or mimic muscular movements and occasionally imitated a word. He was a wild boy, hitting the persons around him. Fröschels considered this behavior to be a speech-related behavior, noting that with therapy the aggressiveness diminished. He reported that "after several months of daily exercise it was thus possible to establish a functioning connection between the optical impression and /or his conscious speech movement and the acoustical sound." Thus this boy was taught by lip reading. Gradually the weak inner sound–image mechanism was reinforced. This sound–tone–image mechanism (the black box) was considered to be the key to motor aphasia, the key to poor production of /s/, and at this stage of Fröschels' thinking, a key to stuttering.

Case 8 was presented in terms of the strength of the sound–tone–image mechanism (black box). A cleft-palate boy of 14 years continued to omit the /g/ sound after being fitted with an obturator. He made good progress with his speech and then was unexplainably absent from therapy for three weeks. When asked for an explanation he said *Meine Mutter ist 'estorben* ('my mother died'). He was asked to repeat the sentence several times and always made the same error. Then Fröschels told him to listen, and he repeated the statement incorrectly. The boy at once understood and corrected the error (*meine Mutter ist gestorben*). The point is that the external auditory stimulus is of greater potency than the internal "black box." In other cases, Fröschels frequently used a tactile addition to the visual and auditory stimulation. His devotion to what he called the optical–tactile method was strong: "It almost astonishes anyone who has never seen it before in cases of both aphasia and hearing muteness." One is left to assume that in the therapies that followed the diagnoses presented here, maximum use was made of optical–tactile stimulation.

Cases 9 and 10 were somewhat parallel, an adult and a child. Both were agrammatical; both used single-word responses to queries as well as in spontaneous speech; both were poor in repetition. The reports permitted Fröschels to illustrate the use that he made of measures of time. He would give a word, requesting that the word be used in a sentence. The lapse between the presentation of the word and the subsequent sentence was as much as 15 seconds.

The report of Case 11 is unusually complete. In this case Fröschels had his best instance of transcortical motor aphasia. He posited, along with the case description, a strong statement that failure in re-repetition is a certain accompaniment of this disorder.

It is pointless to review in further detail the cases that Fröschels discussed. The presentations are the core of the monograph. All readers will note the meticulous care with which he treated case histories; all will note the triads that he treated one by one: an aphasic person, a case of retarded language development, and a didactic discussion of some of the salient points. It is almost impossible to discuss these without simply reproducing Fröschels. However, some of the didactic materials can be emphasized.

The three deaf youngsters who were found to have normal hearing were interesting cases in their own right. They were not feigning deafness; they were simply not responding to aural stimuli. The tests required persistence, patience, and a determination to find the true condition of hearing among the children. Having discovered that they were sensitive to auditory stimuli, the task became one of teaching: attention, discrimination, and language.

In order to hear, an individual must have a normal attitude, be positive and outgoing. This may be countered by inhibition. The child is expected to develop with a normal positive attitude. But in the case of the three "deaf" children, attitude was sublimated by inhibition. The normal outgoing child learns from society to restrict his positiveness; he becomes somewhat inhibited. As an adult he throws off the inhibition and participates freely again in social dialogue. This normal attitude is consonant with babbling, with echolalia, with talking to one's self, and with a continuing conversation. The inhibition is consonant with indifference, withdrawal, muteness, and sensory aphasia. This potential conflict between attitude and inhibition may be read into several of the behaviors that Fröschels discusses.

An emphasis that emerged from a study of the several cases presented is the importance of testing as suggested in the long sequence of tests given to all clients. Fröschels improvised tests. For example, with a case of agrammatism he might ask the client to use a specified word in a sentence, then study the lengths of the lapses between the stimulus words and the responses. Each behavior was treated in the context of a test. The same measure might be used by an experimentalist as a datum. Here it was an indication of the state of a client.

A test for which Fröschels claims credit is the one for cortical motor aphasia: re-repetition. He called it "a confirming test." Although Fröschels presented a test in the context of a single case, he made it clear that its applicability extended far beyond the instance to which it was applied. For example, he hypothesized that the case of a hard-of-hearing boy with missing sound perception (Case 7) might be closely related to the experience of a person who makes /s/ poorly. This person as well as the sensory aphasic (Case 6) may simply not hear himself truly. The same might be the case with the stutterer.

Another emphasis I consider important is the "sound–image mechanism." In Fröschels' time, this "black box" was supposed to lie somewhere in the neurological system. Each auditory experience was stored, and could be treated as an auditory image or a "sound–tone image." This, together with the unknown site of the storage place—presumably in the frontal cortex—constituted the mystery box, the "sound–tone–image mechanism." The mechanism would respond to one's own talking or another person's, and the strength of the image in many cases could be increased, for example through repetition. Fröschels' argument—that the mechanism responds more acutely to outside stimuli than to one's own production of speech (Case 8)—is convincing. Language-laboratory enthusiasts are left to wonder if the boy would have picked up his error from a recording of his own speech.

The building of the sound–tone image requires constant stimulation. Fröschels was a strong proponent of tactile–optical stimulation, a procedure that is recurrently advocated in different schools of speech pathology.

Another emphasis in Fröschels' view of language lay in the relationship between the language of thought and that which emerged as speech. Wepman (1976) wrote, "Language is inextricably related to thought but is not identical with it; language is the product of thought; thought is man's highest mental process, language its maidservant; the ability to think is innate in man, while language is acquired [p. 131]." For Fröschels, the message is always complete and in sentences in the mind of the speaker. The discrepancy between the language and the utterance is unknown to the speaker. Fröschels stressed that communication occurred in sentences, which might have any number of words from one to many, and might incorporate gestures. He probably would have been intrigued with the concept of pivot sentences illustrated in the left-hand column of Table 2.1. There is no hint that he noted that many of the short sentences of children started with the same word or ended with the same word (Braine, 1976).[2]

In Fröschels' view the clutterer is merely omitting and distorting some of the "script" that he has in mind. This hypothetical relationship between script and utterance is not only present in clutterers and aphasic persons who omit materials and give one-word sentences, but is also present in children who are acquiring speech–language. Fröschels would be in accord with Braine (1976), who elaborated some short sentences of children into complete scripts (Table 2.1).

Not only did Fröschels view the language of the script as being complete in the speaker's mind, but he saw each fragment of the script as a sentence. A string of words in a sentence could convey a variety of meanings depending on the relative stress that was given to its parts. Although *the book belongs to me* can be spoken to indicate a number of meanings, Fröschels did not waver in his conviction of the integrity of this sentence as a unit in speech production. However, he admitted some contradictory evidence that is hard to explain away. Records were made to show visually the breathing of young speakers. In some instances, inhalation accompanied practically every word. This would indicate a word-by-word development of an utterance, not a cohesive oral product to be called spontaneous speech and to be visualized as the rendition of a "script."

The priority of the sentence in talking did not carry over to speech perception. A sentence, spoken normally, might be comprehended by a listening child. The same child, however, might get no message from a similar sentence in which one syllable was spoken unusually loudly. It is as though the loud syllable masked the perception of the sentence. This recalls a concept put forward by Kurt Goldstein (1948) called *dedifferentiation*. In work with sensory aphasic individuals, he found that a common fault was their failure to distinguish between "ground" and "figure"—important terms in the then current gestalt psychology. In

2. Note is taken of Braine's revision of the pivot concept and acknowledgment of a revised formula that includes constant plus variable ($c + v$) structure as well as variable plus constant ($v + c$) structure; also to substitute the concept of groping for rigid pivots.

TABLE 2.1.
Meaningful Elaboration of Children's Utterances

UTTERANCE	SITUATION OR GLOSS
No mama	I don't want to go to mama. (Andrew I)
ə no chair	She doesn't want the lambs to sit on the chair. (Kathryn I)
More car	As the car parks after a drive; wants to keep driving. (Andrew I)
More page	Requesting the adult to turn over book page. (Andrew II)
More outside	Asking to go out in the yard again. (Andrew II)
[*Gia more read book*]	Picking up book that she and L. had read previously. (Gia II)
. . . more book	Gives L. label and truck, to put label on truck again. (Gia II)
More train	Looking for a second wire-man to put on the train. (Gia II)
Mommy jacket	Pointing to her drying jacket that mother had washed. (Gia II)
Lois baby record	Asking L. to play "baby record" for her. (Gia II)
Kathryn ə bear	Giving a raisin to the toy bear. (Kathryn I)
Mommy ə Muffin Man	Apparently asking mother to sing the song. (Kathryn I)
Mommy oops	Mommy said "oops." (Kendall I)
Melissa car	Melissa was getting into Kendall's family's car. (Kendall I)
Daddy teeth	Daddy brushing teeth. (Kendall I)
Kendall spider	Kendall looked at a spider. (Kendall II)
Daddy work	Daddy had just left to go to work. (Jonathan II)
Jonathan tree	Jonathan climb tree. (Jonathan III)
Jonathan up sky	Craning his head back looking up at the sky. (Jonathan IV)
Betty head	Betty was moving a tractor along the top of Stevie's head. (Stevie)
Cindy bottle	Cindy is bringing in a bottle of milk. (Stevie)
Odi hallo	Response to "What are you doing?" She is telephoning. (Odi)
Tipu mama	Chick eating food. (Seppo)
Tati mama	Lady serving food to bear. (Seppo)

Source: Children's First Word Combinations, Martin D. S. Braine. Chicago: University of Chicago Press, 1976. With permission from The Society for Research in Child Development, Inc. © 1976.

speech perception, an instance might be the identification or discrimination of words in a background of noise. For young listeners, the unusually loud syllable in a string of words masked an entire sentence, forward and backward, making speech perception impossible.

Each reader will name his own high points in Fröschels' discussions. In this section, I have tried to make a few extrapolations of Fröschels' interesting materials without repeating him unduly.

MORE REMOTE ANALOGIES

Three instances of abnormal development of communication will be discussed in the wake of Fröschels' treatments of related cases, his cases of aphasia and of delayed development of communication. These are, "The savage boy of Aveyron," taught by Itard; Isabelle, taught by Marie Mason; and Genie, taught by Victoria Fromkin and her associates.

The story of Victor, the savage of Aveyron, is legendary. It had been interestingly retold by Harlan Lane (1976). His work is based on numerous sources including 28 that bear the authorship of Itard, the teacher of the savage. Lane discovered some lost material and reproduced it for the first time. Presumably the wild boy had been abandoned at the age of 4 or 5 years and captured at about the age of 12. He became a charge of Itard who subsequently extended his experience into a vast program of education of the deaf.

Itard, like Fröschels, was a painstaking observer of a client. He viewed his task as one of teaching sensory responses, of developing motivational procedures, and teaching verbal material. He would proceed in the order of taking up sensory work, language, thought, and medical pedagogy. His mute subject cherished his freedom and resisted all restraints. His behavior of resistance was a temper-tantrum sometimes including biting. Itard's objectives were to achieve in Victor an interest in social life, to awaken nervous sensibility (emotions), to extend Victor's range of thinking and ideas, to achieve speech through imitation, and ultimately to teach simple mental operations such as arithmetic.

Itard was able to improve Victor's touch, taste, and smell, but not his sight and hearing. These became first-order targets. To improve sight required the development of attention. This, Itard achieved with a shell game and chestnuts. Chestnuts were one of Victor's favorite foods. With practice he could follow the switching of the nut from shell to shell readily. Thus his attention and sight were improved. Audition was sharpened, but slowly. Victor learned to differentiate /a, i, and e/ but not /o and u/.

After being among people for 9 months, Victor uttered the syllable "*o.*" This led Itard to give Victor his name, a word that in the French pronunciation seems to center on the second vowel. Subsequent utterances within the first 18 months included the words for *water* and *milk* and syllables that might be construed as fitting the name *Julie* ('o–d–uh' was interpreted by Victor's governess as remindful of her frequent use of *o–dieu*). Despite much work on language acquisition, Victor developed no sounds /p/ or /b/.

Lane calls attention to the fact that in Skinner's terminology, Victor's verbal behavior was controlled by antecedent events, or was *tacting.* After milk was put in Victor's view he would say the word. He never used *manding,* as in asking for milk.

Victor was effective with gestures. Itard was taking him into society, into fashionable restaurants. Victor would ask for a second helping by putting his plate beside the food he wished. In the event the gesture failed he deftly filled the plate with his hands, taking food from the main dish.

Itard may have set the pattern for Fröschels and subsequently for Montessori in the use of large visual objects, colored cutouts, and various performance tasks. He started by hanging pictures in a particular order on the wall and expecting Victor to replace the pictures in the same order. This occurred; he then used wooden cutouts—a circle, a triangle, a square, perhaps painted red, blue, and black, respectively. The objects were returned to their proper places. The board was reversed, and still the objects were placed correctly. Then Itard gradually reduced distinctions, increasing the difficulty of the task. Fits of anger resulted, and became a controlling behavior. Finally, Itard punished Victor by holding him out of a high window, head downward over a deep chasm. The frightened boy returned to cooperative behavior. An alphabet was cut out of a board, and Victor replaced the letters in proper order. Letters of wood, paper, and metal were properly matched.

Victor was blindfolded, then asked to raise a thumb on hearing *a* and successive fingers on hearing *e–i–o–u*. Responses to *a* and *o* were positive. Itard next turned to touch. Victor was required to distinguish chestnuts from acorns; with long practice he succeeded. Physical qualities were taught—for example, big and little; parts were taught—for example, parts of a book, parts of the body. Also, the delay between stimulus and response was timed—a procedure Fröschels was to adopt later.

The socialization of Victor was relatively unsuccessful. Instances can be found to indicate that moral development (medical pedagogy) occurred. These instances—some of them rare—reflected gratitude, affection, sadness, pleasure, and recognition of injustice. In order to achieve these at the pinnacle of the pyramid of successes and failures with Victor, Itard used many instructional devices. Lane lists the following:

a plank painted black on which everyday objects were placed and their outlines chalked; the same objects suspended underneath their designs; letter cutouts to form names; a vertical board displaying a red disk, blue triangle, and black square, and the corresponding cardboard cutouts hung from nails; similar boards with the same forms in one color, or circles or contrasting colors, or kindred geometric forms, or circles of similar hues, or irregular patches of color; a board with twenty-four slots containing two-inch letters printed on cardboard; the corresponding letters in metal; a board with two equal circles, each having six points on the circumference for placing letter cutouts; drum, bells, shovel, drumstick; various sweets, drinks, snuff; a narrow-neck vase containing hot and cold nuts, acorns, stones, a penny and a die, metal letters; a blindfold; goblets, books, nails, a skewer, chalk, various household objects [p. 166].

In 1806, after 5 years of work with Victor, Itard gave up. The boy goes down in the "annals of education" as retarded and autistic. Perhaps in reverse behavior modification, Victor shaped the life of Itard, a devoted teacher of deaf individuals.

It is uncalled for to compare Fröschels and Itard on the basis of Fröschels' selected cases and the single assigned case of Victor. Perhaps Fröschels was more pliable than Itard, who seemed not to join the wave of popularity of the new sign language for the deaf in France. Fröschels, choosing his own ground, seems at every turn to be pliable and to respect the possible strengths of his students. Lane writes of the possibility that Itard could have used more of the techniques of behavior modification. Using the spurious line of reasoning, "This is true because you cannot prove it otherwise," he supports the notion that Victor could have been taught to communicate verbally and to use manding if he had been instructed by using the procedures of the 1970s. The ones of 1912–1918, available to Fröschels, would lead to the same outcome that Itard found; however, it is unfair to time-bind Fröschels to the period of his book. He was innovative with the cases that he presented. More importantly, he did not present the case of any child who was beyond the alleged age of language acquisition (Lenneberg, 1967).

The second case is vastly different. In different accounts she has the names Isabelle and Annabelle. The child's unknown paternity led her grandparents to consider that she was something to be concealed. The only other person she saw was her partially blind, deaf-mute mother. Isabelle was discovered in 1938 when she was 6½ years old. The same small-town newspaper that covered the area to the south of the Ohio city of 15,000 in which she lived also covered the village to the east in which I lived. The newspaper described Isabelle as being reared in seclusion; in fact, closeted. Mason, who was to take over the language training of the child, described the circumstances as, "During the period of pregnancy, and for 6½ years after the child's birth, the mother and child had apparently been locked in a room behind drawn shades [p. 295]." The child developed rickets and bowlegs, and was scarcely ambulatory. Through contact with her mother, the child knew affection. She was, however, antisocial; she was frightened and responded with a scream when Dr. Mason first approached her bed with a friendly "Hello, there, Isabelle." Later the same day she showed an inquisitive interest in Dr. Mason's watch and ring.

On the second day. Dr. Mason took Isabelle a toy watch, a toy ring, and a doll, each wrapped separately. On the same day, she began teaching Isabelle the names of objects, possession of objects, and body parts such as the eye, ear, nose, etc.

Isabelle's lack of experience made testing difficult. Soon, however, hearing ability was established and sensory aphasia ruled out. Next Dr. Mason gave Isabelle a ball. Isabelle had no idea what to do with it; she only stroked Dr. Mason's face with it. It was, however, an object of attention and led to her first vocalization after one week, *ba;* next the stimulus "car" elicited *ah.* Nouns were introduced by objects, and verbs were presented through gestures. Discriminating among the names of different objects began on Day 10. Dr. Mason reported, "While it is true that her earliest vocalizations, vocal utterances, were those of a child of a year and a half or two years, it is also true that she passed through each successive stage more rapidly than the normal child [p. 300]." Dr. Mason provides a detailed chronology of the progress.

11/16/38:   Admittance to Children's Hospital, Columbus, Ohio.
11/17,18/38:   Cried almost continuously; would not partake of food except milk and crackers; showed either recoil, disinterest, or fear of everyone with whom she came in contact.
11/19/38:   My first visit, described above.
11/20/38:   My second visit. Isabelle showed interest in the watch, ring and doll which I brought her. Partook of some food when seated at a small table.
11/22/38:   Gesture communication between mother and child before and during psychological examination. No attempt at vocalization.
11/25/38:   First vocalization. Attempt to say the words *ball, car,* and *bye* ('good-bye'). Described above.
11/26/38:   Repeated the words *baby* and *dirty* in imitation of words spoken to her in the form of play. *Baby* was the most distinct articulation to date.
11/30/38:   Said *flower, one, two.* Jabbered succession of nonsense syllables in imitation of my rather lengthy explanation to Jane that she should not appropriate Isabelle's toys.
12/3/38:   Isabelle began to associate the word with its object; does not associate individuals with their names, but recognizes her own name when spoken.
12/5/38:   Said voluntarily the words *mama, fat, pretty, hot;* used *bye* spontaneously to everyone.
12/8/38:   Said *watch, ring, blue, car, ball, lady, bell, bow-wow, dog, hot, cold, warm, one, two, three, red, dirty, pretty, baby.*
12/13/38:   Surgical operation.
1/4/39:   Repeated for student teacher (J.H.) *dog, baby, pretty, hair, one, two, three, Jane, good-bye, girl, boy, paper, cut, locket.*

1/13/39:	Repeated: *house, eye, red, green, yellow, purple.* Distinguished yellow from the other colors and said *yellow* voluntarily.
1/31/39:	Said for student teacher (B.O.), *penny, purse, dime, open, all right, come again.*
2/8/39:	Says the following sentences voluntarily: *That's my baby; I love my baby; open your eyes; close your eyes; I don't know; I don't want; that's funny; 'top it—'at's mine* (when another child attempted to take one of her toys).
2/11/39:	New words: *milk, soup, coat, fur.* Sentences: *I want the scissors; I want a balloon; want some soup; Pick it up, Dorothy*—indicating something that had fallen on the floor. She now associates people with names.
2/18/39:	Says, *Give me a penny.*
3/2/39:	Isabelle said, *Say please,* when I asked her to hand me something. Later she said, *I'm sorry,* when she accidentally hurt another child's finger.
3/4/39:	Isabelle said, *I love you, Miss Mason.*
3/9/39:	Identified printed form of the words, blue and yellow, and matched the word with the color.
3/10/39:	Isabelle matched the printed forms of cow, sheep, dog, and cat with corresponding pictures.
3/11/39:	*Stay, I don't want you to go home.*
3/13/39:	Isabelle pointed to pictures in her book saying: *This is a boy, This is a baby,* etc. Said, *I'm sleepy.*
3/22/39:	Said, *I see a purple flower; I see a pretty flower.*
3/27/39:	Isabelle voluntarily sang, *I see you, tra la, la-la, la-la.*
4/1/39:	Isabelle goes about humming nursery rhymes, *Here we go round the mulberry bush,* and *baa, baa, black sheep.*
5/2/39:	Isabelle got her first formal lesson in reading—a book called *Play and Read*—and said *Where's my book?*

After one year of effort:

1. Isabelle has shown considerable progress in word recognition in preparation for reading readiness. She identifies the printed forms of many words and of whole sentences.
2. Her speech has improved noticeably. Her vocabulary is much increased. However, in expressing herself, unless cautioned, she is likely to run her words together. This may be accounted for by her inability to form all of her sentences correctly from the standpoint of grammatical construction and, in her attempt to speak her thoughts, her mental reaction outspeeds her motor speech reactions and a resultant jabber is noticeable.
3. Isabelle's writing has taken on splendid form. She writes with a steadiness and character which might do credit to an older child.

4. She now comprehends numerical concepts, which, at first, were extremely difficult for her. She counts to 20 readily, sometimes beyond. She has acquired a knowledge of addition to 10.
5. Isabelle listens attentively while a story is read to her. She retells the story in her own limited vocabulary, bringing out the main points.
6. She is much interested in her rhythmic activities. She can interpret the tempo of a musical selection in various ways, and she can march and dance. Isabelle is anxious for Santa Claus to come. She says she wants a bicycle and a "real baby" and "Jingle Bells" [Mason, 1942, pp. 301–303].

A summary dated June 1940, after a year and a half training, including items from my own notes and those of five student teachers, may give the reader an idea of Isabelle's vocabulary of nouns, adjectives, verbs, etc., and her use of question forms:

1. Vocabulary between 1500 and 2000 words. (List of five student teachers)
2. Questions asked by Isabelle: (B.J., student teacher). Why do crayons break? Why does the hand move around the clock? Why does the paste come out if one upsets the jar? Do you go to Miss Mason's school at the University? Are you going to church tomorrow? Does your dog sleep in your bed? What did Miss Mason say when you told her I cleaned my classroom?
3. Isabelle now tells in detail the story of Little Black Sambo. (D.B., student teacher)
4. Isabelle recited Baa, Baa, Black Sheep. (M.V., student teacher)
5. Isabelle made up a story, using it in a puppet show. (I.S., student teacher)

After 22 months of training Isabelle was aggressive, often to the point of stubbornness, and under certain conditions she showed extreme negativism, recalling situations reported by Itard and Fröschels. Positively, the child was described as highly imaginative and as having an acute sense of the dramatic; as being affectionate, having an excellent sense of humor, and being a "tease." This contrasts with an early description of "unsocial behavior which betrayed itself in antagonistic and often animalistic reactions."

It may have been important that Isabelle was within the age range hypothesized as allowable for the development of a first language. Genie, however, was pubescent at the time of her discovery at an age of 13 years 9 months. From the age of 20 months she had apparently been isolated in a small closed room, tied into a potty chair, where she remained at day and sometimes at night. Her description upon admission to the hospital, "pale, thin, ghostlike, apathetic, mute, and socially unresponsive," reminds us of what might have been written of Isabelle upon her admission to the hospital. Genie made no sounds other than "spitting," except for a kind of "throaty whisper" (see Fromkin *et al.*, 1974). She might repeat, in the manner of echolalia; for example, the sentence *The puppet will fall* might be followed by *fall*.

The available accounts of Genie understandably emphasize her linguistic development. After 3 years of training it was reported: "Among the grammatical structures, Genie now comprehends single–plural contrast of nouns, negative–affirmative sentence distinctions, possessive constructions, modifications, a number of prepositions (including *under, next to, beside, over,* and probably *on* and *in,* conjunction with *and,* and the comparative and superlative forms of adjectives)." Using "point to" responses, Genie was unable for 20 months to discriminate between single and plural nouns. Then this suddenly changed to 100% correct responses.

Genie as a child was punished for making noises, including speech. The effect of this probably contributed to her inability to speak. As she struggled in the attempt even at the age of 15 years, her development in sentence structure from two-word sentences to longer sequences was one that would have fitted Fröschels' stock of case histories. At 15 Genie was not normal in her speech–language development. The case is contemporary and will doubtless be reported in more detail than it has been. In any event, if one accepts the hypothesis that age 2-to-puberty is the range in which a person can learn a first language, one would not expect Genie to reach normal standards at any age. This is not an instance that fits Fröschels' collection of chosen cases.

CONCLUSIONS

The question remains, what was Fröschels doing? *Child Language and Aphasia,* which he modestly calls a monograph, reflects Fröschels' time. Compartmentalization of disciplines and professions was soon to be the rule. Fröschels, however, was in keeping with the Viennese tradition in which scholarship knew no boundaries. His circle of associates included all branches of learning and therapy. At the same time it was a period and place where exactness of measures and detail in description were stressed. Fröschels exemplifies both. The great wave of American graduate students in Germany had passed, and the United States was to reap the products of this subsequent era through the influx of refugees.

The linkage that Fröschels made between aphasia and the acquisition of one's first language was loose and acknowledged to be one of analogy. Whether or not he chose to strengthen this linkage in subsequent years I do not know. Despite the fact that Jakobson appealed to the authority of Fröschels in presenting his position, there seems little resemblance between the strong, detailed position taken by Jakobson, and the tongue-in-cheek figurative one taken by Fröschels with selected cases. There are many behaviors among aphasic patients that do not lend themselves readily to the viewpoint of any analogy. The aphasic patient may upon learning the name of one fruit suddenly come forth with the names of other fruits; upon learning the name of one animal, recall the names of other animals. Such associations, based upon the patient's experiences, are hardly to be expected from the youngster who is learning a language noun by noun. He may, however, be expected to follow shortcuts as he formulates and applies generalized rules of syntax. It is enough to say that Fröschels did not make the relationship between aphasia and the acquisition of language a complete one.

Fröschels at 33 was preparing a broad base that would later be refined. The sound–image mechanism would contribute to the *F*-method and would recur in his emphasis on a successful oral experience.

I draw my own analogy between Fröschels and his Viennese twin, Sperber. Both were influenced by Freud. Both agreed on the power of emotional content in language and speech. After fleeing to the United States in 1933, Sperber bent his energy to a dictionary of *American Political Terms,* hoping that an understanding of the terms would reduce their emotional impact. This was a refinement of a life-long interest. Fröschels, too, fled to the United States in 1938. His refinements of his work before 1918 contributed to more than 20 books and more than 300 papers.

APPENDIX:
THE SPEECH AND VOICE CLINIC, VIENNA
BY ESTI D. FREUD

Here is the description of the Speech and Voice Clinic in Vienna during the time I worked there (1926–1938). The official title of the clinic was *Ambulatorium für Sprach- und Stimmstörungen.* Its medical director was Dr. Emil Fröschels.

The Ambulatorium was part of the University of Vienna's Department of Otorhinolaryngology, whose attending professor was Dr. Heinrich Neumann. The entire medical complex was located in the *IX. Hof des allgemeinen Krankenhauses* (ninth court of the General Hospital), *Spitalgasse, Wien IX*. To get to the clinic one had to cross a bridge-like corridor, which in allusion to some therapeutic procedures at the clinic was baptized: *Die Wiener Seufzerbrücke* (The Vienna Bridge of Sighs).

Patients at the Speech and Voice Clinic were recruited from many sources. Dr. Fröschels was medical supervisor for *die Sonderklassen für Sprachgestörte Schulkinder* (special classes for speech-disturbed schoolchildren). Every morning, five days a week, teachers trained in the specialty brought groups of children to the clinic. The children were examined and the nature of their problems discussed. During these examinations, Dr. Fröschels' students and assistants sat in a semicircle to the right and left of him. It was his habit to request one of us to make a diagnosis and suggest therapy. The impairments of these children consisted of a wide variety of functional and organic speech, language, and voice disorders.

A second group of patients were referred from the ENT Clinic. These were usually cases of persistent hoarseness secondary to laryngeal surgery. Dr. Fröschels was greatly interested in speech improvement of cleft-palate cases. Together with Dr. Schallit—a dentist—he invented and constructed the meato-obturator.

Aphasia patients were sent by the Department of Neurology for language rehabilitation.

The fourth category of patients, mostly self-referred, were what I shall call "voice professionals." They were teachers, ministers, actors, opera singers—many of them world famous—who suffered from functional voice disorders. When I became lecturer in 1932 for *"Sprechtechnik" der Philosophischen Fakultät der Universität Wien,* I referred those of my students who manifested voice or speech defects to the clinic, where they were examined and treated.

Dr. Fröschels, twice a week, lectured on such topics as aphasia (he still belonged to the school of diagram makers), stuttering (it was during one of these lectures that he suddenly presented his now famous chewing method), and the philosophy of consciousness (during which he attacked Freud). Thrice weekly, we students had seminars, at which one student was assigned to give a "Referat" on a specific subject, for example, the history of the education of the deaf, testing hearing acuity in infants, methods of treating stuttering, the theories of Kurt Goldstein, Arnold Pick, Henry Head, and others on aphasia. A general discussion followed these seminars.

A great majority of Dr. Fröschels students and disciples were women, and in Vienna we were called the "Fröschels girls." Dr. Fröschels had a stimulating personality and was a strict and conscientious teacher. The

12 years I was a member of his staff was the most memorable, important, and interesting period of my life.

REFERENCES

Bein, E. S. *Psychological Analysis of Sensory Aphasia.* Dissertation, Academy of Medical Science, Moscow: 1950. In Martha Taylor Sarno (Ed.), *Aphasia: Selected Readings.* New York: Appleton-Century-Crofts, 1972.

Black, John W. Communication behaviors: Acquisition and effects. In Robert K. Kibler & Larry L. Barker (Eds.), *Conceptual Frontiers in Speech-Communication.* New York: Speech Association of America, 1969.

Braine, M. D. S. *Children's First Word Combinations.* Chicago: University of Chicago Press (Society for Research in Children Development), **41**(1), 1976.

Brodnitz, Friedrich S. Necrology: Emil Fröschels. *American Speech, Language, and Hearing Association (ASHA),* 1972, **14**, 231.

De Laguna, Grace. *Speech: Its Function and Development.* New Haven: Yale University Press, 1927.

Eisenson, Jon. Language rehabilitation of aphasic adults: Some observations on the state of art. *Folia Phoniatrica,* 1977, **29**, 61–83.

Fromkin, Victoria, Krashen, Stephen, Curtiss, Susan, Rigler, David, & Rigler, Marilyn. The development of language in Genie; a case of language acquisition beyond "the critical period." *Brain and Language,* 1974, **1**, 81–107.

Fry, D. B. The development of phonological system of the normal and deaf child. In Frank Smith & George A. Miller (Eds.), *The Genesis of Language.* Cambridge: Massachusetts Institute of Technology Press, 1966.

Goldstein, K. *Language and Language Disturbance.* New York: Grune & Stratton, 1948.

Head, H. *Aphasia and Kindred Disorders of Speech, Vols. I & II.* New York: Hafner, 1963.

Itard, J. *The Wild Boy of Aveyron.* New York: Appleton-Century-Crofts, 1962.

Jackson, J. H. An affectation of speech from disease of the brain. *Brain,* 1879, **1**, 304–330.

Jakobson, R. *Child Language: Aphasia and Phonological Universals.* The Hague: Mouton, 1968.

Jordal, Jytte. Treatment of severe language disorders in children. *Folia Phoniatrica,* 1977, **29**, 22–60.

Lane, Harlan. *The Wild Boy of Aveyron.* Cambridge: Harvard University Press, 1976.

Lenneberg, E. *Biological Foundations of Language.* New York: Wiley, 1967.

Luria, A. *Traumatic Aphasia.* The Hague: Mouton, 1970.

Mason, Marie K. *The Ohio State University Monthly,* 1940 (April), **XXXI** (7).

Mason, Marie K. Learning to speak after six and one-half years of silence. *Journal of Speech Disorders,* 1942, **7**, 295–304.

Nakajima, S. A. A comparative study of the speech development of Japanese and American English in Childhood. *Studies Phonologica,* 1962, **II**, 27–46.

Perello, J. *The History of the International Association of Logopedics and Phoniatrics.* Barcelona: Editorial Augusta, 1976.

Sperber, Hans. *Uber den Affekt als Ursache der Sprachveranderung.* Halle, 1914.

Sperber, Hans. The tyranny of words—can it be broken? Unpublished lecture, delivered May 1, 1955, upon his retirement from Ohio State University.

Sperber, Hans, & Trittsckuh, Travis. *American Political Terms: An Historical Dictionary.* Detroit: Wayne State University Press, 1962.

Stern, William. *Psychology of Early Childhood.* New York: Henry Holt and Company, 1924.

Vignolo, Luigi A. Le sindromi afasiche. In Franco Angeli (Ed.), *Neuropsicologia Clinica.* Milano: Angeli, 1977.

Weiss, Deso A. Emil Fröschels on his 85th anniversary. *Folia Phoniatrica,* 1969, **21,** 240–253.

Wepman, J. M. Aphasia: Language without thought or thought without language? *American Speech, Language, and Hearing Association (ASHA),* 1976, **18,** 131–136.

Wepman, J. M. Approaches to the analysis of aphasia. In *Human Communication and Its Disorders,* NINDS Monograph No. 10. Washington: U.S. Department of Health, Education, and Welfare, 1970. Cited in Jon Eisenson, "Language rehabilitation of aphasic adults," a review of some issues as to the state of the art, in Marsha Sullivan & Mary S. Komers (Eds.), *Rationale in Adult Aphasia Therapy.* Kansas City, Kansas: University of Nebraska Medical Center, 1977.

Wepman, J. M., & Jones, L. V. Five aphasias: A commentary on aphasia as a regressive linguistic phenomenon. In D. M. Rioch & E. A. Weinstein (Eds.), *Disorders of Communication.* Baltimore: Williams and Wilkins, 1964.

Chapter 3

APHASIA IN CHILDREN

Joel Stark

My purpose here is to react to some aspects of Emil Fröschels' work, completed earlier this century, with a view toward its relevance for the contemporary student of language disorders. Thus, I have chosen to comment on some of Fröschels' observations, interspersed with my own biases as they have evolved over the past two decades.

We are somewhat closer to an understanding of the nature of aphasia in children than we were earlier this century when Emil Fröschels was describing the behaviors he observed. We have expanded our repertoire of testing procedures. We can examine intellectual potential in more creative ways, often using match-to-sample procedures with forms, blocks, pictures, objects, and other presumably functional stimuli. We have developed well-standardized tests for auditory discrimination of speechlike and nonspeechlike sounds in CVC words and longer units. There are instruments designed to determine the child's ability to imitate strings of words embedded in units of increased syntactic complexity, and well-standardized tests to measure both the child's lexicon and his ability to understand and/or produce complex syntactic utterances. One has only to visit the commercial exhibits at any major convention of psychologists or examine the catalogues of major publishers to realize how far we have come since Fröschels wrote his book on childhood language development and its disorders.

Yet our understanding of the mechanisms responsible for language

33

deviance in children is still limited. Even our ability to differentiate among various kinds of aphasic behaviors in children is often primitive. I will use the term "aphasic" throughout to apply to children whose language problems are developmental or congenital rather than acquired. The term, which has been abandoned in that particular usage by most clinicians, is synonymous with what others call "dysphasia," "developmental aphasia," "congential aphasia," and "aphasoid." I will also use it to include children labeled "language impaired, deviant, or disordered." Admittedly this is a waste-basketing of terminological confusion. However, the current state of the art does not permit us to do much more. Certainly, the attempt to find a point-to-point correspondence between the language behavior and the neurological abnormality is futile. The overwhelming number of children who are labeled aphasic do not present hard neurological signs or evidence of neuropathology. For most, the presence of "organicity" must be based upon evidence of some problem in the pre- or paranatal history in conjunction with "soft" signs of neurological dysfunction (e.g., gait disturbances, difficulty with alternating movements, etc.). The aphasic problem is cognitive–linguistic in nature. Each aphasic child presents a unique and highly individual combination of symptomology.

While there have been some new theoretical explanations, and a more sophisticated and exhaustive list of symptomology has been made, some of Fröschels' observations on language behavior have relevance for the contemporary student of childhood language disorders. To comment on them here, I have taken some of Fröchels' statements out of context, and thus they may imply much more than Fröschels would have wanted them to. Hence, some of the following issues may well be more of what I want them to be rather than what Emil Fröschels intended.

Fröschels indicated that *"aphasia researchers must pay the closest attention to the transformation of thought into language in the case of children who are still mute* [p. 32]." This statement can be broadly interpreted to form the basis for all treatment programs. When we teach nonverbal children (a contemporary term for "mute"), we provide a responsive environment for the child so that he can experience moving, seeing, feeling, and hearing. We teach semantic relationships, or how objects interact with people, and vice versa. Hopefully, the child is "thinking" about what he is experiencing. We also provide language to enable the child to code his thoughts. The question of how the nonverbal child thinks defies a ready answer. Presumably, his repeated experiences with the physical attributes of the environment provide some mode for his behavior. Whether one can thrust a language stimulus onto this behavior and say that it is now accompanying the child's thought, or whether language, behavior, and thought can ever develop independently is an interesting question.

Fröschels said that *one must never overlook the pragmatic aspect of language.* While he did not use the term "pragmatics," he does allude to ways in which suprasegmental features might change meaning and the functions of language. Contemporary interest in pragmatics has great relevance. The volume on the subject of childhood language disorders by Bloom and Lahey (1978) presents a creative model which describes language disorders in terms of form, content, and use. Thus, some children will be primarily deficient in the form, or syntactic aspects; others will present primary problems in what they talk about or the content of their language; still others will have major impairment in the way that they use language. While aphasic children present major problems with language forms, they are also likely to use language inappropriately and may have content deficits.

It is easy to understand how these disorders interact and why they rarely appear in isolation. The language-impaired child, who has marked problems in the comprehension of syntactic forms, is often not exposed to an enriched verbal environment designed to enhance his concepts. Thus, the basic disorder of form has a maintaining effect on the child's environment. It may lead to a content disorder and ultimately a problem with the use of language. Put another way, since the child continues to manifest difficulty in comprehending and producing language, he finds it all the more difficult to initiate and maintain discourse. Hence, he withdraws from verbal interaction or becomes an inappropriate communicator. Some of these children may have adequate vocabularies and be able to produce and understand most sentence types. Yet, they do not know when to talk or how to respond appropriately in social discourse.

Attention to pragmatics emphasizes the functions of language, long overlooked in our study of language disorders. Even the tests we have developed place inordinate emphasis on certain aspects of language to the virtual exclusion of others. As Rees and Shulman (1978) point out,

> The available clinical measures of children's comprehension of spoken language do not systematically tap their ability to determine the speaker's intended meaning when different from the literal meaning, or relate a sentence to its linguistic and nonlinguistic context. These quite ordinary abilities that language users demonstrate in colloquial discourse are not assessed in routine clinical tests of comprehension [p. 217].

No one uses the kinds of language that we see in most receptive language tests (e.g., *Show me the happy little girl jumping, The wolf is keen to bite, Touch the blue circle with the red square, Point to she brings the boy the girl*)—especially not aphasic children.

In addition to the many tests that assess syntax and vocabulary, there are even more which measure a host of perceptual abilities in both visual and auditory modalities (e.g., digit repetition, identifying and copying designs). Yet, there is no reliable evidence to suggest that these skills are precursors to language ability. While there are positive correlations between scores on perceptual tests and language tests, there are many children who present perceptual deficits in the absence of language impairment, and vice versa. Skill at repeating digits or copying visual designs does not ensure skill with oral or written language.

According to Fröschels, children who appear to be deaf, but are not, may manifest an "acoustic unexcitability [p. 63]." They may have an "optical restlessness"—a term which Fröschels equated with a tendency to fixate on the visual environment. Fröschels emphasized the need to use many modalities by pointing out that "there is a possibility of stimulating the missing or delayed speech development by energetically utilizing the patient's sense of sight and touch for the absorption of the spoken model [p. 55]." He appropriately suggested that training must reduce distractibility and highlight the stimuli being taught. He described some children as "auditory amnesics," suggesting that "the more [the] restlessness (optical) decreases, the more he pays attention to the surroundings [p. 69]." Therapeutic success was achieved when the child was optically starved and had to attend to auditory stimuli. The notion of completely eliminating visual stimulation when we wish to increase our awareness of the auditory is very common even in the normal adult, who may close or avert his eyes when he is listening to something complex.

Fröschels describes the tendency of some children to cling to the visual as if this system were hypertrophied: "While hard to stimulate acoustically, without being hard of hearing, they keep clinging to optical impressions. . . . [There is] a defective excitability of the part of the brain involved [p. 81]." Many language-impaired children present behaviors that have been described with terms such as "stimulus-bound," "attentional problem," and "organically driven." It seems very plausible to suggest that "optical starvation" would be a viable approach.

BEHAVIOR PROBLEMS

Fröschels notes that many of the children who are mute have "wild behavior," a phrase which is certainly as accurate a delineation of the behaviors we describe as such terms as hyperactivity, impulsivity, and distractibility. Consistent with contemporary observations of how a child's behavior changes once he acquires the ability to use language to direct his environment, Fröschels indicates that "... wild behavior diminishes almost without exception with the progress of speech development during therapy [p. 117]."

The behavioral aberrations associated with aphasia in children have been described in many different ways, and often with terminology borrowed from the literature on the brain-damaged adult. Most common are symptoms which have become known as the "Strauss" syndrome (i.e., distractibility, hyperactivity, impulsivity), based upon the work of Alfred Strauss and his colleagues (1947, 1955). Certainly, aphasic children manifest a high degree of behavior problems, possibly because of their frustration in being unable to comprehend or produce language, or for any number of other reasons. It is challenging to hypothesize about the possibility of certain brain mechanisms controlling certain kinds of behaviors. However, the fact is that there is no mystical mechanism responsible for hyperactivity or other abberant behaviors. Indeed, these may be learned or related in some way to hormonal, metabolic, or electrochemical factors.

Behavior problems are frequently concomitant with language impairment and serve as a deterrent to learning. It seems that the child who is distractible and hyperactive either does not attend to stimuli or attends to too many stimuli. Hence, those which are supposed to be salient are rarely attended to. For some aphasic children, medication may be useful in achieving behavioral control; for others, it is not. With some, distraction-free environments have been moderately successful. Special study carrels devoid of multicolored pictures or objects presumably help the child to attend to those stimuli he is expected to, rather than to those which are irrelevant. Regardless of the intervention procedures that are used, achieving some control of attending behavior in the aphasic child is essential and often must precede any serious attempt to teach language.

LINGUISTIC CORRELATES

The assessment and treatment of the aphasic child continues to be a very challenging endeavor. My own experience with the problem began more than 15 years ago, in conjunction with a postdoctoral fellowship to study language-impaired children at the Scottish Rite Institute for Childhood Aphasia, directed by Jon Eisenson, then located at the Stanford University School of Medicine in Palo Alto, California. At that time, the literature was fairly sparse. Most of the terminology was borrowed from adult neurology. West, Ansberry, and Carr (1957) referred to an "infantile aphasia," and said little more than to indicate that it was not as clear as the "classical" picture. Myklebust (1954) had proposed a specific list of symptoms which would help clinicians differentiate the aphasic child from other disorders. However, armed with the checklist in hand, this clinician soon learned that the behaviors of most language-impaired children were not readily accessible to checklisting. The nature and degree of the symptomology varied so much from child to child that it seemed futile to have to select one global label from among a few. One early encounter was with a child who was functioning on a retarded level, had a hearing loss, was described as "having a flavor of autism," and eventually was classified as aphasic. It became apparent that the developmental and behavioral histories as well as the evaluation profiles were markedly disparate from child to child.

An examination of the literature of the 1950s and 1960s reveals how much we have grown since then in our understanding of the nature of language deviance in children. Myklebust (1954) used traditional adult classifications and described the disturbances in young children in terms of the reciprocal relationships between inner, receptive, and expressive language. Thus, if the "inner" language (a term I find elusive and mystical) is retarded, it is expected that both receptive and expressive language would be impaired. Similarly, if receptive language were impaired, it would delay development of the inner and expressive language. Barry (1961) suggested that clinicians observe the quality of the responses. "Does the child answer in jargon, gesture, single words, phrases, sentences, telegraphic speech? Are these reversals of syllables, words, phrases? Does he leave off word endings? [p. 8]" McGinnis (1963) delineated one type of aphasia which involved the use of jargon she referred to as "scribble" speech, and another as a "jargon pattern interspersed with intelligible words or phrases relative to a situation or work stimulus in a question to which they cannot give a direct answer [p. 42]."

There was a tendency to adhere to the rigid guidelines of adult aphasia and plant these characteristics onto children. Major emphasis was on the search for neurological, perceptual–motor, and intellectual correlates of language problems in children. Adaptations of instruments like the Bender–Gestalt Visual Motor Test were rampant, and when the Illinois Test of Psycholinguistic Abilities (ITPA) became available, we were able to do a more sophisticated language evaluation. Until that time, we only had our eyes, ears, some common objects, and the venerable Peabody Picture Vocabulary Test.

We did several studies with aphasic children, including the administration of the ITPA (Stark, 1966), finding that for most of these children the auditory–verbal subtests were much too sophisticated and that the children tended to have highly individual patterns even in visual areas. The language characteristics of the aphasic child

> are often similar to those of a young normal child. Thus, he may omit plural endings, confuse verb tenses and personal pronouns. . . . One seven-year-old boy said, *No home Jeannie* (his sister) and *No cartoons on . . . on Rawhide*. He tended to reverse the orders of words, omit the verbs and articles, and produce utterances which were reduced in length [Stark, Foster, Giddan, Gottsleben, & Wright, 1968, p. 149].

Just at the time when we were becoming increasingly frustrated in our attempt to isolate the aphasic syndrome in children, and bogged down with the search for medical and psychological correlates, a new interest in language acquisition was emerging. The work of Chomsky (1957), Brown and Bellugi (1964), Smith and Miller (1966), and others was to have important implications for the language-impaired child. Menyuk (1963), Lee (1966), and Carrow (1968) were among the first to describe the specific nature of the language-impaired child's deviant syntax. Experimental editions of new tests such as the Northwestern Syntax Screening Test (Lee, 1969), Test for Auditory Comprehension of Language (Carrow, 1968), and the Assessment of Childrens Language Comprehension (Foster, Giddan, & Stark, 1969) emerged. Tests such as these and a revised ITPA provided for the many clinicians who were interested in childhood language disorders.

In the 1970s, the more ambitious effort of describing the nature of the language impairment rather than assigning an age-equivalent score took root. At the Institute for Childhood Aphasia, Morehead and Ingram (1973) studied the language of 15 normal and 15 aphasic children, based upon a corpus elicited during free play and interactions with clinicians or the parents. Their results demonstrated that these children did not have qualitatively different language than normally developing children. They postulated a generalized representational deficit, à la Piaget, whose work was also becoming increasingly popular. They also noted that the aphasic child failed to use language as creatively as a normal child. This kind of research led to the development of more formal language sampling procedures (Tyack & Gottsleben, 1974), and had a significant effect on the assessment and management of the language-impaired child. To illustrate, the following is excerpted from the file folder of a 6-year-old aphasic child whom we have been seeing at the Queens College Speech and Hearing Center for more than 3 years:

> Analysis of a language sample according to the Tyack–Gottsleben procedure indicated that K's word–morpheme index was 5.29 placing him within linguistic level V.

Sentence length ranged from 2–13 morphemes. Forms such as auxiliary (*is, are, were*), copula (*is*), pronouns (*they, he*), demonstratives (*those*) appeared inconsistently and the following forms at or below the assigned linguistic level did not appear:

LEVEL	FORM
III	Plural -*ez*
IV	Present tense, third singular, -*s*, -*z*, -*ez*
IV	Possessive—'*s* (*z*)
IV	Copula—*are, am, 'm*
IV	Modals—*will, could, shall*
V	Pronouns—*our, her* (possessive), *her* (object), *its*
V	Prepositions—*down, off, over, under, near, like, through, by*
V	Modals—*won't, gotta, would, may, might*

The child (K) has been improving consistently but still manifests difficulties in syntax and articulation. During the current semester, work on the contracted negative copula and auxiliary forms (*isn't, aren't*) was continued. This training was done in the context of communication games and eventually moved to activities where more spontaneous usage was required. K's error in the use of negative involves omission of the copula (*It not big*) or auxiliary (*They not riding*) and, at times, confusion between singular and plural forms. In general, K has responded well to training and seems to be aware of the rules for forming the negative. At this point, it would be appropriate to return to work on the copula and auxiliary forms (*is, are, was, were*) in affirmative sentences and to further explore K's understanding of singular–plural agreement in this area. (Training on the copula and auxiliary has been done indirectly while teaching other syntactic forms, such as the present progressive.)

This excerpt is merely a portion of an end-of-semester report, but it does demonstrate that our procedures for describing language behavior in 1978 are very different from those of 20 years ago. We have learned much about child language during the past two decades, and the continuing search for efficient ways to describe and modify deviant language in the aphasic child continues to have highest priority.

PERCEPTUAL DEFICITS

It has taken considerable thought to know how to deal with the perceptual characteristics of the language-impaired, perhaps because they are so obviously a part of the syndrome. The old "chicken or egg" question can be easily applied to the issue of the relationship of perceptual impairments to language disorders. The evidence that auditory perceptual problems are very common in children with language disorders is overwhelming. There have been dozens of clinical and controlled laboratory studies demonstrating that aphasic children have deficits in skills such as auditory discrimination, memory, sequencing, closure, figure–ground, and so on. Some investigators have posited that these deficits are responsible for the language impairment.

The search to discover perceptual aberrations has characterized the assessment of children with language and learning disabilities for many years. Rather than examine the language per se, there are extensive batteries designed to uncover deficits in peripheral skills. We may assess the child's responses to nonlinguistic stimuli, such as tones that vary in frequency and intensity, meaningless sounds or digits. While some of the tasks include so-called linguistic stimuli such as discriminating between minimally different word pairs or guessing the word from individually produced phoneme segments, they have not dealt with the ability to discriminate language—which is more than isolated tones, words, and sounds.

In a study of the auditory processing abilities of aphasic children, Lowe and Campbell (1965) demonstrated that these children needed significantly more time to process nonlinguistic auditory stimuli such as sequences of high and low tones. Their performance on standardized tests of sequencing ability was also deficient (Stark, 1967), and there was increasing support for the clinical observation that these children had primary deficits in the temporal ordering of speech. In effect, they would seem to transpose sounds and words, and be unable to imitate sentence strings in the correct order. Stark, Poppen, and May (1967) reported an experimental study in which these children had difficulty sequencing words that were presented auditorily. Even when the response mode was modified so they could press panels that displayed the items visually, their ability to remember the correct order in which the words were presented was markedly different. McReynolds (1966) studied the sound discrimination abilities of these children under optimal conditions in an environment that included a lever-press response and continuous reinforcement. She found that the aphasic children required more trials to reach criterion and had most difficulty discriminating phonemes when they were embedded in context. Hence, while the child was able to discriminate among two sounds in isolation, when the same sounds were placed in a phonetic context in which only those sounds varied, there was significantly more difficulty.

With such variables as the nature of the stimuli (e.g., linguistic versus nonlinguistic) and the length of the interstimulus interval to consider, Rosenthal (1972) studied the responses of aphasic children to synthesized linguistic stimuli (fricative–affricate pairs) and nonlinguistic stimuli (tone–noise). He found that the aphasic children performed poorly at the ordering of the stimuli regardless of the length of the interstimulus interval. Further, he found that the temporal distinctions provided most difficulty. The most comprehensive series of studies of the discrimination and sequencing abilities of aphasic children were done by Tallal and Piercy (1973, 1974, 1975) and Tallal (1976). They used linguistic and nonlinguistic stimuli in many different experimental conditions to demonstrate that the aphasic child does have a variety of auditory processing deficits, the latest of which is related to the rate at which these stimuli are being presented.

It is easy to become disenchanted with the continued search for perceptual problems in the light of the overwhelming amount of evidence that they do exist. All too often, we see only that part of the elephant which we touch, and much of the correlational research that continues to pervade the literature is somewhat regressive.

CONCLUSION

Happily, many innovative and constructive approaches to the diagnosis and management of the language-impaired child are emerging. As already mentioned, we are becoming increasingly disenchanted with the standardized test in our assessment procedure. Many clinicians are investing their time in more naturalistic language-sampling procedures. There is a healthy respect for the many variables that operate to facilitate language growth, including the role of the parents, teacher, siblings, and peers. Language ability is seen as part of a dynamic communication process, and there is increased emphasis on what a talker accomplishes with his utterances. The sterility of highly programmed syntax teaching kits and the artificiality of the language that characterizes most clinical sessions has become apparent. Sophisticated clinicians who work with language-impaired children are beginning to appreciate the importance of having the children experience meaningful encounters with the environment. They are attempting to address language learning as a process that evolves from intensive and genuine human interaction—a highly individual endeavor that requires a tremendous investment of time and energy. We have indeed come a long way since Fröschels wrote his book, but we still have a long way to go.

REFERENCES

Barry, H. *The young aphasic child: Evaluation and training.* Washington, D.C.: Alexander Graham Bell Association, 1961.

Bloom, L., & Lahey, M. *Language development and language disorders.* New York: Wiley, 1978.

Brown, R., & Bellugi, U. Three processes in the child's acquisition of syntax. *Harvard Educational Review,* 1964, **34**, 133–151.

Carrow, M. A. The development of auditory comprehension of language structure in children. *Journal of Speech and Hearing Disorders,* 1968, **33**, 99–111.

Chomsky, N. *Syntactic structures.* The Hague: Mouton, 1957.

Foster, C., Giddan, J. J., & Stark, J. *Assessment of children's language comprehension.* Palo Alto, California: Consulting Psychologists Press, 1969.

Lee, L. Developmental sentence types: A method for comparing normal and deviant syntactic development. *Journal of Speech and Hearing Disorders,* 1966, **31**, 311–320.

Lee, L. *Northwestern Syntax Screening Test.* Evanston, Illinois: Northwestern University, 1969.

Lowe, A., & Campbell, R. Temporal discrimination in aphasoid and normal children. *Journal of Speech and Hearing Research,* 1965, **8**, 313–315.

McGinnis, M. *Aphasic children: Identification and education by the association method.* Washington, D.C.: Alexander Graham Bell Association, 1963.

McReynolds, L. Operant conditioning for investigating speech sound discrimination in aphasic children. *Journal of Speech and Hearing Research,* 1966, **9**, 519–528.

Menyuk, P. Syntactic structures in the language of children. *Child Development,* 1963, **34**, 407–422.

Morehead, D., & Ingram, D. The development of base syntax in normal and linguistically deviant children. *Journal of Speech and Hearing Research,* 1973, **16**, 330–352.

Myklebust, H. *Auditory disorders in children.* New York: Grune & Stratton, 1954.

Rees, N., & Shulman, M. I don't understand what you mean by comprehension. *Journal of Speech and Hearing Disorders,* 1978, **43**, 208–219.

Rosenthal, W. Auditory and linguistic interaction in development aphasia: Evidence from two studies of auditory processing. *Stanford University Papers and Reports on Child Language Development,* 1972, **4**, 19–35.

Smith, F., & Miller, G. (Eds.) *The genesis of language.* Cambridge: M.I.T. Press, 1966.

Stark, J. A comparison of the performance of aphasic children on three sequencing tests. *Journal of Communication Disorders,* 1967, **1**, 31–34.

Stark, J. Performance of aphasic children on the ITPA. *Exceptional Children,* 1966, **33**, 153–161.

Stark, J., Foster, C., Giddan, J., Gottsleben, R., & Wright, T. Teaching the aphasic child. *Exceptional Child,* 1968, **35**, 149–154.

Stark, J., Poppen, R., & May, M. Effects of alterations of prosodic features on the sequencing performance of aphasic children. *Journal of Speech and Hearing Research,* 1967, **10**, 849–855.

Strauss, A. A., & Kephart, N. C. *Psychopathology and education of the brain-injured child* (Vol. II). New York: Grune & Stratton, 1955.

Strauss, A. A., & Lentinen, L. E. *Psychopathology and education of the brain-injured child* (Vol. I). New York: Grune & Stratton, 1947.

Tallal, P. Rapid auditory processing in normal and disordered language development. *Journal of Speech and Hearing Research,* 1976, **19**, 561–571.

Tallal, P., & Piercy, M. Developmental aphasia: Impaired rate of nonverbal processing as a function of sensory modality. *Neuropsychologia,* 1973, **11**, 389–398.

Tallal, P., & Piercy, M. Developmental aphasia: Rate of auditory processing and selective impairment of consonant perception. *Neuropsychologia,* 1974, **12**, 1–11.

Tallal, P., & Piercy, M. Developmental aphasia: The perception of brief vowels and extended stop consonants. *Neuropsychologia,* 1975, **13,** 69–74.

Tyack, D., & Gottsleben, R. *Language sampling, analysis and training: A handbook for teachers and clinicians.* Palo Alto, California: Consulting Psychologists Press, 1974.

West, R., Ansberry, M., & Carr, A. *The rehabilitation of speech.* (3rd ed.) New York: Harper Bros., 1957.

Chapter 4

STROKES IN CHILDHOOD I: COMMUNICATIVE INTENT, EXPRESSION, AND COMPREHENSION AFTER LEFT HEMISPHERE ARTERIOPATHY IN A RIGHT-HANDED NINE-YEAR-OLD

Maureen Dennis

INTRODUCTION

Cerebral damage sustained in childhood, after language has developed but before it is fully mastered, causes a disruption of linguistic function. The language of children with post-infantile focal injury could reveal how the brain modulates a volatile and partially acquired linguistic system. What must first be understood is how the component skills of language disintegrate and re-form in a brain where a temporally ordered developmental process is superimposed on a topical lesion.

Some consensus exists about the general nature of the language disruption after post-infantile cerebral damage. Expressive problems, ranging from mild articulation difficulties to mutism, are common but comprehension disorders are rare (Bernhardt, 1885; Freud, 1897; Guttmann, 1942; Byers & McLean, 1962; Alajouanine & Lhermitte, 1965; Benson, 1972; Geschwind, 1972; Assal & Campiche, 1973).

Interpretation of the consensus is not obvious. The first problems are ones of interpretation and definition. The reported dissociation between expression and comprehension has usually been given a circular or post hoc explanation. Alajouanine and Lhermitte (1965), for example, argue that expression is of "greater complexity" (p. 657) than comprehension, but present no independent evidence for this assertion aside from the observations of which the explanation is a summary, that is, the greater

45

incidence of expressive problems in their sample of childhood aphasics. In most instances, the measures of expression and comprehension are not specified; even in recent studies (e.g., Hécaen, 1976), there is no attempt to assess the relative difficulty of the comprehension and expression measures.

A more basic problem is conceptual. The usual frame of reference for describing language performance in children with post-infantile focal lesions is the adult aphasic syndrome, rather than the language system with which the child operated at the time of the trauma. Statements such as the following one by Assal and Campiche (1973)

> A la relative monotonie de l'aphasie traumatique de l'enfant s'oppose la symptomatologie diversifiée de l'adulte où tous les grands syndromes classiques et parfois des formes dissociées très pures s'observent . . . [p. 403].

imply that brain damage rather than degree of linguistic development is responsible for the differences in lesion-induced symptoms between the child and the adult. One might reasonably ask why brain damage could be expected to produce the aphasias of adulthood in a child whose language system possessed a different set of dissociations from that of an adult at the time of the injury.

Exactly how the child's brain is organized for language is not clear. The existing evidence is at least superficially inconsistent. Some authors argue that similar problems are found regardless of within- and between-hemisphere lesion localization (e.g., Assal & Campiche, 1973), while others present variations in language symptomatology depending on the site of the injury (e.g., Hécaen, 1976). This discrepancy may be more apparent than real, reflecting only the heterogeneous etiologies and lesions in the childhood aphasic samples studied. Hécaen (1976) and Alajouanine and Lhermitte (1965) both sum trauma, tumor, meningitis and arteriopathy cases in calculating their percentages of language-disordered children; yet the etiology of the lesion has been shown to be significant in predicting long-term language status in childhood aphasics: both Guttmann (1942) and van Dongen and Loonen (1977) report that children with vascular lesions recover language less well than those with traumatic injuries. There is even less a priori reason to assume that the effects on language of slow-onset lesions like tumors would be identical to those of acute-onset strokes and trauma. The reported childhood aphasia cases, further, vary widely in how well their cerebral lesion has been identified. Those studies with clear evidence of lesion localization do in fact show a functional representation of language similar in at least some aspects to that in the adult brain. Hécaen (1976), for example, reported disorders of auditory verbal comprehension only in cases with temporal lobe lesions.

A further problem in attempting to describe the post-infantile neural systems of language is that questionable inferences are drawn about the language representation in the child's brain based only on the analogy with clinico-pathological correlations in the adult. Assal and Campiche (1973), for example, juxtapose the three premises that (1) children show expressive language problems regardless of lesion site, (2) adult left-handers show expressive problems regardless of lesion site, and (3) adult left-handers have diffuse representation in the brain; then draw the inference that children may have a diffuse cerebral organization of language. The point is not whether either the premises or the inference is factually true, but rather whether language in the child's brain can best be understood by a process of analogy with adult language symptoms and adult lesion sites.

What need to be defined are, first, the characteristic dimensions of language at different points throughout childhood; and, second, the conditions under which focal cerebral injury can shift each language component below that performance which would represent normal age expectation. Of particular interest is the nature of language comprehension in children who have sustained lesions that would disrupt this function in the mature brain.

A most clearly defined and conceptually sophisticated view of comprehension after early childhood aphasia comes from Fröschels (1918).[1]

Are we dealing with a complete disappearance of phenomena stemming from erstwhile infantile perceptions, that is, in the words of Semon, with a destruction of the engram; or are we only facing the inability to pronounce the engram? But even here the distinction should at least be made as to whether the patient succeeds in experiencing the engram within himself but is unable to communicate it, or whether this function also can no longer be activated.

Conforming to nature even before the occurrence of comprehension, some concepts of understanding must exist in the child's brain.

Comprehension certainly also depends again on a certain affective selection process by the inner person, whereby the need for expression may take charge.

An impetus of feeling "attitude" or "situation of consciousness" is inherent in the formulation of speech as well as in the interplay of thought.

In Fröschels' framework, expression is separated from the comprehension of what is expressed, and both are dissociated from communicative

1. The following extracts are from the translation found in this volume.

intent. One notes both the methodological soundness of evaluating different aspects of the same utterance, and the curiously modern tone of the interest in pragmatic communication.

My purpose in this chapter is to apply to the language of a 9-year-old girl, victim of an aphasic stroke, a slightly more modern cast of Fröschels' questions. Does her comprehension function at a higher age level than her expression? Can she understand, in some tacit sense, the correct structure of her own agrammatic utterances? Which pragmatic schemata can her disordered language system succeed in communicating?

CASE HISTORY OF A NINE-YEAR-OLD GIRL

Onset of Symptoms

JM, a right hander, showed a normal educational–developmental course until the age of 9 years, 9 months, when she suddenly collapsed while playing. Although there was no loss of consciousness, she was noted to be trembling and speaking in a garbled manner. Within an hour, the trembling abated but the right side of the body was limp. After a 10-day stay in a country hospital with the diagnosis of hysterical conversion reaction, JM was admitted to the Hospital for Sick Children in Toronto. Examination revealed the right hand to be held in semi-flexion by the left, and a wide-based gait involving circumduction and drop of the right foot. Speech was garbled, and she appeared to have clinical difficulty in both understanding and using language.

Investigations

A brain scan demonstrated an increased area of uptake on the left side. Computerized axial tomography showed a large area of cerebral edema located in the left temporo-parietal region, a finding felt to be consistent with infarction. Bilateral internal carotid arteriograms revealed arteriopathic changes involving the left side of the brain: the vessels involved were the supraclinoid portion of the middle cerebral artery and the horizontal portion of the left anterior cerebral artery; and there were also small branch occlusions involving the peripheral smaller vessels in the region of the frontal, parietal, and occipital areas. A large thrombus involving the left angular artery was also observed. The EEG showed poorly organized activity but no focal

or epileptogenic features. Visual fields appeared to be intact. JM was diag-
nosed as a case of acquired expressive and receptive aphasia with right
hemiparesis due to arteriopathy of the left cerebral hemisphere.

LANGUAGE FUNCTION

The Neurosensory Center Comprehensive Examination for Aphasia
(Spreen & Benton, 1969) was administered on two occasions, the first 2
weeks and the second 3 months after the onset of speech and motor
symptoms. Figure 4.1 shows JM's performance in each session on the 20
subtests, plotted against the scores of normal children of different ages
(Gaddes & Crockett, 1975).

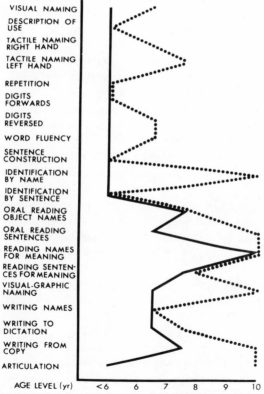

Figure 4.1. *Profile of scores on the Spreen–Benton aphasia battery 2 weeks (solid line) and 3
months (dotted line) after onset of speech and motor symptoms. The age level refers to the scores in the
normative sample. (From Gaddes & Crockett, 1975.)*

Two Weeks Post-Stroke

Most oral language functions have deteriorated to a level below that of a 6-year-old. Naming to visual confrontation is below the 6-year-old level, with phonemic paraphasias (*brush* → /brɛt/), semantic paraphasias (*padlock* → /ki/), and random misnamings (*shoelace* → /lif/). Tactile naming is poor in both hands. It is evident that this is not an asterognosia, however, since JM is accurate in performing tactile–visual matches of the objects she is unable to name. Tactile naming shows the error pattern typical of visual naming: phonemic paraphasias (*scotch tape* → /skeks/), semantic paraphasias (*cup* → /bɒtl/), and random misnamings. Throughout the naming tasks, JM was perseverative, producing /ki/ as the response to several successive items. Word fluency and sentence construction are both at a 6-year-old level. In consequence of her impairment in formulating sentences, JM is also poor at providing descriptions of the use of common objects. The error pattern suggests that hers is an aphasic rather than agnostic disturbance (e.g., *plate* → /bir/). In addition, JM showed a tendency to use emotional expressions in lieu of functional description (e.g., she described the use of a pistol as /pa ʊ/). JM had difficulty in articulating single words and in repeating sentences, and her repetitions show phoneme omissions, substitutions and confusions (*tall*→/tod/); *notice*→/nots ɪ/; *service*→/d ɜʊ ɪ/; *shoulder*→/ ʃod ɚ/). Comprehension of the names of simple objects and identification by sentence (the Token Test commands) are impaired to the same extent, in relation to age, as the expressive language skills of naming and repetition.

Written language functions are relatively better preserved than oral functions. JM's capacity to write names for visually presented objects, to read names and sentences for meaning, and to write to dictation are all at a higher level than the oral processing of the same content. Oral output was in fact disruptive of reading. When JM was asked to read some simple commands (e.g., *Show me a circle*) and execute them, she became confused and bothered if she read the command aloud: oral output impaired her performance of the task.

On the basis of her language performance, JM shows a significant degree of expressive and receptive aphasia in relation to the language skills expected of a 9-year-old. The capacity to generate phoneme sequences, to produce names, and to provide use descriptions are all impaired. In situations where comprehension depends upon the processing of nonredundant oral information, JM also performs poorly in relation to age expectations. Written language is less affected than oral functions in terms of the age levels to which performance corresponds. When visual linguistic material uses oral output channels, as in oral reading, JM is disturbed because her productions fail to match her internalized word. The visual representation of language appears to be functionally separate from the oral, in the sense that it operates at a higher, more intact level.

JM obtains an age score of 7 years 6 months on the Porteus Mazes Vineland Revision, a test of visually guided route-finding. The test was done with her impaired right hand.

Three Months Post-Stroke

There has been an improvement in naming to visual confrontation. The bilateral tactile anomia is now resolved to a milder form, evident mainly on the right hand. Articulation has improved dramatically, and JM is now able to pronounce many phonemes and blends that she could not manage before. She is still not properly fluent, and continues to have difficulty in repeating sentences. There is no measurable improvement in the ability to construct simple sentences from target words. JM is now able to understand single words and short commands, but her comprehension of longer nonredundant oral commands is still quite impaired.

Written language abilities are relatively well-preserved. Oral reading of simple sentences, reading names for meaning, reading short sentences for meaning, visual–graphic naming, writing to dictation and writing from copy are all functioning at an age-appropriate level.

Three months after her stroke, JM shows an improvement in the oral processing of single words and short utterances. Her expression and understanding of more complex language information has still not recovered. Comprehension and expression appear to reform in parallel, as evidenced by the age levels of the scores.

On the Porteus Mazes Extension Series, JM obtained a score of 9 years.

JM'S METALINGUISTIC JUDGMENTS OF HER OWN AGRAMMATISMS

JM shows a comprehension deficit which appears to parallel her impaired expressive language. This raises the broader question of the extent to which she has some tacit knowledge of the correct structure of those utterances she produces imperfectly. To address this issue, she was asked to make metalinguistic judgments of the interrelationships of words in sentences she had produced.

A sample of spontaneous speech was taken during the Three Months Post-Stroke language assessment. The examiner told JM the fairy tales of Little Red Riding Hood, The Frog Prince, and Goldilocks, using puppets to represent the characters in the stories (e.g., Little Red Riding Hood, The Wolf, and Grandmother). JM was allowed to manipulate the puppets provided that she retold the story. By increasing the motivational value of speaking and by allowing her to bring to the task both information in the examiner's tale and any other memories she possessed of the story, the test format maximized speech productivity and helped to overcome her tendency to avoid speech situations.

Nine utterances were selected from the transcripts of her spontaneous story retelling. Three had been produced correctly (*Where're you goin'?*, *He goes to bed*, and *He's puttin' on the tat*). Three had been agrammatic on at least one occasion but produced correctly at other times (*Too hot*, later produced as *It's too hot; Someone is my bed*, later produced as *Someone is in my bed;* and *Frog come*, later produced as *The frog came*). Three had been agrammatic and were never correctly produced (*Big ears you have, She want sittin' in the chair*, and *Now carry him bathroom*). These three clusters of utterances were termed, respectively, Full Productive Control Sentences, Partial Productive Control Sentences, and No Productive Control Sentences.

JM was asked to make relatedness judgments for pairs of words from all the 3-word left-to-right triads of the correct form of each utterance. She first read the written sentence, which was then placed in view throughout the test. The task, as in Zurif, Caramazza, and Myerson (1972) and Dennis and Whitaker (1976), was to judge which pair of the triad was most related and which least related. Two test sessions were given, 1 month apart, and the judgments from each session pooled for the analysis. The similarity judgments were tabulated as a word-relatedness matrix and an algorithmic scaling procedure used to induce a phrase-structure tree (e.g., Zurif, Caramazza, & Myerson, 1972; Martin, 1970). The minimum distance tree graphs are shown in Figure 4.2.

A linear strategy appears to have been developed by JM for some relatedness judgments. The 4-word sentences are perceived as two 2-word groupings. This strategy is used in Full Productive Control Sentences (*Where are you going?*, *He goes to bed*), Partial Productive Control Sentences (*It is too hot*) and No Productive Control Sentences (*She wanted to sit*). The linear strategy is used for making similarity groupings regardless of how grammatically the sentence was produced in context. In

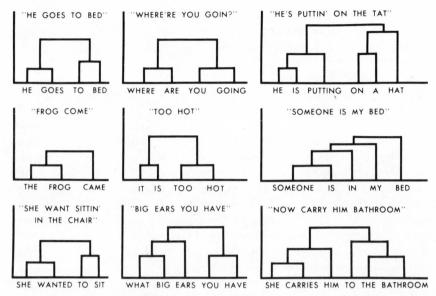

Figure 4.2. *Hierarchical clustering of sentences from JM's spontaneous speech.*

consequence, the fact that a link is perceived between the infinitive and verb stem in the cluster, *She wanted to sit*, is not evidence that JM has tacit awareness of the structure of infinitives which she omits in spontaneous speech. One of the 5-word sentences, *Someone is in my bed*, also seems to be perceived on the basis of some aspect of spatial and/or temporal (she could both see and hear the sentence throughout the task) surface word order. The tendency to respond to the surface features of the sentence regardless of its structure is also evident in the 6-word utterances, where the first and second words tend to be judged as the most related.

Some of JM's utterances were agrammatic because telegraphic. *The, It is,* and *What* omitted from *Frog come, Too hot,* and *Big ears you have* are not really critical to the message. The hierarchical clustering data, however, do not simply reflect a poor perception of elements peripheral to the core of the utterance. For example, there is a perceived link between the determiner *the* and the noun in *She carries him to the bathroom* and *The frog comes.* The status of the indefinite *a* is uncertain. In *He's putting on a hat,* JM fails to cluster the article and noun. Because of an erroneous initial transcription of her tape, she had been required to judge the indefinite determiner rather than the *the* she actually produced. JM tended not to produce *a* and *an* in speech, and she appears to show little metalinguistic control of this form. Nevertheless, the fact that she has control over one determiner does suggest that the role of at least one of the structures omitted in her spontaneous speech is better understood than her output would indicate.

There are limits to the generalizability of the hierarchical clustering data. Similarity judgments were not made in the same session as the spontaneous production of the utterances being judged. By selecting the sentences from her speech rather than from a priori linguistic dimensions, a systematic look at JM's metalinguistic comprehension is not possible. The constructions in some of the fairy tales, further, are infrequently encountered in speech (e.g., *What big ears you have!*). Nevertheless, the hierarchical clusters do not support the hypothesis that JM's agrammatisms represent a purely productive problem. She sometimes shows poor metalinguistic understanding of structures which she can produce correctly (e.g., she did not perceive the relatedness of the adjective and noun in *What big ears you have!*) and, perhaps aside from one determiner, she seems to have adopted simplified, surface or linear processing strategies for many types of complex utterances.

A STORY GRAMMAR FOR JM'S SPEECH

What kinds of information does JM's disordered language system succeed in communicating? Are there indications of a normal communicative intent discernible through her impoverished spontaneous speech? Which schemata above the level of the sentence can be observed to underlie her fragmented and sometimes agrammatic sentence structures?

Little Red Riding Hood Story

To answer these questions, a more detailed analysis was made of some of the connected speech in JM's Three Months Post-Stroke language assessment. She had been read the following story, omitting the proposition numbers.

LITTLE RED RIDING HOOD TEXT
[*adapted from a 1729 story in Opie and Opie, 1974*]
1. *Once upon a time there was a little girl.*
2. *Her mother made her a red riding hood;*
3. *after that, everybody called her The Little Red Riding Hood.*
4. *One day her mother said to her, "Go and see how your grandmother is*

5. *and take her some cake."*
6. *Little Red Riding Hood put the cake in her basket*
7. *and left to see her grandmother.*
8. *As she went through the wood,*
9. *she met a wolf.*
10. *He said, "Where are you going?"*
11. *Little Red Riding Hood said, "I'm going to see my grandmother*
12. *to take her some cake."*
13. *"Where does she live?" said the wolf.*
14. *"On the other side of the mill in the first house in the village."*
15. *"I'll go and see her too," said the wolf.*
16. *"You go this way*
17. *and I'll go that way*
18. *and we'll see who gets there first."*
19. *The wolf ran to grandmother's house the shortest way.*
20. *Little Red Riding Hood dawdled*
21. *and went by the longest way.*
22. *The wolf got there first.*
23. *He knocked at the door.*
24. *"Who's there?" said grandmother.*
25. *"Little Red Riding Hood," said the wolf.*
26. *"Oh, come in," said grandmother.*
27. *And the wolf came in,*
28. *locked grandmother in a cupboard*
29. *and put on all her clothes.*
30. *Then Little Red Riding Hood came to the house*
31. *and knocked on the door.*
32. *"Who's there," said the wolf.*
33. *Little Red Riding Hood thought her grandmother sounded funny*
34. *and she wondered if she had a cold.*
35. *"It's Little Red Riding Hood," she said.*
36. *"Come in," said the wolf.*
37. *Little Red Riding Hood came in the door*
38. *and went to the wolf in the bed.*
39. *She thought her grandmother looked funny.*
40. *"Oh, grandma, what big arms you've got!"*
41. *"All the better to hug you with!"*
42. *"Oh grandma, what big legs you've got!"*
43. *"All the better to run with!"*
44. *"Oh grandma, what big ears you've got!"*
45. *"All the better to hear you with!"*
46. *"Oh grandma, what big eyes you've got!"*
47. *"All the better to see you with!"*
48. *"Oh grandma, what big teeth you have!"*
49. *"All the better to EAT YOU UP!!"*
50. *And the wicked wolf jumped out of bed,*

51. *grabbed Little Red Riding Hood,*
52. *and then what happened?*

The following is the text of JM's retelling of the story, including interactions with the examiner, SK.

JM'S LITTLE RED RIDING HOOD TEXT

SK *So now, how does the story go, What happens?*
JM *The wolf comes*
SK *Oh, you have to say something first. How does the story start?*
JM *Look at my little basket, my mum made this, and this, and this, and my ribbon*
SK *She comes along and . . .*
JM *And say somethin'*
SK *What do they say, what does he say?*
JM *Hi, Little Red 'n Hood, where you going?*
    To Grandma's
    Well, I'm goin' too. You go this way and I'll go that way
SK *OK, then what happens?*
JM *Umm.. Come*
    Knock
    Come in
    Ahhh!
SK *What does he say?*
JM *Nothin'*
SK *Nothin? What does he do? Tell me, what's he doing?*
JM *And then he goes to bed, and then Little Red . . .*
SK *But what's he doing now? What's he doing now?*
JM *He's puttin' on the tat*
SK *And what does he do when he gets there? What else does he do?*
JM *I don't know*
SK *He puts on grandma's clothes, right? Then what happens?*
    We'll just pretend . . . OK, here, let's take this . . . What happens after he puts on grandma's clothes?
JM *He goes to bed*
    KNOCKS
    Oh grandma, you, you have big eyes!
    Say something!
SK *No, you tell me what he says. What does he say?*
JM *I don't know*
SK *She says, Oh grandma, what big arms you've got!*
JM *I know!*
SK *And what does the wolf say?*
JM *To hug you with!*

SK *Right!*
JM *Oh grandma, you have big eyes, eyes, eyes, eyes!*
SK *And what does he say?*
JM *He says, "Shut up!"*
SK *He doesn't say shut up. What does he say?*
JM *He says, um, I don't know*
SK *He says, "The better to . . .*
JM *To see you with!*
SK *Right!*
JM *Oh grandma, big ears you have, to, uh, hear you with! Oh grandma, how big is your mouth!*
SK *What does he say?*
JM *Nothin'*
SK *Oh yes he does! He says something important*
JM *To somethin' eat you with!*
SK *Right! And then what happened?*
JM *Um, somethin' ate 'im*
SK *Something ate him? Something ate who?*
JM *Her*
SK *Why'd he eat her, who's this?*
JM *A wolf*
SK *The wolf ate her, right, the wolf ate her up. And then what happened?*
JM *The, the somethin' come, the woodcutter came*
SK *And what did the woodcutter do when he got there and he saw that the wolf had eaten up Red Riding Hood?*
JM *No, she didn't*
SK *No? Oh, he didn't get a chance to eat her, did he?*
JM *No*
SK *What did the woodcutter do when he got there and saw what was happening?*
JM *He shoot him*
SK *He shot the wolf, right?*
JM *And then he'll never come again!*
SK *That's right. And what about poor granny, what happened to granny?*
JM *Granny came out*
SK *Granny came out of where?*
JM *the clothes hozeh, the closet. The closet!*
SK *Boy, its a good thing that guy came along and shot that wolf, eh? My goodness, he would've eaten both of them up, I think*
JM *Yes, all bastard!*

Story Grammar for Little Red Riding Hood

A story grammar refers to the representation of the parts of a story and how they relate to each other. Recent developments in cognitive processing suggest that the story schema determines what is encoded during comprehension and what is retrieved during recall (e.g., Thorndyke, 1977). Parsing a story divides it into levels and components. The parsing system, which consists of a set of rewrite rules, constitutes the story grammar. By applying the rewrite rules to a particular story, a tree structure representing the story schema can be obtained. This technique is one mode of access to the underlying constituents of a story, even when these are expressed imperfectly in spontaneous speech.

The story grammar written for the Little Red Riding Hood text, part of a larger story grammar study (Dennis & Lovett, 1980), is based directly on the rewrite rules of Mandler and Johnson (1977). These are summarized as follows:

Fable	→	Story and Moral
Story	→	Setting and Event Structure
Setting	→	$\begin{cases} \text{State* (and Event*)} \\ \text{Event*} \end{cases}$
State*	→	State ((and State)^n)
Event*	→	Event (($\begin{cases} \text{and} \\ \text{Then} \\ \text{Cause} \end{cases}$ Event)^n) ((and State)^n)
Event Structure	→	Episode ((Then Episode)^n)
Episode	→	Beginning Cause Development Cause Ending
Beginning	→	$\begin{cases} \text{Event*} \\ \text{Episode} \end{cases}$
Development	→	$\begin{cases} \text{Simple Reaction Cause Action} \\ \text{Complex Reaction Cause Goal Path} \end{cases}$
Simple Reaction	→	Internal Event ((Cause Internal Event)^n)
Action	→	Event
Complex Reaction	→	Simple Reaction Cause Goal
Goal	→	Internal State
Goal Path	→	$\begin{cases} \text{Attempt Cause Outcome} \\ \text{Goal Path (Cause Goal Path)}^n \end{cases}$
Attempt	→	Event*
Outcome	→	$\begin{cases} \text{Event*} \\ \text{Episode} \end{cases}$
Ending	→	$\begin{cases} \text{Event* (and Emphasis)} \\ \text{Emphasis} \\ \text{Episode} \end{cases}$
Emphasis	→	State

From Mandler and Johnson, 1977, p. 117.

SETTINGS introduce the main characters and/or the time and location of the story. EPISODES consist of three causally connected nodes, a BEGINNING, a DEVELOPMENT, and an ENDING. The BEGINNING initiates the episode. The DEVELOPMENT elaborates it, by means of a reaction on the part of the protagonist, followed by either a simple ACTION or a more complex GOAL PATH according to the extent of purpose and planning in the protagonist's behavior. A GOAL PATH consists of an ATTEMPT at goal attainment together with the OUTCOME of this attempt. The ENDING concludes the episode or the story, sometimes with a dramatic touch or EMPHASIS. Sub-episodes may be embedded in the BEGINNINGS or ENDINGS of broader episodes, or in the OUTCOMES of GOAL PATHS. Higher-level structures rewrite as terminal EVENTS and STATES. The connections between terminal nodes may be that of co-occurrence (AND), sequence (THEN), or causality (CAUSE). A fuller elaboration of the definitions of the story grammar rules is found in Mandler and Johnson (1977).

The Little Red Riding Hood tree structure, shown in Figure 4.3, was derived from the application of the rewrite rules to the Little Red Riding Hood text. Numbers in the tree structure refer to propositions in the text.

The setting of the story introduces Little Red Riding Hood and explains how she got her name. The basic or supraordinate episode takes the form of a long story (Story Episode), beginning with the mother's request that Little Red Riding Hood visit grandmother, developing the tale of the visit and ending with whatever the child supplies (Proposition 52: *And then what happened?*). The development of the Story Episode subdivides further. It involves Little Red Riding Hood's decision to accede to her mother's request and her setting off for grandmother's house. The outcome of this is a sub-episode (Wolf Episode) describing her interaction with the wolf. From the simple beginning in which she meets the wolf, the sub-episode develops in a series of goal paths forming the wolf's plan to visit grandmother, the outcome of which is that he locks grandmother in the closet. The ending of the Wolf Episode is another sub-episode (Grandmother's House Episode) covering Little Red Riding Hood's adventures at grandmother's house. The beginning itself rewrites as a sub-episode (Arrival and Doubts Episode) covering Little Red Riding Hood's anxieties about grandmother's anomalous voice, a situation resolved by her decision to enter the house. The development of the Grandmother's House Episode concerns the clarification of Little Red Riding Hood's doubts and her questioning of grandmother's identity. These activities culminate in Little Red Riding Hood's decision to ask the critical wolf-verification question (*Oh grandma, what big teeth you have!*) rather than her previous grandmother-verification questions about eyes and ears. The ending of the Grandmother's House Episode reveals the wolf's identity and character.

Using the Mandler and Johnson rewrite rules, a tree structure was

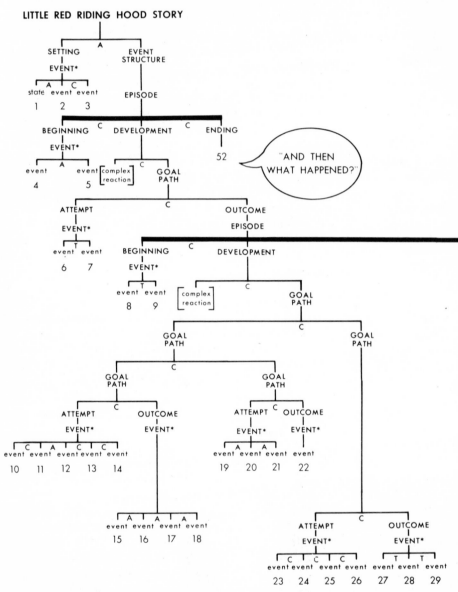

Figure 4.3. *Tree structure derived by applying Mandler–Johnson rewrite rules to canonical Little Red Riding Hood text.*

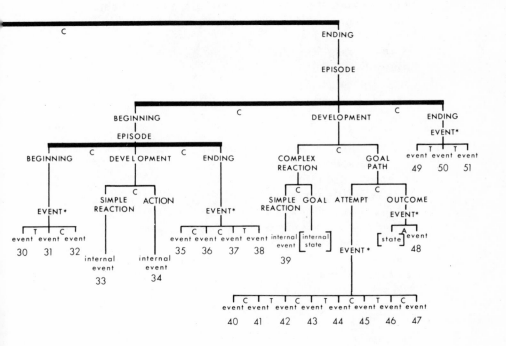

derived for JM's Little Red Riding Hood text. The propositions contained in her story were extracted from the text and numbered consecutively. It was necessary to distinguish spontaneously produced propositioins from those prompted (*What did she do? What did she say?*) or supplied (*She says, "Oh grandma, what big arms you've got!"*) by the examiner. In the following list, spontaneously produced statements are in *italic,* prompted propositions are in **bold face,** and supplied propositions are in ***bold italics.*** The numbers in brackets refer to the corresponding propositions in the canonical text.

JM'S PROPOSITION LIST

1. *The wolf comes* (9)
2. **Look at my little basket,**
3. **my mom made this, and this, and this, and my ribbon** (2)
4. *and say something, "Hi, Little Red'n Hood, where you going?"* (10)
5. *"To Grandma's"* (11)
6. *"Well, I'm going too"* (15)
7. *"You go this way* (16)
8. *and I'll go that way"* (17)
9. *Come* (22)
10. *Knock* (23)
11. *"Come in"* (26)
12. **And then he goes to bed and then Little Red** (38)
13. **He's puttin' on the tat** (29)
14. **He goes to bed** (38)
15. *KNOCKING* (non-verbal) (31)
16. *"Oh grandma, you, you have big eyes!"* (46)
17. ***"Oh grandma, what big arms you've got!"*** (40)
18. **"To hug you with"** (41)
19. *"Oh grandma, you have big eyes, eyes, eyes, eyes!"* (46)
20. **He says, "Shut up!"**
21. **"To see you with!"** (47)
22. *"Oh grandma, big ears you have!"* (44)
23. *"to, uh, hear you with!"* (45)
24. *"Oh grandma, how big is your mouth!"* (48)
25. **"To somethin' eat you with!"** (49)
26. *"Um, somethin' ate 'im"* (Q) Her (Q) A wolf (Q) No she didn't (52+)
27. *The, the somethin' come, the woodcutter come* (52+)
28. **He shoot him** (52+)
29. *And then he'll never come again* (52+)
30. **Granny came out. The clothes hozeh, the closet. The closet!** ((52+)

31. ***Boy, it's a good thing that guy came along and shot that wolf, eh? My goodness, he would've eaten both of them up, I think!"***
32. *Yes, all bastard!* (52+)

In relation to those in the canonical story, JM's propositions are semantically impoverished. Most are reduced or incompletely specified ("overgeneralized" in Fredericksen's [1975] terms). There are no clear instances of inferred or of pseudodiscriminated (more specific than the canonical form) propositions: the *Yes, all bastard!* might be argued to be an instance of inferential processing, but one could assert equally that it is an answer to the Proposition 30 supplied by the examiner; Proposition 31 is more specific than the canonical Proposition 29 (*and put on all her clothes*), but this could have been because the grandmother puppet has a lace hat which the wolf puppet dons as part of his disguise.

The tree structure formed by the application of the rewrite rules to JM's propositions is shown in Figure 4.4.

In the formation of a tree structure, the subject is not penalized for agrammatic utterances or for imperfectly expressed propositions. Credit is given for the proposition if its content is identifiable. Even under a system which makes very weak demands of the semantic and syntactic quality of utterances, JM has produced a simplified story, in which the internal structure is disordered in several ways.

Although simplified in structure, it cannot be concluded that JM's story is merely reduced to that of a younger child. First-graders' schemata for telling stories emphasize settings, the outcomes of action or the internal events motivating action: they recall settings and outcomes better than attempts (Mandler & Johnson, 1977). JM, by contrast, omits outcomes, ignores settings, and produces no internal states.

It might have been expected that JM would produce a spontaneous setting for her story, purely on the basis of the overlearned "Once upon a time" framework which is always followed by a setting. It was necessary, however, that her setting be prompted. JM has encoded the story without reference to its embedded episodic structure. The only episode in the canonical story that she produced was the overall episode, which involves the most general communicative plan (girl visits grandmother, wolf tricks girl, girl is avenged). The other episodes are produced by JM not as episodes but as a series of goal paths, the middle-level structures in the grammar hierarchy. Even the goal path structure was produced only once without prompting. Unless the examiner provided a prompt for the outcome, JM tended simply to concatenate events. Since the prompt meant that the whole exchange could then be written as a goal path, the

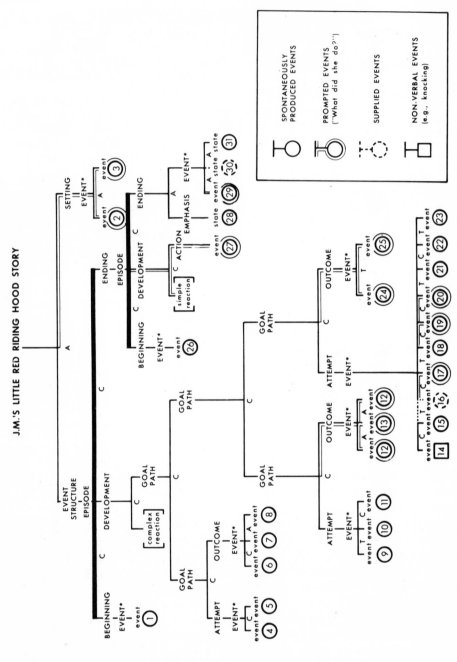

Figure 4.4. Tree structure derived by applying Mandler–Johnson rewrite rules to JM's Little Red Riding Hood text.

tree structure in Figure 4.4 certainly overestimates the complexity of JM's middle-level schemata.

In general, the more a component structure requires an overall plan for its generation, the less likely is JM to produce it spontaneously: she misses three of the four episodes in the story and four of the five attempt–outcome structures, but is able, albeit in a semantically constricted manner, to produce a fair percentage of the story events.

DISCUSSION

All three aspects of JM's language system—communicative intent, comprehension, and expression—have been disrupted by her left hemisphere arteriopathy. The deficit, demonstrably, is not exclusively one of output. JM rarely understands utterances she cannot produce, she does not have tacit comprehension of the correct structure of her agrammatic utterances, and the schemata guiding her spontaneous speech do not appear to be significantly more complex than her output.

The demonstration of parallel impairments in expression, comprehension and pragmatics suggests that language performance in the 9-year-old brain is an excellent mirror of the cognitive structures producing that language. This conflicts with earlier proposals that, since only expression is affected by brain damage in children, the child's language represents something other than her thoughts (Alajouanine & Lhermitte, 1965). Quite aside from any theoretical conclusions, the expression–comprehension dissociation does not account for JM's language on a purely descriptive level.

Two other functional dissociations, however, do characterize her language performance. The first is hierarchical. Lower-level structures (simple, single-element commands, one–two word sentences for repetition, simple determiner–noun relationships, the events in simple propositions) are relatively better preserved than more complex structures involving supraordinate schemata, embeddings, and plans. Her deficit appears to be hierarchical, but not in the simple sense of a regression to globally earlier or lower levels of function. Although some clinical measures of JM's language correspond to the overall performance of a younger child, other pragmatic structures guiding her output are disordered in a qualitatively different way.

A second dissociation is that of stimulus modality. While JM certainly could not read passages of complex verbal material, she did show a relative preservation of visual linguistic material which she could not process in its oral form; and she was easily able to read all the sentences in the hierarchical clustering test—sentences that she had previously produced agrammatically. Written language, in relation to oral, may be processed less rapidly, is less bound to stimulus sequence and provides the opportunity for reprocessing of elements missed earlier in the stimulus sequence. Whatever the reason, the visual is easier than the auditory modality for simple language material. The data provide no evidence for a necessary dependence of reading on intact auditory processing (e.g., Alajouanine & Lhermitte, 1965). Neither do they support the view that the restoration of language occurs at the expense of some nonlinguistic visual functions (e.g., Byers & McLean, 1962): JM's visually guided route-finding was back to age-appropriate levels by 3 months after the stroke. Her impairment is one of auditory linguistic processing.

Such impairments would commonly follow the same etiological process and the same lesion in an adult brain. What this indicates is a general functional parallel rather than an identity of mechanism in the way language is represented across the age range of language users. In the neural processing of language in children and adults, similar linguistic constituents may prove to be affected differently by the same etiology and lesion; different components may yet be impaired to a similar extent by diverse etiologies and lesions.

Impaired language results from temporo-parietal lesions in a child whose language is partially developed. The prior acquisition of language need not have been mediated by the same neural system shown to be necessary for sustaining it, once established. And a brain lesion that disrupts partially developed language may, in addition, truncate the end stages of acquisition. The present tests were made at the time of JM's brain insult and 3 months afterwards; it remains to be shown that she does recover normal language with respect to both linguistic skills operating at a time of the stroke and those which, in a normal developmental course, would be acquired only after the age of 9. Until this is established, it is premature to speculate about the neural mechanisms mediating recovery (for example, to guess that recovery should involve language shifting [Benson, 1972] to the right hemisphere). Whatever its long-term result, it cannot be disputed that the short-term effect of JM's stroke has been to change the fundamental organization, not just the output mechanism, of her language.

ACKNOWLEDGMENTS

This research was supported by an Ontario Mental Health Foundation Scholarship and by Ontario Mental Health Individual Award Grant No. 704. I thank C. R. Fitz for discussing the radiological material, Judith Sugar for help with the data analysis, and Stewart Cameron for drawing the tree structures. I am grateful to Maureen Lovett for her assistance with the story grammar text and structures, and to Sally Kuehn, without whose skill in eliciting spontaneous speech there would be none.

REFERENCES

Alajouanine, T., & Lhermitte, F. Acquired aphasia in children. *Brain,* 1965, **88,** 653–662.

Assal, G., & Campiche, R. Aphasie et troubles du langage chez l'enfant après contusion cérébrale. *Neuro-Chirurgie,* 1973, **19,** 399–406.

Benson, D. F. Language disturbances of childhood. *Clinical Proceedings Children's Hospital of Washington,* 1972, **28,** 93–100.

Bernhardt, M. Ueber die spastiche Cerebralparalyse im Kindesalter (Hemiplegia spastica infantilis), nebst einem Excurse über "Aphasie bei Kindern". *Archiv für Pathologische Anatomie und Physiologie und für Klinische Medicin,* 1885, **102,** 26–80.

Byers, R. K., & McLean, W. T. Etiology and course of certain hemiplegias with aphasia in childhood. *Pediatrics,* 1962, **29,** 376–383.

Dennis, M., & Lovett, M. Story schemas in the isolated left and right hemispheres of children with hemidecortication in infancy. (1980, in preparation).

Dennis, M., & Whitaker, H. A. Language acquisition following hemidecortication: Linguistic superiority of the left over the right hemisphere. *Brain and Language,* 1976, **3,** 404–433.

Frederiksen, C. H. Effects of context-induced processing operations on semantic information acquired from discourse. *Cognitive Psychology,* 1975, **7,** 139–166.

Freud, S. *Infantile Cerebral Paralysis.* 1897. L. A. Russin (Trans.), Coral Gables, Florida: University of Miami Press, 1968.

Gaddes, W. H., & Crockett, D. J. The Spreen–Benton Aphasia Tests, normative data as a measure of normal language development. *Brain and Language,* 1975, **2,** 257–280.

Geschwind, N. Disorders of higher cortical function in children. *Clinical Proceedings Children's Hospital of Washington,* 1972, **28,** 261–272.

Gold, A. P., Challenor, Y. B., Gilles, F. H., Hilal, S. P., Leviton, A., Rollins, E. I., Solomon, G. E., & Stein, B. M. Strokes in children. *Stroke,* 1973, **4,** 1009–1052.

Guttmann, E. Aphasia in children. *Brain,* 1942, **65,** 205–219.

Hécaen, H. Acquired aphasia in children and the ontogenesis of hemispheric functional specialization. *Brain and Language,* 1976, **3,** 114–134.

Mandler, J. M., & Johnson, N. S. Remembrance of things parsed: Story structure and recall. *Cognitive Psychology,* 1977, **9,** 111–151.

Martin, E. Towards an analysis of subjective phrase structure. *Psychological Bulletin,* 1970, **74,** 153–166.

Opie, I., & Opie, P. *The Classic Fairy Tales.* London: Oxford University Press, 1974.

Shillito, J. Carotid arteritis: A cause of hemiplegia in childhood. *Journal of Neurosurgery,* 1964, **21,** 540–551.

Spreen, O., & Benton, A. L. *Neurosensory Center Comprehensive Examination for Aphasia* (Edition A, Manual of Instructions). Victoria: Neuropsychology Laboratory, University of Victoria, 1969.

Thorndyke, P. W. Cognitive structures in comprehension and memory of narrative discourse. *Cognitive Psychology,* 1977, **9,** 77–110.

van Dongen, H. R., & Loonen, M. C. B. Factors related to prognosis of acquired aphasia in children. *Cortex,* 1977, **13,** 131–136.

Zurif, E. B., Caramazza, A., & Myerson, R. Grammatical judgments of agrammatic aphasics. *Neuropsychologia,* 1972, **10,** 405–417.

Chapter 5

THEORIES OF READING AND LANGUAGE DEVELOPMENT: AN INTERPRETIVE REVIEW

Eric R. Brown

INTRODUCTION

Emil Fröschels' contributions to the study of childhood aphasia (see this volume) were substantial and are still of theoretical interest today. As other authors in this volume observe, although the terminology has evolved, Fröschels' insights remain fresh, and a number of topics he raised have yet to be explored. In this chapter two contrasting theories of reading and language development are presented; the consequences of assuming either of these theoretical interpretations of normal function bear directly on the interpretation of childhood dysphasia and dyslexia. As we shall see, the latter of these two positions, the mediated approach, is particularly germane to Fröschels' ideas on childhood aphasia.

On the walls of Hayden Planetarium, appropriately enshrined, is the following quotation attributed to the American astronomer Harlow Shapley: "A hypothesis or theory is clear, decisive, and positive, but it is believed by no one but the man who created it. Experimental findings, on the other hand, are messy inexact things which are believed by everyone except the man who did the work." Until quite recently, theory making has been a noticeably absent activity in basic research on reading. I think it fair to say that experimental psychology earlier in this century had abandoned reading to educational researchers on the grounds that it was a far too complex human activity to be amenable to the learning

69

theory paradigms of American academic psychology. And the educational researchers had in turn engaged in a seemingly endless round of doubtful methodological comparison studies on the best way to teach reading, culminating in the monumental U.S. Office of Education first-grade reading studies of the mid 1960s, which generally concluded that it was the "teacher variable" that was significant in successful reading programs.

Most philosophies of science would maintain that this was a strange state of affairs, given the importance of reading to society as a whole. Normally progress in a scientific area is marked by the vital interaction of theory and methodology, neither advancing very far without the other. Thus by about 1966 the literature on reading was filled with calls for new integrative theory that would break the deadlock on further progress towards universal literacy and alleviate severe reading disabilities by reexamining the basic reading process itself.

At about the same time there was a rapid growth of interest in the relatively new interdisciplinary field of psycholinguistics. Psycholinguistics, which is concerned with the basic processes of language, has its historical roots at least as far back as the 1953 Seminar on Psycholinguistics organized by Thomas Sebeok at the University of Indiana, but it was the infusion of Noam Chomsky's linguistic theory in the latter part of that decade which gave impetus to the rapid development of psycholinguistic studies in the early and mid 1960s. John Carroll, Charles Osgood, George Miller, and Roger Brown are important figures in cognitive psychology who were instrumental in capitalizing on the availability of this theory to bring about major paradigm shifts in the psychological study of language acquisition and language performance.

Without detailing the nature of Chomsky's theoretical contribution here, we may note that there was suddenly available a significant body of explicit theory on the syntactic structure of English. Furthermore, Chomsky claimed that his theoretical constructs ought to be relevant to psychological investigations of how we produce and understand language in general. With this elaborated theory, experimental psychologists were willing to work with fewer numbers of subjects than is traditional in experimental psychology, and to entertain the possibility that elaborated hypothetical or mental mechanisms could contribute to the explanatory power of crucial experiments on language. Cognitive psychology, like reading studies, had been in a period of almost total eclipse until the rapid growth of interest in psycholinguistic paradigms. But as testimony to the invigorating influence theory has had in cognitive and language studies, in the past half-dozen years an equal number of new scientific periodicals have appeared which are devoted to these issues in experimental psychology.

It was then perhaps inevitable that this infusion of linguistic theory into cognitive and developmental psychology should eventually filter down to the more applied problem of reading. In February 1967, Kenneth Goodman first presented a paper entitled "Reading: A Psycholinguistic Guessing Game" at the American Educational Research Association annual metting in New York. I happened to attend that session and remember well the enthusiastic response of the audience to his presentation. It was a new and immediately appealing theory of reading that was easily interpretable at the level of classroom instruction. Goodman's ideas have since undergone the inevitable process of further articulation and elaboration, but they still retain much of their original appeal among teachers of reading.

By 1970 there were a number of competing theories or models of the reading process, including work of my own (Brown, 1970, 1971), which made use of linguistic and psycholinguistic theory to varying degrees. A reasonable sampling of that work can be found in Singer and Ruddell's *Theoretical Models and Processes of Reading,* first published in 1970 and reissued in an expanded format in 1976. Increasingly these theories and models were typed as "information-processing," or "psycholinguistic" models of reading because first, they all argued that reading could be studied by considering initially the adult reading process as a complex event in time; and second, they generally agreed that models of this process must include a linguistic component which was compatible with contemporary linguistic theory. By the middle of the present decade, reading had once again become a fashionable area of cognitive-experimental research in psychology,[1] and this development, too, I believe is attributable to the availability of theory in a complex human learning problem area which was previously inaccessible to traditional experimental techniques.

It might be noted here that none of these recent theories made any attempt to deal with reading disability in a serious or direct manner. This may be attributed to a primary concern for first delineating the normal process in the competent reader before sorting out all the peripheral issues, including the more complicated and vexing problem of why the function should fail to develop normally. The theoretical-psycholinguistic work which did exist on this problem came from

1. See for example, Gibson, E. & Levin, H. *The psychology of reading.* Cambridge: MIT Press, 1975; or Massaro, D. (Ed.) *Understanding language: An information-processing analysis of speech perception, reading, and psycholinguistics.* New York: Academic Press, 1975.

another perspective, the neuropsychological–neurological consideration of dyslexic and/or learning-disabled children. As we shall see, the minimal intersection of these concerns with psycholinguistic theories of reading, led to differing emphases on visual–perceptual, linguistic, and cognitive processes.

This brings us to the present status of psycholinguistic or information-processing theories of reading. I believe that there are at least two distinct types of theories within this broad classification. Each can make quite legitimate claims as a "psycholinguistic theory of reading," and yet each has proposed a different set of implications for the basic educational problems of reading instruction and, to a lesser extent, reading disability. Both begin by attempting to model the normal adult reading process as a basis for making such educational inferences. I will call them "direct" and "mediated" theories of reading (see Figure 5.1) and will discuss each in turn.

DIRECT MODELS OF READING

The "direct" theory of reading argues that at least for the mature and competent reader there can be an almost direct transition from visual perception to the underlying meaning, or semantic representation, of the material read. This transition occurs with minimal recourse to oral language processes or verbal mediation. The directness of this link-up is theoretically feasible because reading is viewed as a *primary* natural language process which can be largely *parallel* to oral language abilities. Therefore it would be possible, although unlikely, for a child to learn to read with minimal oral language abilities, as occasionally happens in cases of congenitally deaf children. Normally a child would learn to read

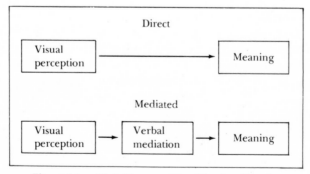

Figure 5.1. *Block Diagram of Two Theories of Reading.*

with oral as well as visual and semantic cues as to the meaning of a reading passage. However, this would certainly not be true for the adult reader, who has long since abandoned oral language mediation as an inefficient and redundant level of processing for the recovery of meaning.

The transition from the visual perceptual act to the underlying meaning of a passage is usually stated in terms of a "mapping" from visual to semantic features. That is, the mature reader, making use of his extensive knowledge of language, selects some subset of distinctive visual features in the text and translates them directly into corresponding semantic features in a hypothetical conceptual network. The task of the child learning to read is to learn these correspondences, using a sample of visual cues in the text to identify the author's intended meaning. The visual features are customarily described as binary in form, and represent the minimal set of abstracted visual features necessary to differentiate letters, words, and eventually phrases. As a reader becomes more proficient, he will need fewer features to recognize words and phrases, because he will be able to anticipate the author's intended meaning as a result of his reading experience, and thus require fewer visual cues for the identification of meaning.

The semantic features, in turn, are aspects of a highly organized metalinguistic representation of meaning. This conceptual network is most recently thought of as associative, propositional, or hierarchical in form, which means that semantics is more fundamental than syntax or language itself. Our ability to paraphrase sentences shows how sentences, once understood through interpretation in a semantic system, can be recast into equivalent but syntactically different sentences. Generative semantics (Steinberg & Jakobovits, 1971), within the literature of theoretical linguisitics, has proposed that language must commence and terminate in some such system of semantic productivity— that semantics comes first. Furthermore, much recent linguistic and psycholinguistic research has shown that the interpretation of sentences is quite limited, if indeed possible at all, without direct access to nonlinguistic general knowledge structure. This structure makes the interpretation of sentences possible, as in the case of presupposition or entailment, under the general heading of pragmatics. By proposing that an abstract semantic system is only part of more general knowledge structures, a number of these potential problems of semantic interpretation can theoretically be avoided. This is particularly important for a model of reading which proposes that comprehension or understanding is fundamental to any viable definition of the reading act.

This approach to reading is probably most clearly delineated in the work of Frank Smith, but other researchers, such as Kenneth Goodman, T. G. Bower, Paul Kolers, and Eleanor Gibson would share aspects of this approach as well. Most of these theoreticians would agree that Huey (1908) was the first to give a detailed accounting of the reading process as a whole from a cognitive, comprehension-based orientation. Indeed, some would say there has been little improvement on his original account.

As was earlier stated, Kenneth Goodman (1967, 1976) was the first writer in reading education to make use of psycholinguistic theory to propose a theory of reading which was comprehension-based. Frank Smith (1971, 1973, 1975) elaborated upon Goodman's idea of reading as a "psycholinguistic guessing game" in a number of technical ways. In particular, he made this concept precise by proposing that reading is a visual-to-semantic feature transition. T. G. Bower (1970) and his earlier collaborator Thomas Bever stated that very rapid reading was only possible if it could proceed as a parallel and somewhat independent process from oral language, therefore encouraging the development of strictly "visual" readers. Paul Kolers (1970, 1976) concluded from his series of experiments that reading comprehension involves the detection and retention of textual–graphic information in addition to linguistic cues. And finally, Eleanor Gibson (1972, 1975) and her occasional collaborator, Harry Levin, has studied the process of visual–perceptual learning necessary for the acquisition of reading. Her particular contribution is the development of the binary visual feature coding for the perception of letters and words.

This type of theory then places an extra emphasis on perceptual and cognitive features of reading. As was earlier stated, reading is viewed as a natural language process *parallel* to oral language abilities. Its efficiency is related to the reader's knowledge of the world, or the degree and type of cognitive structuring he possesses. Reading depends more on the reader than the text or the quality of the interactive process itself. For the knowledgeable reader is constantly generating semantic hypotheses about what he is yet to read, and the reading act itself is limited to *sampling* the text with these hypotheses in mind—confirming, denying, or in other ways modifying them on the basis of the available textual evidence. The picture then is of a finite set of messages that the writer intends to communicate, and the reader's task is to select which message was intended from a corresponding internalized list of his own.

The historical antecedents of this theoretical premise can be found in information theory and its application to modeling communication, a phenomenon of the early 1950s.[2] In this probabalistic conception of

---

2. See Miller, G. What is information measurement? *American Psychologist,* 1953, **8**, 3–11.

language, the listener, or in this instance the reader, actively construes the unfolding message on the basis of prior context and knowledge of the converging structural constraints of English sentences. Frank Smith (1971) has analagously discussed reading as a process of "reduction of uncertainty" concerning the intended message. Less formally, Kenneth Goodman (1967) speaks of reading as a "psycholinguistic guessing game" in which the reader is constantly forming semantically motivated hypotheses about the meaning of the passage on the basis of pertinent cues from the text and his knowledge of the structure and content of the material. As he aptly puts the case, "Skill in reading involves not greater precision, but more accurate first guesses based on better sampling techniques, greater control over language structure, broadened experiences and conceptual development."

In this type of theory, the reading act itself is almost completely defined in terms of comprehension or understanding. Silent, "meaningful" reading is the standard by which all other aspects of reading are to be judged. As Figure 5.1 clearly shows, for the mature reader there is no necessary auditory or even verbal mediation between perception and comprehension. The mature reader samples the text under the control of an intentional comprehension process, whose purpose is to understand the material at some predetermined level. Since understanding is never complete, sampling the text to confirm semantic hypotheses can proceed at varying rates, depending upon the redundancy of the material and the reader's purpose in reading. Indeed, very rapid reading (400–500 words per minute or more) has some advantage from this point of view in that it encourages a rapid direct assimilation of meaning without recourse to such slower mediating processes as subvocalization or verbal mediation. T. G. Bever and T. G. Bower, in a paper prepared for Project Literacy in the late 1960s and later published by Bower (1970), "propose that reading can and should be taught as a visual skill, enabling readers to analyze written sentences into their fundamental psychological structure directly, without auditory mediation." It is sometimes said elsewhere in the reading education literature, that were children not taught an early heavy reliance on letter–sound correspondence, or decoding skills, they would read faster and with greater comprehension.

The substantive experimental evidence for the "direct" model predictably groups around perceptual and cognitive issues. Gibson (1972, 1975) and her colleagues at Cornell have shown that the visual perceptual processes involved in letter and word recognition develop as a series of approximations to adult perception in preschool and primary-aged children. These developmental perceptual processes are best described as the learning of the relevant features of an alphabetic display. The features, in turn, have been systematized by Gibson into sets of visual distinctive features for the differentiation of various linguistic units. It follows that one of the beginning reader's first important tasks is the learning of this code. Gibson has studied this process in great detail.

In the mature reader this process of visual-feature abstraction appears to continue with increasingly more complex displays of text. Frank Smith (1971, 1973, 1975) reports the consistent experimental finding that short phrases can be as readily recognized as individual letters. Indeed, the recognition of individual letters is aided by a linguistic context. Further, it has been noted that fluent readers do not "see" everything on the printed page (McConkie, Rayner, & Wilson, 1973), but instead scan the text with selective eye fixations, sampling the material in a smooth inductive process. Smith argues that very rapid reading is only possible because readers are able to recognize distinctive features of sentences. This reduced need for visual information rests on the mature reader's increasing reliance on his own knowledge of the meaning of the passage, therefore requiring fewer visual cues to confirm semantic hypotheses. Smith formalizes this to state that reading can be an abstract visual-to-semantic feature transition, thus making it the most efficient medium of communication.

In this connection, the slow rate of oral reading is another line of experimental evidence that is frequently cited by "direct" theorists. If reading were to involve some type of auditory-based mediation, how could one explain the rapid rates achieved by some individuals in silent reading? For example, the average rate of adult oral reading is approximately 165 words per minute (Miron & Brown, 1968, 1971). This is far too slow as a mediating process to allow for quite common silent reading rates of 400–600 words per minute. Only a more direct and efficient process could accomodate this rapid reading phenomenon.

The cognitive experimental work compatible with the "direct" position is of two kinds. First, there is some evidence that aspects of language registration and interpretation are retained for a significant period of time when presented visually, even though the subvocal mechanisms are occupied with other irrelevant tasks (Scarborough, 1972; Peterson & Peterson, 1959). Furthermore, Kolers (1976) has shown that visual aspects of the typographic display can be retained and recognized again over long periods of time when the primary task is simply reading and understanding the material. This is still a sharply debated issue, and many experimenters in psycholinguistic research would maintain that any linguistic material which must be retained is coded from visual to auditory–articulatory representation for rehearsal and memory (Sperling, 1970). While the preponderance of evidence is presently in favor of the latter point of view, work on the hypothesis that a strictly "visual" retention of language is possible has only a recent history and appears to be growing, especially with investigations of language in the deaf.

The second line of cognitive experimental work which is compatible with the "direct" model is concerned with the organization of memory (Meyer & Schvaneveldt, 1976). Beginning in the late 1960s, advances in the experimental paradigm for the investigation of semantic memory led to an inductive model of semantic "priming" in the recognition and retrieval of lexical items in memory. Reaction-time studies have shown that prior semantic context can influence the speed and ease of recognition and interpretation of subsequent lexical items. This work can be interpreted as suggesting that how and what we comprehend while reading is largely determined by the current organization and priming of our lexical memory. Recent work in artificial intelligence has emphasized much the same point (Winograd, 1972). Organized lexical and general knowledge schemes are the basis for any computer-based language interpretation device. For new information to be understood, it must be interpreted with reference to a preexisting linguistic and factual model of the world. Thus for a model of reading which largely defines reading as comprehension, this type of cognitive experimentation has special significance.

Implications for Instruction

This last statement is incidental to a more general set of hypotheses about the teaching of reading that can be identified with this theory. Reading and oral language development are thought of as parallel activities, and while normally interrelated in a number of ways, they can also be relatively independent. Gibson (1972) has pointed out that scribbling may be an appropriate precursor to reading and writing activities, just as babbling invariably precedes the first utterances of the child. When children are first learning to read, Goodman (1967) has observed a strong well-motivated bias towards semantic substitutions in their oral reading errors; that is, the children tend to substitute synonymous words or phrases for the text as written, despite the visual–oral decoding emphasis given to much early reading instruction. Within a comprehension-based reading theory there is no reason to think of such "miscues" as errors in the reading process.

Furthermore, with a deemphasis of the importance of letter–sound correspondences, larger, more natural, units of language such as phrases and sentences have been proposed as first reading materials. From the point of view of this type of theory, using natural language contexts to teach reading would have the additional benefit of telling the child from the first that the point of reading is not reading aloud, but silent comprehension. And by deemphasizing oral reading as well, the child would be encouraged to adopt more efficient and hence "direct" strategies which are not limited by the rate of inner speech. In short, this type of theory takes a more "natural" approach to initial reading instruction, stressing the parallels between child and adult reading comprehension, and giving less attention to the more traditional teaching paradigm of having children learn to be accurate in establishing letter–sound correspondences as a first step in reading.

Reading Disabilities—Perception and Cognition

As for the problem of severe reading disabilities, or dyslexia, the "direct" models of reading generally emphasize perceptual and cognitive issues. If reading is a parallel activity to oral language competence, then following the analogy from speech perception problems in the aural domain, one would expect to find dysfluencies and immaturities in the visual perceptual process. And indeed, much of the research by Gibson, Smith, and Kolers, cited earlier in the chapter, is concerned with visual perceptual learning. Furthermore, if one surveys the specialized research literature on severe reading disabilities over the past two decades, the dominant theme has been investigations of visual perceptual and cross-modal processes. Especially in the late 1960s, perceptual training was widely recommended by educators for younger children who were experiencing difficulty in learning to read. These activities were generally, and often mistakenly, based on theories of visual perception and reading (Masland & Cratty, 1970).

The "direct" models of reading might also argue that subtle cognitive deficits or immaturities would account for a significant proportion of reading difficulties. Goodman and Smith in particular argue that deficiencies in conceptual development are a major deterrent to reading comprehension, and hence, under the assumed model, to reading itself. For if reading is dependent upon the reader's ability to generate semantic hypotheses which are compatible with the writer's intention, then the reader's "knowledge of the world" largely determines his ability to make such predictions. This concern is reflected in the reading educator's traditional admonition that "concept development" is one of the most important activities in the teaching of reading. Ramifications can also be found in the recent upsurge of research interest in relating stages of cognitive development and reading ability (Elkind, 1976), and in the artificial intelligence problem of constructing text-comprehending devices. This type of reading theory might suggest that selective retardations in overall intellectual functioning would account for many of the more resistant forms of reading failure.

MEDIATED MODELS OF READING

The "mediated" model of reading argues that all normal readers of alphabetic languages, whether child or adult, make use of an intermediate level of oral-language-based verbal mediation within the reading act. This verbal mediation occurs between visual perception and semantic interpretation (see Figure 5.1, page 72). Reading is seen as a *secondary*, oral-language-dependent process rather than as a *parallel* activity to oral language development. In this type of theory, reading ability is directly related to oral language competence and awareness of abstract oral language units. Reading therefore is defined as a fairly direct transition from letters and letter patterns to a corresponding level of oral language representation, and skill in reading per se consists of learning these correspondences. In this way, the reader can make use of the same oral-language understanding system in both reading and listening, and thereby avoid the redundancy of constructing a parallel system for reading alone.

Some of the theoreticians, in historical perspective, who might share a least a part of this set of assumptions include: (*a*) Leonard Bloomfield (1942), an earlier structural linguist who proposed the syllabary as an appropriate method for teaching the letter–sound correspondences of English; (*b*) Richard Venezky (1967), who catalogued the range of correspondences in the late 1960s; (*c*) Noam Chomsky (1968, 1970), who suggested a correspondence system at the level of abstract oral language segments; (*d*) myself (Brown, 1970), in outlining an information-processing system approach to reading which elaborated upon Chomsky; (*e*) Philip Gough (1972), who demonstrated some of the time constraints in a letter-to-abstract language segment model of reading; and (*f*) LaBerge and Samuels (1974), who have emphasized the shifting of attention in learning to read, from an initial preoccupation with decoding to a later developing comprehension strategy. A reasonable review of the problems of reading surveyed from this perspective can be found in the 1972 Kavanagh and Mattingly (Eds.) publication, *Language by Ear and by Eye: The Relationships Between Speech and Reading.*

Under this set of assumptions reading becomes a translating skill, mapping orthography onto oral-language-based phonemic or articulatory features; and like any skill, once learned, we are almost totally unaware of its automatic functioning. The translation process requires oral language competence, knowing the code (the letter–phonological segment correspondences), and access to the same ability to understand language as is true for a listener in an alphabetic language. This rather low-order transition to an oral-language competence system means that the acts of reading and understanding language are no longer viewed as being more or less synonymous. Reading skill becomes a more exact, automated, sequential processing of letter-like material into the more familiar and hence comprehensible oral language equivalents. As we shall see, this has meant that research, based upon this type of theory, has centered on topics related to orthography (the writing system), the lexicon (the reader's knowledge of words and word structure), and the decoding skills linking these two representations of language.

The theoretical bases of the "mediated" model of reading can be found in the nature of alphabetic languages and in more contemporary linguistic theory on the phonological structure, or sound patterns, of English. It is argued that despite its superficial inconsistencies, written English is an alphabetic language with regularized, if somewhat abstract, correspondences between letters and sounds. The invention of the alphabet was a great civilizing step forward in allowing a larger segment of the general population to learn to read. No longer was reading confined to a scholarly class, where years of study were required to learn the thousands of correspondences between one complex visual symbol and one word, as is the case in ideographic systems. Instead, a limited set of symbols (letters) was used to represent a limited set of speech sounds. Leonard Bloomfield, the great American structural linguist, proposed teaching these correspondences in a systematic fashion by using a syllabary in the late 1930s. His proposals were met by such universal opposition from comprehension-oriented reading educators that the method and material could not be published until 1951 (*Let's Read: A Linguistic Approach*), some 10 years following his death.

A second important theoretical linguistic fact was the development of generative phonological theory by Noam Chomsky and Morris Halle in their publication, *The Sound Pattern of English* (1968). In this theory Chomsky and Halle propose that lexical (vocabulary) items are coded in human memory by their *unique* phonological properties—those aspects of articulation and sound that are not predictable by general rule. Those aspects of the phonetic speech stream which *are* regular and predictable are determined by the syntactic surface structure and a set of phonological rules. Chomsky and Halle note that these lexical items in their abstract form, prior to the application of phonological rules, bear a striking resemblance to English spelling patterns. In other words, for the mature reader, the correspondence in reading is from orthography to phonological base forms at the first level of abstraction in the sound system of English. One might infer that from this point forward, in the process of understanding, reading and listening are very similar if not identical. However, for children first learning to read, this level of lexical abstraction may be relatively inaccessible. Further explanation of this model of reading can be found in my own work (Brown, 1970, 1971, 1976, 1977), or with a somewhat different interpretation, in Carol Chomsky (1970).

The substantive experimental psychological research on understanding language has also motivated mediated models of reading. It has been very difficult to experimentally verify a substantive memory of any duration for language that is primarily visual in character. While there are literally thousands of experiments on auditory short-term memory for language, there are very few in the corresponding visual realm. This is because the human language system appears to be especially adapted to auditory stimulation (Liberman, Cooper, Shankweiler, & Studdert-Kennedy, 1967), and when language appears in a visual format, most experiments suggest that it is quickly converted into auditory or articulatory equivalents so that it can be retained. In Sperling's (1970) experimental model of visual perception of letters, he demonstrates that the brief visual impression we have of letter-like material in rapid reading, normally lasts only about ¼ of a second, and if the information is to be retained, it must be recoded into a form suitable for auditory short-term memory.

A second line of experimental evidence which is relevant to the mediated position on reading is the persistent phenomenon of subvocalization in silent reading. While the traditional wisdom in reading theory and instruction has been that subvocalization is a manifestation of poor reading habits or a carry-over from too great an emphasis on decoding and oral reading in early reading instruction, several major studies (Edfeldt, 1960; Hardyck & Petronovich, 1970; McGuigan, 1970) have shown that all readers engage in this activity to some extent while reading silently, and that subvocalization is greater when the material is difficult or the situation is distracting. It is as if the motoric realization of saying the words to ourselves gave an extra dimension of perceptual salience to the material, perhaps because of the more fundamental and natural character of aural processing, especially if an articulatory–motor theory of speech perception is assumed. For children, while reading silently, vocalization undoubtedly serves an important place-keeping, attentional function, as well as allowing the young reader additional time to disambiguate the structure and meaning of the utterance (Farnham-Diggory & Gregg, 1975). Finally, there is no evidence that reading speeds exceed those of listening to rapid speech. Using an electromechanical process called time-compression, recorded speech can be speeded up with minimum distortion to rates exceeding 400 words per minute; and a study I completed some years ago with Murray Miron (Miron & Brown, 1968, 1971) showed that the most efficient listening rate is in this range. Taken in all, there is little to suggest that mediation, even in its most manifest form (i.e., vocalization) in any way impedes the reading process in children or adults.

Implications for Instruction

As noted earlier in the chapter, the "mediated" model of reading, in contrast to "direct" theories, suggests that early stages in learning to read will likely be devoted to learning the letter–sound correspondences as an exact, left-to-right, sequential processing. There undoubtedly will be considerable stress on achieving a level of accuracy in this decoding process, and that as this skill develops, it should increasingly become more automatic, thus freeing the attention to other, higher, comprehension tasks. This means that learning to read develops in several sequential steps towards fluent comprehension. Early reading materials would emphasize the regularities in letter–speech segment correspondences, and only later treat the more important exceptions. And oral reading would therefore have an important place in early reading instruction, both as decoding practice and supportive motoric correlated behavior.

The child's task is to learn the code that is orthographic–alphabetic English. This may require additional development of a more sophisticated awareness of English, a skill that may not be accessible to all children at age 6 (see Brown, 1976), but there is every reason to believe this approach will succeed with most children. Chall (1967), in her comprehensive study on the merits of various reading methodologies, *Learning to Read: The Great Debate*, concludes that while not all issues are clear, the preponderance of evidence lies with approaches emphasizing early regularized instruction in decoding skills. One can also note that decoding instruction has been the universal first strategy in remedial reading programs, after an initial exposure to reading has failed. Overall, at least as a matter of history, it would appear that a strong decoding emphasis has been recognized by teachers as the most systematic approach to effective reading instruction.

Reading Disabilities—Aphasia and Reading

As for the problem of reading disability, or dyslexia, the "mediated" position on reading has emphasized deficits in central processing or language capacities, rather than visual perceptual or conceptual difficulties as in the "direct" models of reading. The principal hypothesis of a mediated position has been to view severe reading disabilities as instances of aphasia, or sometimes subtle defects in central language processing. My own strategy has been to separate dyslexic children into either developmental or residual types of disorders (Brown, 1976). The developmental disorder is defined as the possibility of differing rates of maturation within the perceptual, linguistic, and cognitive systems; while the residual disability is for the present given a post hoc operational definition as those specific reading disabilities that do not show marked improvement by the time the child has reached age 9–11, hence, an inferred neurological dysfunction. Both types of disorders share the assumption that persistent deficits in primary oral-language-based processing abilities, such as linguistic immaturities and dysnomia, are principally at issue in dyslexia, rather than modality-specific or intellectual dysfunctions.

The linguistic function is obviously robust enough so that most dyslexic children show few overt symptoms of communication difficulties. However, more subtle deficits, such as the inability to become aware of phonemic contrasts and other problems of awareness of abstract language units, may be sufficient to disrupt the normal acquisition of reading (Kavanagh & Mattingly, 1972). In addition, auditory or articulatory short-term memory deficits (Farnham-Diggory & Gregg, 1975), articulatory coding problems (Brown & Opperman, 1977; Eimas, 1975; Shankweiler & Liberman, 1972), and general difficulties in speed and fluency of processing, such as Denckla and Rudel's (1974, 1976) account of dyslexic children's problems in the "cued retrieval" of names, have all been found to correlate with the dyslexic syndrome. These deficits in the abstracted form of primary linguistic ability argue that severe reading disability is a selective dysfunction of blockage of central language processing (Brown, 1976), which in most instances is unrelated to visual perception deficits (Masland & Cratty, 1970) or intellectual–conceptual variation. This conclusion places the "mediated" position on the nature of these disorders at some distance from the perceptual and cognitive preoccupations of the "direct" theory of reading. But as we shall see, this is only one instance where fundamental, almost philosophical, differences about the nature of reading have led to sharply contrasting inferences as to what constitute the research problems themselves.

INFERENCES AND CONCLUSIONS

The many differences between these two types of reading theory, both at the theoretical and experimental levels, can be partially accounted for by their respective first-order definitions of reading. The "direct" theory of reading with its emphasis on comprehension and understanding would almost a priori exclude any explanation of reading which is not semantically motivated. If the point of reading is to understand what is read, this consideration must enter into every level of explanation and research. Thus oral reading, in and for itself, has little fundamental value for understanding the reading process, because comprehension is not necessarily required. Oral reading may be an interesting and valuable performance skill, which may have diagnostic value in reading failure, but it has little intrinsic value as a linguistic level of theoretical interest. Silent reading, with its presumption of comprehension, is a far more interesting phenomenon for investigation. As seen by the "direct" theorists, silent reading is a primary linguistic activity which is more efficient than listening, and which can and ought to replace listening as an information processing medium of communication in all but extraordinary circumstances. Therefore, it follows that children should be encouraged to acquire reading-as-understanding in a more natural fashion, reflecting the assumption that reading is a modern natural language activity. It also follows that failures in reading are basically failures in reading comprehension. If one is not reading well, one fails to comprehend; and failures of comprehension usually mean that the reader lacks an appropriate conceptual frame of reference to make any interpretation.

The "mediated" theory of reading accepts a much more limited definition of reading. While not quarreling with the pedagogic goal of comprehending what one reads, at least some mediated theorists, including myself, argue that what is unique to the reading process is complete by the level of oral reading. Moreover, this level of realization can precede deeper levels of understanding (see Brown, 1970, 1971). In other words, the sometimes difficult-to-learn skill of reading is centered on the problem of decoding from visual to more customary oral-language-based equivalents. From this point forward in the reading process, understanding what we read is more or less the same as understanding what we hear. Reading is a parasitic, secondary activity, normally based on oral language competence. That the skilled reader's attention is usually preoccupied with questions of meaning does not mean that prior levels of skills and linguistic representation are unnecessary for the beginning reader learning this skill, or the mature reader who encounters a particularly difficult reading passage (LaBerge & Samuels, 1974). Indeed, the first few steps in learning to read can be thought of as similar to the first steps in learning any complex skill, such as riding a bicycle, or learning to swim or type. What is unique to reading, as opposed to listening, or more generalized processes of comprehension or understanding, is the additional complexity of deriving a viable level of linguistic representation from the visual display while proceeding with the normal language functions of understanding the message.

In general, the acceptance of these two types of reading theories has coincided with larger historical trends in reading instruction and remediation. The "direct" position has been compatible with the more informal teaching style of the contemporary primary classroom. A relaxation of decoding standards and greater stress on reading comprehension has meant a less rigid and precise teaching schedule for the acquisition of reading skill, with less rote learning. As a natural language activity, reading is introduced in an incidental fashion within the context of a well-prepared classroom environment. The child is encouraged to read to discover information that otherwise might not be available to him. This approach has found wide acceptance with primary school teachers who have been concerned with failures of comprehension in children following the acquisition of basic decoding skills. By stressing comprehension and reading for a purpose from the first, the goal of reading is never lost, and the traditional transition from practice of skills to using reading for some end is eliminated.

All this, however, has left many primary school teachers wondering what if anything they should teach their children concerning the letter–sound correspondences in English. This is an even more difficult situation with children who fail to read following the first several years of formal schooling. Here, I believe, the "direct" position on reading, with its emphasis on perceptual and cognitive issues, has been less successful.

As stated earlier in the chapter, the stress on visual perception and perceptual learning coincided in the late 1960s with the development of perceptual training activities for children who for a variety of reasons did not acquire reading skills on schedule. These materials are based on a theory of stimulus approximation from simple geometric figures to alphabetic letters, words, and phrases, through a series of staged exercises. While I would not want to claim that any of the theorists I have associated with the "direct" position have actually advocated the use of such materials, it was a fairly simple step from theory to implementation for many people more directly concerned with the remediation of reading problems. Unfortunately, the consensus of studies on the effectiveness of these perceptual training activities has been that the perceptual gains fail to generalize to reading itself (Masland & Cratty, 1970); instructional time might be better spent on more traditional *reading* activities.

A more productive line of inquiry may be the recent revival of interest in the role of conceptual variation as an explanation of reading failure (Shuy, 1977). Sociolinguistics and pragmatics are current linguistic topics which emphasize the sociological and cognitive context in which a statement can be understood. Presumably, without an appropriate personal context, children are unable to respond to the teaching situation or reading materials, and consequently comprehend very little. This point is reinforced by artificial-intelligence research on the comprehension of natural language (Winograd, 1972). As cited earlier, this work shows that without an appropriate internalized context or knowledge state, computerized programs are incapable of responding appropriately to verbal inquiries at even the most rudimentary level. One could predict that basic research work on these topics will find a ready audience among reading educators, since the "concept readiness" theme has been an important part of the reading education literature for the past three decades. In such basic teaching paradigms as the Directed Reading Activity, no reading material is introduced without assurances that the child has an appropriate linguistic and conceptual context for what he is to read.

In contrast, the acceptance of the "mediated" position by a significant minority of the reading education community has never been in doubt. A loosely defined version of this position is compatible with the phonics movement and all such code-oriented instructional programs stretching back to the historical roots of formalized instruction in reading. While phonics is today more likely to be associated with "back to the basics" teaching regimens, more sophisticated "linguistic" approaches to code breaking are found in many school systems, especially those in low socioeconomic areas. Code-oriented instructional programs are liked by some teachers because they give an easily structured, teachable curriculum of limited duration. In 2 year's time a child can theoretically be taught all of the letter–sound correspondences necessary for oral reading; after this, the child is more or less on his own. Oral reading therefore assumes again an important role in the acquisition of reading, indicating for the teacher and child a minimal level of reading competence. This also reasserts the literary meaning and pleasure of reading aloud, which was relegated in the "direct" model to a phonological "recoding" of assimilated material.

Unfortunately, not all children respond well to this regimen of intensive decoding instruction in the first several years of school. The rules and regularities of pattern drills may be too abstract and intrinsically uninteresting for some children to respond. Furthermore, less mature children may experience difficulty perceiving and combining the various isolated elements of English speech sounds.

A linguistically more sophisticated version of the "mediated" position suggests that the level of phonological realization to which letter patterns correspond may be so abstract that it cannot be isolated or taught directly at all (Gough, 1972). Instead, one must wait for the child's phonological system to mature to the point that with proper encouragement the child can work out these correspondences for himself. An increased awareness of oral language properties through "enrichment" activities would be the first reading task for such children. In an interesting way, this set of inferences is in quite close agreement with the traditional "language arts" teaching philosophy of the primary-school classroom. Here the child is exposed to literature and discourse in the oral domain, leading quite naturally to reading and writing activities. It is indeed curious that in an era when reading, like so many other learning activities, has become a professional specialization, that a rather sophisticated contemporary theory of reading should align so well with the language arts curriculum of the primary classroom.

A much stronger case can be made for the acceptance of mediated theory when the problem of reading failure or dyslexia is considered. As was noted earlier in the chapter, the almost universal strategy for remedial instruction in reading is the introduction of a systematic program in decoding skills; this normally means some variant of phonics. The first assumption of most remedial reading teachers is that the child simply was not taught the rudimentary reading skills; the task of the teacher is to discover what it is that the child does not know, and then teach it to him. If the child does not respond to this regimen, then with additional supportive activities, which are largely motivational, he is put through the same type of curriculum again, but at a much slower pace. Perceptual training has been shown to have definite limits; and learning individual words by sight is a tedious method for developing reading skill, beyond acquiring the most rudimentary reading vocabulary. Moreover, cognitive issues are difficult to put into therapeutic practice, except for the quite obvious observation that the child should be reading material which is interesting to him and which he would understand if presented orally. This leaves the remedial reading teacher few alternatives except slow and often painful progress through some type of decoding, or "word attack," curriculum. At this basic level, reading is stripped to its most fundamental definition—acquiring the alphabetic principle.

My biases in characterizing these two types of reading theories are quite apparent; I classify my own work as typical of the "mediated" position. I believe that this type of theory is more intrinsically interesting, has greater potential for development as theory, and provides a better account of a broader range of significant reading problems. While

I have not elaborated upon the technical complexities of this theory here (see Brown, 1970, 1971, 1976, 1977), the assumptions, basic mechanisms, and problems addressed in this and the "direct" position are generally represented in the context of this chapter. Therefore, it must also be clear that there are major differences on the most fundamental questions which separate these two positions, for example, how the normal reading process functions, how children learn to read, and why some children experience extraordinary difficulty in learning this intellectual skill. These divisions will very likely continue to exist into the indefinite future. They should at least serve as an admonishment against making premature claims that the "psycholinguistic theory of reading" has been or is being discovered. We have not yet reached a consensus.

What unites the two positions is the desire for better explanatory models of reading, a belief in better research on basic problems in reading, and an acceptance of the value of negative knowledge as a first step in understanding a process as complex as reading. As Roger Brown said a few years ago at a psycholinguistics conference when asked about the positive value of psycholinguistic experiments:

> There are such things as negative effects. Psycholinguistics helps to control simplistic notions about language deprivation in certain groups, and notions about how to enrich the linguistic environment—which sweep society and are held by people who don't know what language is. It's not unlikely that eventually psycholinguistics will have some usefulness in language learning.[3]

ACKNOWLEDGMENTS

The research leading to this paper was supported by a grant from the Spencer Foundation, National Academy of Education.

REFERENCES

Bloomfield, L. Linguistics and reading. *Elementary English Review*, 1942, **19**, 183–186.
Bloomfield, L., & Barnhart, C. *Let's read: A linguistic approach*. Detroit: Wayne State University Press, 1961.
Bower, T. G. How to read without listening. In J. Williams & H. Levin (Eds.), *Basic studies on reading*. New York: Basic Books, 1970.
Brown, E. The bases of reading acquisition. *Reading Research Quarterly*, 1970, **6**, 49–74.
Brown, E. Implications of a theory of reading. In F. Greene (Ed.), *Reading: The right to participate*. Milwaukee: National Reading Conference, 1971, **20**, 355–367.

3. *The New York Times*, August 7, 1971.

Brown, E. Neuropsychological interference mechanisms in aphasia and dyslexia. In R. Rieber (Ed.), *The neuropsychology of language: Essays in honor of Eric Lenneberg.* New York: Plenum Press, 1976.

Brown, E. An information-processing model of reading with special reference to dyslexic disorders. Invited address to the New York Academy of Sciences, New York, January 1977.

Brown, E., & Opperman, P. Phonological regression in short-term memory and the prediction of oral reading errors in beginning readers. Unpublished manuscript, New York University, 1977.

Chall, J. *Learning to read: The great debate.* New York: McGraw-Hill, 1967.

Chomsky, C. Reading, writing, and phonology. *Harvard Educational Review,* 1970, **40,** 287–309.

Chomsky, N. Phonology and reading. In J. Williams & H. Levin (Eds.), *Basic studies on reading.* New York: Basic Books, 1970.

Chomsky, N., & Halle, M. *The sound pattern of English.* New York: Harper & Row, 1968.

Denckla, M., & Rudel, R. Rapid "automatized" naming of pictured objects, colors, letters, and numbers by normal children. *Cortex,* 1974, **10,** 186–202.

Denckla, M., & Rudel, R. Naming of object drawings by dyslexic and other learning disabled children. *Brain and Language,* 1976, **3,** 1–15.

Edfeldt, A. *Silent speech and silent reading.* Chicago: University of Chicago Press, 1960.

Eimas, P. Distinctive-feature codes in the short-term memory of children. *Journal of Experimental Child Psychology,* 1975, **19,** 241–251.

Elkind, D. Cognitive development and reading. In H. Singer & R. Ruddell (Eds.), *Theoretical models and processes of reading.* (2nd ed.) Newark, Del.: International Reading Association, 1976.

Farnham-Diggory, S., & Gregg, L. Short-term memory function in young readers. *Journal of Experimental Child Psychology,* 1975, **19,** 279–298.

Gibson, E. Reading for some purpose. In J. Kavanagh & I. Mattingly (Eds.), *Language by ear and by eye: The relationship between speech and reading.* Cambridge, Mass.: MIT Press, 1972.

Gibson, E., & Levin, H. *The psychology of reading.* Cambridge: MIT Press, 1975.

Goodman, K. Reading: A psycholinguistic guessing game. Paper presented at the American Educational Research Association, New York, February 1967.

Goodman, K. Behind the eye: What happens in reading. In H. Singer & R. Ruddell (Eds.), *Theoretical models and processes of reading.* (2nd ed.) Newark, Del.: International Reading Association, 1976.

Gough, P. One second of reading. In J. Kavanagh & I. Mattingly (Eds.), *Language by ear and by eye.* Cambridge, Mass.: MIT Press, 1972.

Hardyck, C., & Petronovich, L. Subvocal speech and comprehension level as a function of the difficulty level of reading material. *Journal of Verbal Learning and Verbal Behavior,* 1970, **9,** 647–652.

Huey, E. B. *The psychology and pedagogy of reading.* New York: Macmillan, 1908.

Kavanagh, J., & Mattingly, I. (Eds.) *Language by ear and by eye: The relationship between speech and reading.* Cambridge, Mass.: MIT Press, 1972.

Kolers, P. Three stages of reading. In H. Levin & J. Williams (Eds.), *Basic studies on reading.* New York: Basic Books, 1970.

Kolers, P. Pattern-analyzing memory. *Science,* 1976, **191,** 1280–1281.

LaBerge, D., & Samuels, J. Toward a theory of automatic information processing in reading. *Cognitive Psychology,* 1974, **6,** 293–323.

Liberman, A., Cooper, D., Shankweiler, D., & Studdert-Kennedy, M. Perception of the speech code. *Psychological Review,* 1967, **74,** 431–461.

Masland, R., & Cratty, B. The nature of the reading process, the rationale of non-educational remedial methods. In E. Calkins (Ed.), *Reading forum.* Washington: NINDS Monograph No. 11, 1970.

Massaro, D. (Ed.) *Understanding language: An information-processing analysis of speech perception, reading, and psycholinguistics.* New York: Academic Press, 1975.

McConkie, G., Rayner, K., & Wilson, S. Experimental manipulation of reading strategies. *Journal of Educational Psychology,* 1973, **65,** 1–18.

McGuigan, F. Covert oral behavior during silent performance of language tasks. *Psychological Bulletin,* 1970, **74,** 309–326.

Meyer, D. E., & Schvaneveldt, R. W. Meaning, memory structure, and mental processes. *Science,* 1976, **192,** 27–33.

Miller, G. What is information measurement? *American Psychologist,* 1953, **8,** 3–11.

Miron, M., & Brown, E. Stimulus parameters in speech compression. *Journal of Communications,* 1968, **18,** 219–235.

Miron, M., & Brown, E. The comprehension of rate incremented aural coding. *Journal of Psycholinguistic Research,* 1971, **1,** 65–76.

Peterson, L. R., & Peterson, M. J. Short-term retention of individual items. *Journal of Experimental Psychology,* 1959, **58,** 193–198.

Scarborough, D. L. Memory for brief visual displays of symbols. *Cognitive Psychology,* 1972, **3,** 408–429.

Shankweiler, D., & Liberman, I. Misreading: A search for causes. In J. Kavanagh & I. Mattingly (Eds.), *Language by ear and by eye: The relationship between speech and reading.* Cambridge: MIT Press, 1972.

Shuy, R. (Ed.) *Linguistic theory: What can it say about reading.* Newark, Del.: International Reading Association, 1977.

Singer, H., & Ruddell, R. *Theoretical models and processes of reading.* (2nd ed.) Newark, Del.: International Reading Association, 1976.

Smith, F. *Understanding reading.* New York: Holt, Rinehart & Winston, 1971.

Smith, F. (Ed.) *Psycholinguistics and reading.* New York: Holt, Rinehart & Winston, 1973.

Smith, F. *Comprehension and learning.* New York: Holt, Rinehart & Winston, 1975.

Sperling, G. Short-term memory, long-term memory, and scanning in the processing of visual information. In F. Young & D. Lindsley (Eds.), *Early experience and visual information processing in perceptual and reading disorders.* Washington: National Academy of Sciences, 1970.

Steinberg, D., & Jakobovits, O. (Eds.), *Semantics: An interdisciplinary reader in philosophy, linguistics and psychology.* London & New York: Cambridge University Press, 1971.

Venezky, R. English orthography: Its graphical structure and its relation to sound. *Reading Research Quarterly,* 1967, **2,** 75–106.

Winograd, T. Understanding natural language. *Cognitive Psychology,* 1972, **3,** 1–191.

Part II

A Translation of
Kindersprache und Aphasie

Kindersprache und Aphasie.

Gedanken zur Aphasielehre auf Grund von Beobachtungen
der kindlichen Sprachentwicklung und ihrer Anomalien.
(Berücksichtigung der modernen Psychologie.)

Von

DR· EMIL FRÖSCHELS,

Privatdozent an der Universität und Arzt für Sprachstörungen
in Wien.

Mit 5 Abbildungen im Text.

BERLIN 1918
VERLAG VON S. KARGER
KARLSTRASSE 15

ACADEMIC PRESS, INC.
111 Fifth Avenue, New York, New York 10003

United Kingdom Edition published by
ACADEMIC PRESS, INC. (LONDON) LTD.
24/28 Oval Road, London NW1 7DX

Originally puplished as *Kindersprache und Aphasie,*
by Emil Fröschels. Berlin: Verlag von S. Karger,
1918.

PRINTED IN THE UNITED STATES OF AMERICA

80 81 82 83   9 8 7 6 5 4 3 2 1

CHILD LANGUAGE AND APHASIA

*Thoughts on Aphasia Based on
Child Language Development
and Its Anomalies*

Emil Fröschels

The University of Vienna

Edited by

R. W. Rieber

Translated by

Bernard M. Porhoryles

and

*Ruth M. Economos
Leonard M. Tompakov*
Pace University in the City of New York

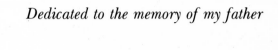
Dedicated to the memory of my father

CONTENTS

PREFACE

The attempt undertaken in the following text to approach an understanding of certain forms of aphasia through a detailed description of speech development—and its obstruction—in children must be interpreted in a very definite sense. By no means do I go so far as to accept the total equation of incompletely developed speech with destroyed speech. I believe, rather, that with the precise knowledge of the structure of speech which results from studying various stages of infantile speech the prospect for clearing up fine points in aphasia research might well improve. If one becomes acquainted with the individual stages of functional development, and if one subscribes to the opinion that these stages, in their entirety, continue to exist in a more or less changed form, then one will look for them even where function has been disrupted by some damaging event. It is very likely that these individual stages will appear in a different form from what they were prior to their subsequent evolution. They have probably undergone a shaping, maturing, and polishing process precisely because of active linkage with other stages, so that the partial function, if isolated through illness or even exposed in one of its aspects, will no longer present the same picture as it did in childhood.

I have, however, also tried to utilize the teachings of modern psychology and linguistics in an attempt to illuminate the nascent thinking–speaking process. But if the results indicate another gradual process showing many similarities with the phylogenetics of speech development in infantile speech, then this latter process, along with modern psychology and linguistics, could probably bring further support to this area. It is evident too, that experimental phonetics must not be neglected in the present treatise, in view of its close relationship to psychology on the one hand and aphasia research on the other. Special reference should be made here to a publication by Kruger[1] which is fundamental in this area.

The theory of speech as a multilevel structure, however, also postulates that the elimination of a deep-seated level upsets the whole structure in such a way that the observer thinks he is dealing with the process at a higher level, or with a whole structure in general decay. Here again, studying the development of infantile speech has shed some light by bringing out similar phenomena that were accessible, thanks to the fact that one deep structure still continued to exist.

I think it appropriate here to clarify a personal matter. Arnold Pick, in his broadly conceived work *Agrammatical Speech Disturbances*,[2] recommended in general terms using not only a psychological approach to various forms of aphasia, but, more specifically, the observation of infantile speech development. It might appear then, as if I have adopted an idea originating with Pick as one of my own. Outside of the fact that Pick's work was intended only as a stimulus, it is clear that any pertinent study which can withstand criticism will only fall within the scope of his bold project. However, I can point to various earlier publications in which I myself have already presented the train of thought which guides this text.

Finally, it is my hope that this study may contribute to solving the question of the various forms of aphasia, a question that so deeply affects the fields of psychology, philosophy, linguistics, and medicine.

Many thanks are due to Dr. F. Rosenthal for his help in proofreading the book.

Vienna, Fall 1917   E. FRÖSCHELS

1. *Beziehungen der experimentellen Phonetik zur Psychologie. Bericht uber de II. Kongress fur experimentelle Psychologie in Wurzburg 1906* (Leipzig, 1907).
2. *Die Agrammatischan Sprachstorungen* (Berlin: Springer, 1913).

Chapter 1

PSYCHOLOGICAL INTRODUCTION ON THE QUESTION OF THE PSYCHOLOGY OF ASSOCIATION

Attitude

In studying the literature of aphasia of the last decades and endeavoring to acquaint oneself with modern psychology, one will find that psychologists do indeed try to use the results of aphasia research for their discipline; whereas many physicians dealing with aphasia do not appreciate the teachings of psychology to the same extent. Perhaps this disparity may be due partially to the fact that modern experimental methods of psychology require complicated equipment which hospitals almost never have at their disposal. How urgently a remedy is needed is shown by the words of Wolfgang Köhler, who insists that cases of amusia [inability to hear musical tones] or sensory aphasia respectively should be referred to a psychologist for detailed examination, since physicians lack the methodology for examinations of a psychological and acoustic nature. Indeed, interest in questions of psychology is already widespread in medical circles, a fact which, together with the above-mentioned lack of opportunity for sufficient accord, with psychological methodology, leads to the curious phenomenon of aphasia researchers frequently resorting to a psychology that has only a loose connection with professional psychology.

Since the historic discoveries of Broca and Wernicke, if I understand correctly, the basic tendency of aphasia research and the investigations of the psychology of speech connected with it consist above all in using the crude symptoms of loss to clarify relevant questions. Basically the old Wernicke–Lichtheim scheme, modified more recently in a very functional way by Liepman in accordance with a growing understanding of the role of sound–tone images, is appropriate only for forming an idea of the mechanism of the most severe forms of aphasia. However, in those cases which are much more frequently encountered in practice—cases of small changes in normal speech—the scheme has really failed us from the start and has even had a damaging effect insofar as it was considered the mold into which one was obliged to pour. For instance, it was too easily decided, without any further ado, to explain the case of a patient who, after temporary aphasia, soon spoke well again, by assuming that Broca's region had temporarily been put out of commission by an embolism that was later reabsorbed. It did not seem to occur to anyone that even in ordinary life an individual has various types of speech expressions at his disposal which differ, for instance, in conversation with friends and superiors. Basically, the emotional situation in each case is of great importance for the developing form of expression, and Sperber[3] even established the principle that the entire development of human speech appears as a struggle between its two main functions: conveyance of information and expression of emotion.

For the sake of illustrating the need for a psychological foundation in aphasia research, I should like to insert statements by psychologists and linguists here and there which may serve as sidelights, even though the applicability of the idea in question for aphasia research may not be explained in more detail in each individual case. Otherwise, the potential scope of this study would have to be greatly extended on the one hand; nor is it yet possible, on the other hand, to assign psychological aphasia research its rightful place at this current stage. That is, doing so would be something like assigning to each stone in advance the place that would seem suitable for it in the construction of a building. In this connection, let me quote some statements by Sperber:

> The fact that one word is supplanted by an emotionally stronger one does not create any definite condition. The more the new word gains ground, the more frequently it is therefore pronounced; the more the emotions which were originally clinging to it disappear, the sooner the point is finally reached at which it has supplanted the old word completely. It has become so colorless itself that in the struggle with a newly emerging carrier of emotions it must in turn be the loser. . . . Just as speech emotions must be held responsible for a large part of the shifts of meaning and level affecting individual words, so these emotions also play a part in the history of syntax.

The reference to the ingenious experiment of Elise Richter[4] to look for the effect of these emotions—especially by way of tracheal pressure—and to study their influence on the change of the Romance languages, vulgar Latin, and Romance itself, may, at this point, shed some further

3. Über den Affekt als Ursache de Sprachveränderung. Halle a. S., 1914.
4. "Der innere Zusammenhang in der Entwicklung der romanischen Sprache," in Beihefte zu Gröbers *Ztschr. f. Roman. Phil.*, 1911.

light on the intimate relations of psychology to phonetics, and of both these subjects to our topic.

If these theories of historical linguistics are brought into accord with Freud's book *On the Psychopathology of Everyday Life,* one realizes how fruitless must be the attempt to lock the language of an individual inside a celestial dome. Here, too, everything is in constant flux; and whenever the stream, which may have disappeared after the drying up of a source, apparently reappears some time later, it would be hasty to assert without further examination that it was nourished by the former source, or that it was in fact the old river. Indeed, quite possibly it might have received its nourishment somewhere else. The aphasic who at some later time speaks again would first have to be examined most closely as to whether he was really in possession of his entire former vocabulary. Naturally, one will often encounter great difficulties in establishing this fact, unless the people around the aphasic had previously noticed a change in the way in which he expressed himself. At present it is not possible to direct these subtle probings along an exact path, but perhaps one cannot completely dismiss the thought that upon accurate establishment of the vocabulary on the one hand and the psychological type on the other, data will emerge which point to the fact that the patient owes this or that expression of everyday colloquial speech perhaps more to his potential than to his actual sensory type of disposition.

The question of sensory types has indeed been playing an important role in aphasia research for a long time. Strictly by the Wernicke–Lichtheim pattern, people have frequently taken refuge in the concept of types of representation. But here too, one did not keep up with modern psychology; and the process of distinguishing between the type [of representation] with which a person forms an idea (actual type of representation) from that with which he is able to form an idea (potential type of representation) (Meumann, William Stern, St. Paul, Baerwald) has not been sufficiently considered. How necessary it has become to acquaint oneself here, too, with modern experimental psychological methodology may be substantiated by several sentences from Baerwald's study:[5]

> The fact that people who are visually and acoustically oriented are frequently able to discover their factually existing motorial–representational elements only with difficulty was recognized as one of the reasons why the completion of the method of self-observation by that of the memory of instinctive accompanying movements suggests itself to us.

5. *Zur Psychologie der Vorstellungstypen* (Leipzig, 1916), p. 388.

He also explains to us the following apparent contradictions:

> When learning to read, the word image and speech-movement are so closely as-
> sociated with each other that children and illiterates are unable to read without an
> accompanying silent whisper. This association remains permanent; therefore, in case
> of illness of the motor speech center, reading ability is often affected. Consequently,
> Lichtheim in such cases assumes a spreading of the illness to the reading center. It is
> more probable that one disturbance conditions the other, because the cooperation of
> the speech–movement concept is permanently indispensable to reading [Goldstein].
> Thus the connection between reading image and speech–movement concept is con-
> sidered by many psychologists to be of the very closest nature, even closer than that
> between reading image and word–sound concepts [Ballet]. Nevertheless, even some
> strong believers in the motor theory, people whose customary thinking is accom-
> plished mainly through internal speech, do not become at all aware of any participa-
> tion of kinesthetic word concepts in the reading activity.

In connection with the foregoing, the question must also be clarified as
to whether it is altogether justified to make the general claim that an
aphasic learns to speak again all by himself, or whether the daily conversation of his environment is not to be interpreted as practice therapy.
For this purpose it is probably useful to keep in mind the various ways by
which people attempt to bring back to speaking those aphasics who do
not regain speech without extensive practice therapy. Since a more detailed knowledge of the pertinent bibliography (Kussmaul, Gutzmann,
Fröschels, Liebmann, Mohr, Küchler, Dejerine, and others) may be assumed, only a few examples need be quoted. A motor aphasic, for instance, is not capable of repeating an *a*. In that case the doctor sits down
with him in front of a mirror, shows him the mouth position for the *a*
and lets him imitate it under visual control. Furthermore, the physician
places one hand of the patient on his throat, the other one on the throat
of the patient himself, in order to let him feel in this manner the rhythmical vibrations which are produced by the vocal chords and transmitted
to the throat in the pronunciation of *a*. Thus, as a rule, the production of
the sound is successfully achieved. If we ask aphasics who learned to
speak again "by themselves" whether they were not watching the speakers' mouths a great deal, we often receive an affirmative answer! Are we
not confronted here with a case of practice therapy? For ordinarily the
eye, at least as a rule, only plays a minor role, to be sure, in the child's
process of learning how to speak. But if we think about what kind of
psychological and physiological conclusion can be drawn from such behavior,[6] we shall have to admit that a precise psychological analysis of the
means of reacquisition of speech is necessary even in the cases of

6. Fröschels, "Über den zentralen Mechanismus der Sprache." *Deutsche Zeitschr. f. Ner-
venh.*, Bd. 54.

aphasics not treated by physicians specialized in speech. Furthermore, it is now a sufficiently well-known fact that nearly all aphasics still have a word or a short sentence at their disposal here and there; and if we now assume that an *a* was contained in it, it is clear that we cannot affirm without qualifying the statement that the patient forgot the *a*. Rather we would first have to determine what this word is supposed to mean. Are we dealing with a complete disappearance of phenomena stemming from erstwhile infantile perceptions; that is, in the words of Semon, with a destruction of the engram, or are we only facing the inability to pronounce this engram? But even here the distinction should at least be made as to whether the patient succeeds in experiencing the engram within himself but is unable to communicate it, or whether this function also can no longer be activated. On the basis of modern psychological research all these possibilities must be answered in the affirmative. That the first possibility, which we might call total forgetting, cannot be dismissed out of hand, is already demonstrated by the fact that it has to be assumed under normal circumstances. James[7] states the following:

> All of these facts show that the volume of what we can remember is larger than we may ordinarily assume, and that in certain cases apparent forgetting is no proof that, under different conditions, a recollection could not indeed take place. But they will not support the exaggerated interpretation according to which no part of our experience can be forgotten.

What these conditions might be under pathological circumstances has been a matter of great interest to aphasia research for many years. Based on clinical observations, we really came close to the true situation by assigning an important role to emotion. Broca, Wernicke, Kussmaul, and other earlier researchers did not overlook the fact that in a state of joyous or sorrowful excitement, aphasics pronounce words and sentences of which ordinarily they no longer have any fractional parts at their disposal. Especially instructive here is a case transmitted by Jackson from Lengdondown's observation that a speechless idiot in a feverish delirium made his debut as a speaker. Jackson also points out that idiotic children mastering only a few words produced additional words in a sung form under the influence of musical stimuli. It may be permissible to deduce from this very example something about the difference between the older type of aphasia research and the psychologically oriented type. In this connection it must be emphasized, however, that Jackson, as Pick points out in a monograph which will be subject to further detailed evaluation, must be recognized as the pioneer of

7. *Psychologie* (Leipzig, 1907), translated by Dürr.

modern psychological aphasia research. Nothing would be simpler than to state, in keeping with the theory of extreme localization stipulating a separate central area for sung words, that the engrams in this central area were stored more abundantly than in the speech center, and that this was the reason why the idiots were able to sing more words than they could speak. The study of the emotional situation at any given time for the purpose of explaining the phenomenon results, however, neither in such a simple explanation nor in such a simple possibility of localization. But it does offer the basis for understanding—or at least for the possibility of understanding—far more numerous phenomena and is far more consistent, in the light of modern psychology, than the extreme theory of localization utilizing only engrams. We would, however, miss the mark by far, if we were to assume that it is the intent of this study to dispute the significance and even the fundamental importance of localizing physical, mental, and physical activities in the central nervous system. Indeed, a portion of the frontal brain has been claimed even for parts of the speech function that are of a purely emotional nature, such as intention and restraint (Edinger, Brotmann, Hartmann, Quensel, Goldstein), and I myself have had occasion to observe soldiers with gunshot wounds that have made this assumption plausible. Therefore, this monograph does not intend to deny the localization theory, but merely combines it with modern psychological views and limits it to the extent that localization does not occur in the all-too-narrow confines of individual sections of the brain. Frequently, however, people have pictured emotion as something appearing occasionally, like a deus ex machina, in order to be instilled for a moment into the fallow speech function. Today we must hold an essentially different view. If I understand correctly, this is one of the main points which Arnold Pick[8] wanted to bring to our attention. Insofar as we may talk about the "Studies for Psychological Foundation of Aphasia Theory"—the subtitle of the book—it is a guideline for a sequel to which we must look forward with the greatest of interest; a sequel which might partially move in this very direction. If we consider how greatly the success of practice therapy depends on the frame of mind of the patient, so that the physician time and again must take the initiative of encouraging him, then an additional indication of the importance of emotions for the understanding of aphasia may be found here. Let us again give the floor to modern psychologists in this important question.

Müller-Freienfels[9] agrees with the assumption that consciousness of

8. *Die agrammatischen Sprachstörungen* (Berlin, 1913).
9. *Das Denken und die Phantasie* (Leipzig, 1916).

feeling is the component of special physical processes different from external sense-stimulation. There exists, as is frequently assumed, not only the one and only pair of feelings, "desire and lack of desire," but a whole multitude of types of feelings, such as the subjective experience of being known, of being new, of strangeness, largeness, smallness, and many others. By no means can they be expressed as concepts; for what concept can be formed of how something new appears to me? He cites Hoffding, who proved that the sensation of "recognition" cannot be reduced to a concept but must be considered a special psychical "quality." In particular, he recalls the merit of Theodor Lipp, who in several studies undertook a detailed classification. We must maintain, above all, the view of Wundt that the variety of sensations is infinitely great. If Müller-Freienfels continues to oppose the word–motion concept, especially in connection with speech movement, by refusing to admit the memory image of an earlier movement, but assumes a state of consciousness directed exclusively towards movements, that is to say an orientation of a nonreproductive type, then I must, in answer to this, at least emphasize the possibility that under pathological conditions such motion concepts do exist. Hoepfner[10] not only explains stuttering by the concept of an excess of motorial speech, but also admits the possibility of a linguistic–motorial concept, perhaps lasting only a few moments under physiological conditions during the development of speech. The motor aphasic reeducated toward speech undoubtedly works for a long time with a concept of the position of the speech organs necessary for a particular sound. This effort is characterized by strained attention. Starting from this point of view, the consideration is only natural that children learning how to speak, especially ones ungifted in the speech–motorial sense, whose condition, however, might very well fall within the framework of physiological types of senses, might likewise work with motion concepts. Whether these childish concepts can now automatically be identified as being of the same type as the concepts of a more mature thinking person is probably only a secondary consideration for this question. It is rather a question as to whether initially we are in the presence of a mere nonreproductive mechanism or indeed a conceptive mechanism. Müller-Freienfels states specifically that he would accept as a concept only something that represented a reproduction, a memory image of external impressions. Here the objection seems justified to me that even among phonetically untrained people there exist sounds and sound combinations that stand out by means of strong kinesthetic com-

10. "Psychologisches über Stottern and Sprechen. Zugleich ein Beitrag zur Aphasiefrage." *Ztschr, f. Psychother. u. med. Psychol., Bd. 3. H. 5.*

ponents. Although I myself am not an excellent motor speaker, I experienced even before my preoccupation with experimental phonetics certain sounds so kinesthetically vivid during their utterances that I was completely clear as to the nature of their motorial origin. *Bl* and *gl* belong to those sounds, and since I recently mastered the tongue-tip *r*, that sound as well; but with these the list is by no means exhausted. Yet a more precise self-analysis shows that in this respect there are gradations, and that on the lowest level there are sounds which in regard to kinesthetics are rather colorless. I would not like to leave this item without having pointed out that it is exactly these different types of kinesthetic evaluation of sounds resulting from self-analysis which have not been taken into consideration in aphasia research up to now.

We still would have to counter the objection that kinesthetic sensations cannot automatically be identified with the motion concept. Outside of the difference of the words sensation and concept, which will be examined more closely forthwith, the objection in question does not seem valid, since the kinesthetic sensation accounts for at least an important part of the concept of motion. Although the terms *sensation* and *concept* in psychological literature are not used in a completely uniform manner, I can surmount this difficulty all the more easily since the terminology of Müller-Freienfels has been utilized here. In keeping with the interpretation of the latter, we must only correct ourselves so far as to talk of kinesthetic *perceptions* instead of kinesthetic *sensations.* By *perceptions,* however, he understands the *entire subjective assimilation which the sensation material undergoes while affecting us. Sensations* can be represented in isolation only in an abstraction; indeed, they cannot be experienced in an isolated manner. What happens is rather always a connection, so to speak, with the entire psychical personality of the moment. *Concepts,* however, are by no means, as the older school of associational psychology assumes, mere reproductions of sensations—a fact that is almost completely valid for the areas of lower senses, namely, senses of smell, taste, and touch, where intentional reproductions hardly ever are successful.

It is true that in the case of the higher senses, reproductions of sensation contents can be proven in somewhat greater number and extent, and, in any case, they are here not quite so unimportant as in the area of the lower senses. Here too, however, we have demonstrated the large part played by auxiliary and substitution phenomena; and at the same time it becomes manifest that in cases where perceptual elements also can be demonstrated, these cannot automatically be designated as reproductions at all; they often are figments of fantasy, and in any case are frequently complete transformations.[11]

11. Wundt, *Phys. Psych.* 6. Auflage. 3. Band. Leipzig, 1911, p. 484.

Since the reproductive, contemplative factor cannot be the essential thing in the complex of different elements, in which the concept manifests itself, we had to assume an additional nonperceptual factor which we named attitude. In a different place I state: "The thing that lends its typical and object-forming character to perception is not concepts (stemming from earlier perceptions) but feelings and attitudes toward activities."

It goes without saying that Müller-Freienfels does not deny the existence of concepts—he merely does not accept them as carbon copies of perceptions. Let us briefly point out the importance of this view for aphasia research in general. The lack of motorial speech concepts which he assumes seem in no way proven to us, as we have already mentioned. We could expecially use against him the argument of the adult's high degree of perfection in the area of speech movements as compared with the clumsiness of the child's. What is advanced here against Müller-Freienfels concerns arbitrary movements in general, such as the statement by Exner[12] that

> A movement to be produced is accessible to the influence of the will only when it calls forth conscious sensations, and thus also conception. . . . Each arbitrary movement causes conscious sensory effects; and a movement, the sensory effect of which cannot be conceived, is outside the domain of the will.

As to judgment, it is, according to Müller-Freienfels, the formulation of a perception, which latter, in turn, is an assimilation of sensations. Judgment serves both the purpose of clear fixation and that of communication to others. *Comprehension* is the formulation of the synthesized elements of perception (since during perception, both an analytic function that selects individual parts from a multitude of data and a synthesizing function that recondenses the selected parts into a new unity, are both manifest). Judgment, therefore, is always an action— either a reactive one resolved by an emotion, or a preconceived one accompanied by a certain intent; that is to say, an act of will.

Another orientation of our topic, namely, the relation of modern psychology to aphasia research, may well be successful in connection with statements by Müller-Freienfels of a specifically psychologistic nature, which developed, as he notes frequently, through a partial endorsement of other authors (Wundt, Mach, James, Avenarius, Münsterberg, H. Gomperz, Bolzano, Brentano, W. Stern, Paul, and others). It is sufficiently known that the prototype of speech-thinking is the one-word

12. *Entwurf zu einer physiologischen Erklärung der psychischen Erscheinungen* (Leipzig and Vienna, 1894).

sentence, and that, according to Meumann, it is emotional in nature. The utilization of a single expression for several only superficially similar objects is an additional well-known phenomenon of the early speech of children. Meumann points out that a sentence is never a mere stringing together of words but a unit firmly welded together. (Even the sentence: "I understand the content if I react to it in some manner, and if the words somehow stimulate my own mental activity," does not seem without meaning with regard to sensory aphasia.) "It is misleading in the highest degree when in traditional logic the concepts, that is the words, are illustrated by circles. It would be much more correct to represent the words by lines pointing in definite directions."

There is a great deal of affinity here with James's theory of "fringes" to which we shall return in detail. That memory images of sentences could be reproduced like sentences learned by heart, is, of course, not according to fact. This is a realization which, among other things, makes us understand that aphasics frequently repeat a sentence with different words without realizing that they did not use the same terms as the doctor. Müller-Freienfels opposes the old theory of association in his section "The Course of Consciousness" by stating: "The real problem is: why does only *b* enter into consciousness after *a*, and not *c* or *n*, since as a rule *a* is in contact not only with *b*, but with many other areas of meaning?"[13] Indeed, a problem exists here which belongs to the everyday occurrences of aphasic research. Why, for instance, does the patient read the word "infantry reigment" and not the word "island" presented to him? If in the course of further discussions we now find that here, too, a mental adjustment oriented toward processes of selection and recapitulation was the decisive factor—what French and American scholars prior to Müller-Freienfels called "attitude"—then by accepting this theory we shall be admitting that not much thought was given to anything of the kind in aphasia research up to the present. Recognition of the influence of our state of mind on the thinking process, it might be pointed out, is by no means of such recent date; it is only that the attention of aphasia research could not have been attracted to it. As proof for this let us quote Schopenhauer who, in his fundamental book *Concerning the Tenet of First Principles,* expresses himself as follows:

13. Cf. Wundt (*Phys. Psych.* 6. Auflage. 3. Band. Leipzig, 1911, p. 519): "When basing all reproductive processes on the model of successive association, numerous processes are being added to them which have nothing whatsoever to do with successive association.... There is no question anywhere here of the traditional model of association, according to which a direct impression must be followed by any kind of a memory image. Rather the impression immediately combines with reproductive elements to form a single, uniform concept, while at the same time characteristic feelings are tied to this process."

The will influences recognition by forcing it to repeat conceptions, to focus attention on this or that matter, and to evoke any kind of a train of thought. Thus it also acts upon the association of ideas, which is nothing but the utilization of the tenet in its four forms for the presentation of the mental images in the consciousness (that is to say, the train of thought).

In the same publication, by the way, Schopenhauer points out the inadequacy of the association theory, since in the reproduction process, the concept is different each time, and that could not be possible if only completed concepts were stored. Related to this matter are the words of Otto Liebmann,[14]

It is sheer assumption, however, that the organic structure of the fantasy is being produced through an associational mechanism without any guiding and shaping function of psychic entelechy. In just as trifling a way, the remaining intellectual life can be reduced to a purely logical process, as in Hegel. Man would much rather believe what he wishes.

Concerning this statement, Otto Liebmann says that it refers to the acceptance (as true) or the rejection (as false) not of the act of combination or separation of concept, but rather the nature of combination or separation itself. Finally, let us quote Vaihinger, who in his *Philosophie des Als Ob*[15] created a voluminous and no less informative book, through which the proof for the influence of our psychical life on our thinking runs like a scarlet thread: "The psyche is an organic creative force which independently changes absorbed matter functionally and adapts extraneous matter to itself just as much as it is able to adapt itself to new conditions." The common point of view which these authors, together with numerous and no less important psychologists, express is an attack on the association theory going back to Hume, Harltey, and Priestley. Nevertheless, knowledgeable people need hardly be reminded what great things association psychology has accomplished in science.

14. *Zur Analyse der Wirklichkeit,* 4th edition (Strassburg, 1911).
15. 2nd edition (Berlin, 1913).

Chapter 2

THE THEORY OF THE TRANSITIVE
CONTENTS OF CONSCIOUSNESS

William James in his theory of "substantial" and "transitive" components of the stream of consciousness has furnished additional psychological data which aphasia research cannot pass by without notice. In our consciousness there exist resting places which ordinarily are filled by some kind of visual concepts,[16] the particularity of which consist in the fact that they can be retained by the mind for an indefinite period, and can be observed without undergoing any change. Here, too, the psychology of association will have to take into consideration facts which it cannot cope with, at least not in their original frame of reference, for it is these fluid parts of our stream of consciousness—concerning which James himself says that they are very difficult to recognize by way of introspection for what they really are—which will hardly fit into the scheme of concepts to be associated. Elsewhere James states: "There are still other unknown modifications of consciousness which are as important as the transitive conditions, and which contribute to understanding as much as they do." After quoting other instructive examples James hits upon one of relevance to aphasia research:

Of what does that first lightning-like recognition of a man's disposition consist, which is experienced when, as we ordinarily say, we see right through him? It is certainly a very specific affectation of our mind. *Also, has the reader never asked himself what kind of psychic condition exists when he intends to say something before actually saying it? It is a very definite intention, different from all other intentions, and, therefore, a state of consciousness not to be confused with* any other. . . . The intent to say this or that is the only name that it can be given. It can be assumed that a good third of our psychical life consists of such fleeting, critically effective surveys of chains of thoughts not yet formulated. *How can*

16. *Psych.,* p. 158.

someone read a passage out loud, perhaps for the first time, be immediately capable of stressing all words correctly, if he did not have from the very beginning a consciousness at least of the form of the sentence to follow . . . ? Galton and Huxley took a step forward in rejecting the ridiculous theory of Hume and Berkeley, according to which we presumably have only images of perfect definite objects. A further step is the rejection of the equally ridiculous theory whereby, in contrast to the simple, objective qualities which we recognize in states of consciousness, relations are said not to have any such psychical representation. . . . What must be admitted is the fact that the definite images of traditional psychology account for only the smallest part of our actual psychic life. The view of traditional psychology is rather like a river consisting merely of so many spoons, pails, pitchers, barrels, or other containers full of water. But even if the vessels in question were actually standing in the stream, the free water would still continue to flow through between them. . . . Each definite image in our mind is being moistened and colored by the "free water" flowing around it. The consciousness of its close and distant relations, the fading knowledge of where it came from, and the emerging presentiment of where it is leading, move along together with each image.

Let us call the consciousness of this background of relations surrounding the image its "psychical overtone" or its "fringe." It is not necessary specifically to point out how valuable the insight into aphasia research contained in James's words must become; and if in Pick's excellent monograph we read the abundant literary material, which this widely read researcher gleans from modern linguistics and speech psychology, we shall find there many specialized cases which support James's theory. Related to this are also the statements of Buhler:[17]

Two equal parts of a complex can also stand out without conscious comparison if the observer aims only to find equality. . . . The formation of equal proportions may go on without the need for observing the members of the proportion individually (that is, by the way of non-evident processes of consciousness).

In the interest of evaluating the nonevident parts of consciousness, let us refer to Messer,[18] who actually considers them necessary for the explanation of the evident segment. In view of the fact that two psychologists (Müller-Freienfels, James) have been quoted so extensively here, I believe I must apologize for having neglected to give consideration to other no less highly meritorious researchers due to lack of available space. Although I have found the monograph, as well as both older and more recent publications of Pick most stimulating, I believe I particularly serve the cause of the medical profession by offering a clear presentation of more recent psychological theories. In this connection, I am completely aware that among psychologists themselves many a contradictory view still prevails; or, respectively, that many detailed studies deal with

17. *Die Gestaltswahrnehmungen* (Stuttgart, 1913), p. 175.
18. *Psychologie* (Stuttgart and Berlin, 1914), p. 9.

some parts of the quoted theory in essentially a more specialized manner. Let us recall at this point the Marburg School, and also Külpe, who died so young and who (like Marbe), in various studies, addressed himself directly to physicians, together with their followers. Let us mention Titschener, who made important contributions regarding the influence of types of sense, among other areas; and last but not least, Wundt and his school.

Pick also is justified in mentioning how advantageous the study of logic in Stöhr's psychological presentation[19] must become for our problems; we must not neglect it in the present study either. Of no less interest is his book, *Umriss einer Theorie der Namen.*[20] in which he describes the various psychological processes (and their interrelationship) which bring about the creation of names, a term that should be understood as meaning words in general.[21] Of special interest also are the arguments of W. Poppelreuther.[22] He, too, points out the failure to note that it is precisely the order of reproduction, the chronological course, that must be influenced by processes of the will. He distinguishes four stages of reproduction: (1) the summary total recall; (2) the differentiation of details or gradual explanation of the evident parts of the total concept (and he explicitly states that these details do not reappear at all in the order a, b, c, d, etc., in which they had been perceived); (3) the optimal stage, or the potentially greatest completeness and differentiation; and (4) a stage in which differentiation as well as clearness again decreases. "In spite of these different stages, the event in all its stages is nevertheless always a whole, a more or less complete concept of the event." And elsewhere: "The physiological–sensorial material can be completely divided into elements. That is not the case for comprehension. This always produces a whole, namely a total impression."

19. Leipzig and Vienna, 2nd edition, 1915.
20. Leipzig and Vienna, 1889.
21. Stöhr's *Psychologie* was published only after the completion of this study, and for this reason it unfortunately could not be quoted.
22. "Über den Versuch einer Revision der psychophysiologischen Lehre von der elementaren Assoziation," *Monatschr. f. Psych. und Neur.*, 1915.

ON THE PRECEDENCE OF THE SENTENCE IN CONNECTION WITH INTERNAL SPEECH FORMULATION OF THOUGHTS

Two main points emerge with a certain preponderance from the views of the modern psychologists quoted here: namely, the attitude; and also the nonevident parts of our consciousness (James's "transitive parts" and "fringe"). In view of the close relation of speech to perception, concept, and thinking in general, we cannot be surprised to find very similar and even frequently analogous views held by linguists and speech psychologists. In this connection also, Pick's monograph is a rich source of information to which we shall refer once again. Let me offer, as clearly as possible, merely a brief resume. Not unintentionally, as will become apparent later, I begin with the words of C. and W. Stern:[23]

> Meumann's great achievement consisted in pointing out the strongly volitional-emotional meaning that the first words of children's speech of necessity possess—as opposed to those researchers who conceive of them cognitively as designations of objects.

If we compare this to Stern's general definition of sentences—"A sentence is the expression of a uniform attitude with regard to a content of consciousness"—we shall understand the idea, to be explained later on in greater detail, that infantile speech characteristics may be assumed to be the basis for adult speech. Taking into consideration, on the other hand, one of the two main aspects previously mentioned, Wilhelm Wundt's definition no less belongs at the head of this paragraph: "The whole of the sentence in all its parts at first appears to us as a total

---

23. *Die Kindersprache* (Leipzig, 1907), p. 168.

concept, although we might be only rather dimly aware of it; and this concept structures itself into its parts, if these parts are being perceived one after the other."

I hope not to interrupt, but rather to further the present summary by inserting after these words of Wundt an observation derived from experimental phonetics—regarding which, after this example, one need hardly point out any more closely its importance for psychological aphasia research. To wit, if by one of the current methods—among which I found that of Gutzmann to be the handiest—a pneumogram of a healthy speaker is taken, we can verify the fact that the tested person is out of breath at the end of a sentence, or at least of a coherent part of a sentence. This is all the more remarkable in that it occurs both after very short and after long sentences. It can only be explained by the fact that a normal speaker must have a certain feeling for the sentence's future structure as early as its beginning; whereas, on the other hand, it will be clear to everyone that, particularly in the expression of difficult thoughts, he does not have all words readily at his disposal when beginning the utterance. This may be taken as proof of Wundt's definition. Stern's words could be more closely explained by a quotation from Pick, especially since this quotation leads to another important item, that is, the role of the listener:

> In evaluating the subjective factor introduced into speech we must not allow ourselves to forget a further general aspect. Just as conceptions of objects are not their copied images, but modifications of them through additional ingredients from the ego, the signs (words) also, no matter how conventional their foundations may be, are not the expression of even the somehow modified objects, but have to pass through the modifying object too. Seen from the point of view of the listener, they must even take this road twice, a fact which lends a still more subjective touch to the whole. Therefore, something subjective, reflected to a greater or lesser extent by speech, is attached to the seemingly objective parts of language.[24]

With regard to the listener, I would like to refer to the very precise grammatical expression, *dativus ethicus.* Also let me quote Kretschmer in Pick's monograph: "A speech utterance is a sentence only when the emotion causing it has found its solution, and when the impulse of will underlying it is satisfied." Because of such theories, the pedagogical view[25] now becomes understandable and at the same time furnishes an important clue for the speech-therapy behavior of certain aphasics; that

---

24. Further reference should be made to the 2nd volume of Edmund Husserl's works. *Logische Untersuchungen* 2nd. ed., (Halle a. S., 1913).

25. Gassman and Schmidt, *Die Fehlerscheinungen beim Nachsprechen von Sätzen usw.* (Leipzig, 1913).

"a new concept is best introduced by allowing the child first to grow and feel its way into the entire situation, and then by giving him the name for the concept, or inversely (as for instance in reading) by teaching him to understand an unknown or not sufficiently known word from the context of the situation."

Chapter 4

ON THE QUESTIONS OF
THE IDENTITY OF THINKING AND SPEAKING

Pick clearly recognized the importance for aphasia research, given to the question of the identity of thinking with speaking, and dedicated almost half his book to it. After having become acquainted with the transitive components of consciousness, attitude, and "fringes," it will come as no surprise to us that modern psychology and speech research rejects the identity of thinking and speaking. In this connection the frequently stated phrase of Adolf Stöhr seems to be especially instructive, to wit, that nonsense can only be spoken, but not thought. "Red equals blue," for instance, can be easily said, but cannot be thought. A further base for attack on the theory of identity is contained in Pilsbury's[26] statement that the manner we select for expressing our thoughts depends on the person to whom we are talking: "If thinking and speaking were inseparable from each other and essentially identical, everyone hearing a new sentence also would at once understand its contents." As Sachs[27] also states in his precise fashion, even superficial observation shows that this is not the case. From this realization Pick draws the following very important conclusion:

Through the foregoing it became clear to us that thinking and speaking are neither identical, nor do they show such a precise synchronization that a formal understanding of speech would go hand in hand with that of the corresponding processes of thinking. A further determination is the fact that, in order to obtain an understand-

26. *The Psychology of Reason,* 1910.
27. *Gehirn und Sprache* (Wiesbaden, 1905), p. 63.

ing of the achievement of speech, we must take into consideration both the processes
of speech and thought, and above all, the transmission into speech, which indeed is
the end result of all these processes.

In my activity as a physician specializing in speech disorders I have
had to deal not only with aphasics, but also with all other speech disturbances, especially with the developmental disorders of children's speech;
and I would like to insert here some of my own experiences. Pick is
talking about the transmission of thought processes through language,
and in this connection is thinking of the respective processes of the
accomplished speaker. However, I am not merely playing a game with
the same words when I recommend that aphasia researchers pay the
closest attention to the transformation of thought into language in the
case of children who are still mute. This process, by the way, was already
taken into consideration here and there, especially by Pick. These same
pertinent observations of mine are to be a main topic of the present
study, and I am convinced I can thereby contribute something to the
"psychologizing" of aphasia research. This can be accomplished all the
more easily because I am in a position to offer a rich store of observations on impediments in the development of children's speech. In these
very impediments I see conditions closely related to forms of aphasia.
Consequently, I believe that some understanding of aphasia can be
derived from them. If the deaf child has frequently been useful for
understanding the psychology of speech and also of aphasia, (cf. the
interesting chapters in Reuschert's *Gebärdensprache der Taubstummen und
die Ausdrucksbewegungen der Vollsinnigen*, Leipzig, 1909) is it not all the
more logical to utilize in this application the lack of speech in children who
are capable of hearing?

Erdmann makes a distinction between *formulated* and *unformulated*
thinking. When formulated, it may be either completely or incompletely
so. The former consists in a completely conscious sequence of both the
objective parts of the statement and their connection with words; in the
latter, the contents of meaning become partially unconscious because of
an habitual sequence. In addition, Erdmann names two other forms of
unformulated thinking, i.e., *hypological* and *metalogical* thinking. The
hypological thinking is of special interest to us, since, according to
Erdmann, it occurs in children's speech as well as in the speech of
aphasics: It is characterized by the inability to formulate thoughts. He
defines metalogical thinking as follows:

The more strongly reproduction acts on any areas of conception, the more sharply
the abstracting attention sets in; the more its reproducing power is being fertilized by

an abundance of easily produced potential associations, the less thinking is bound to a symbolism that includes and supports the objects of this attention by way of the word. . . . The intellectual efforts of the businessman, technician, statesman, artist, and philosopher frequently are completed as soon as they attempt to retain what they see, to introduce it into reality, to construct, shape, and formulate it. . . . And all of them feel, even insofar as they have to use language, how rarely they succeed in completely reproducing the richness of something perceived as a certainty.

Chapter 5

THE PATH FROM THINKING TO SPEAKING

If, from the foregoing, it has been sufficiently proved that there are levels of thinking which do not correspond to words, it is of interest to acquaint oneself with the individual stages of the transition from thinking to speaking. H. Gomperz names three stages; The first takes care of the logical structuring of thoughts (referred to as the undetermined speech-form stage). The second is called the potentially determined speech-form stage, in which the logical structuring has advanced so far that only a very distinct form of speech expression remains adequate to it any longer. Finally, in the third stage—that of the actually determined speech-form—the concept of expression is already on hand. How closely related the second stage is to those psychological processes which we have previously met as "attitude" is especially stressed by Pick (*Die agrammatischen Sprachstörungen,* 1913):

> It has been emphasized that in connection with the well-known phenomenon of searching for a word, W. James[28] assumes that, even before it is found, there is an adaption of the word to a scheme. It appears quite likely that the moment for the occurrence of this feeling of suitability or unsuitability also corresponds to that of the situation of consciousness . . . [p. 233].

The attempt made here to draw an analogy between the aspect of a situation of consciousness in this stage and that found while searching for a forgotten word was proved correct by Messer's observation (Principles of Psychology) that

> further judgment as to the suitability of emerging contents of thinking is partially prepared, but also partially replaced by the situation of consciousness of the suitable

28. *Principles* 1, p. 251.

(or unsuitable), of the meaningful (or meaningless), and the correct (or the incorrect, false, or inadequate) [p. 183].

An additional comment by Pick reads as follows:

> How must the transition from thought to sentence structure within the speaker be conceived? It may be permissible at first to use an image for that purpose. We might be able to imagine that the pattern of thought acquired through the processes of thought gives rise to a scheme of speech that we can picture as somewhat analogous to a linear blueprint of a mosaic executed in a basic substance, into the meshes of which the words are "placed" in the stage of word selection which then follows. We can probably draw an analogy of syntax, perhaps, with localization in the basic substance, and of the grammatical structuring occurring simultaneously with the modifying influence which the word elements partially receive from the basic matter, and partially absorb in a reciprocal manner. If the words are to follow one another according to the meaning of the thought, and if they are to mutually adjust to each other in form and arrangement, then we might represent this perhaps by an image of two such schemes [pp. 234-235].

Furthermore, the so-called accents are to be regarded as preliminary steps of the formulation of speech.[29] I shall quote myself here since my view on accents differs radically from that of most other authors. In my treatise *Über die Akzente der deutschen Sprache*[30] (*On Accents in the German Language*), I state the following:

> If we read the words *Das Buch gehört mir* ('The book belongs to me') in the following four stresses: (1) **Dás** *Buch gehört mir;* (2) *Das* **Búch** *gehört mir;* (3) *Das Buch* **gehört** *mir;* and (4) *Das Buch gehört* **mir,** we shall not doubt for a single moment that we are dealing with four statements, each different as to meaning. Somebody pronouncing the quoted words with the stress indicated by the first written version expresses a different thought than if he used one of the three other stresses.

Stress develops through two factors, that is, through a higher pitch compared with the pitch in which the other syllables were spoken, and through an increase of tonal volume compared to the tonal strength of the other elements of the sentence. The first factor is designated as the *musical* accent, the second as the *dynamic*. Furthermore, in one of the

29. Very recently an article by a student of mine, L. Stein, appeared in the *Monatsschrift für Ohrenheilkunde und Rhine-Laryngologie* ("Beobachtungen bein Wiederaufbau der Sprache Aphatischer") in which it was pointed out that motor aphasics, who were taught to speak again by a physician speaking High German, for instance through the optical–tactile method (to be fully explained later), then automatically reverted to their customary dialect. This phenomenon could be made use of by assuming that these elements, which most likely are largely musical in nature, still existed inwardly, although the words themselves, and even the sounds, were missing. In this we might see an indication that they represent a function which, up to a certain degree, is independent from the process of finding words.

30. Passow's and Schäfer's *Beiträge*, 1916.

quoted examples, a speaker may pronounce the stressed syllable more slowly than in another, where the stress rests on another syllable. This phenomenon is called *quantity* or *temporal* accent. However, it is not at all necessary for the three types of accents to fall on one and the same syllable. It is possible, for instance, to say *Daas Buuch geehöört mir.* There is a temporal accent here on the first four syllables and a musical one on the fifth. Later on in the treatise, I show that the musical accent may also consist in a lowering of the pitch, the dynamic accent also in a lessening of the speech volume, and the temporal accent in shortening the syllable. Of the examples given I want to mention just one here. Let us pronounce the verse by Goethe, *Über allen Wipfeln ist Ruh.* The highest pitch is in the first syllable of the word *Wipfeln,* the lowest in the word *Ruh.* If we were to follow the authors quoted there (Minor, Panconcelli-Calcia, Gutzmann, Zwaardemaker, Pipping, Barth, Scripture, but excepting Sievers and Luick) we would have to decide that the musical accent of the sentence rests on the syllable *Wi,* and the dynamic and temporal one on the syllable *Ruh.* Let us now try, in the Goethe verse, to say the words *Über allen Wipfeln ist* in an even, medium-low pitch, and the word Ruh in a still lower one. We can convince ourselves that this will not change the meaning. However, the meaning would change were we to speak the word *Ruh* in a higher pitch than the others. From this we must conclude that the low pitch of *Ruh* is the most important thing in the whole line. In other words, on the word *Ruh* there is a musical accent which consists in lowering the pitch. I conclude the treatise by saying: The importance of stress consists in the fact that the speaker directs the listener's attention to a sentence, a word, or a syllable by pronouncing them in a manner unaccustomed and strange to the listener. It is perhaps due to this definition, which takes both the speaker and the listener into consideration, that the importance of stress in language is now being recognized.[31] Wolfgang Köhler (*Akustische Untersuchungen* III, 3, 112) claims that the spoken sentence possesses no tonal pitch, and this seems to be a contradiction to what has just been said. However, this contradiction actually applies only to nomenclature,[32] and is therefore without importance

31. Wundt, p. 91, points out that whenever we speak following a metronome, the rhythmical beats of which increase in rapidity, we experience the sensation of an increase in emotion, and that even in ordinary speech an increasing tempo is one of emotion. He uses these observations to explain stresses in general, which thus are results of emotional processes. The continuous intervention of emotions also conditions the change not only of the tempo in language, but also in music. Modern music has progressed to notes of a duration of 1/30th of a second.

On the other hand, Wallacchek (*Psychologie und Technik der Rede,* Leipzig, 1914) points out that the listener also feels the musical element before he recognizes the intellectual one.

32. Max Meyer, "Vorschläge zur akustischen Terminologie," *Zeitschrift für Psychologie,* V. 08. No. 1–2, proposes the term "tonality" for "height of tone" (or "pitch"). This may be

here. No less influential than the stresses is the rapidity of speech, or *pace*. As Pick emphasizes: it, too, must be conceded a primacy as compared to word sequence. Since the very disturbance of the speech tempo is a frequent occurrence in cases of aphasia, I would like to pause a little here, especially since I am able to offer some analogy from my other logopedic experience, which is of interest since it seems to be suitable for clarifying the value of more precise psychological analyses connected with speech disturbances in general. There is a speech disorder designated by the term *poltern* (cluttering) or *paraphrasia praecox*. At first glance, it is outwardly characterized by the fact that the patients speak hurriedly, often to the point of incomprehensibility. Sometimes they even get stuck, in which case one syllable is repeated several times, or else the speech organs are engaged in a peculiar struggle with two sounds which they want to produce simultaneously. Suddenly the patient is sitting there with his mouth wide open, and we have the distinct impression that he has lost his connecting thread. These people's thoughts seem to burst forth with such speed that one thought appears to overtake the other before it is even pronounced. The same applies to parts of a single thought, and manifests itself in speech by the previously mentioned symptoms; It also manifests itself in that some individual words are completely omitted or "swallowed," that occasionally words appear which consist of parts of different words, and finally that sounds and words emerge at too early a stage. In case histories of such patients I have recorded the words *Sun sky* developed from "sunshine in the sky", and *Glonnenglanz,* instead of *Sonnenglanz* ('radiance of sunlight'). Similar symptoms can frequently be found in aphasics, and may be illustrated here by two stories and their rendering by a "polterer" ('clutterer')—Case 1, which has previously been published elsewhere.[33]

CASE 1: THE "CLUTTERER"

First Story: The Game of Billiards

The First Consul had received as a present two very beautiful horses, which he had brought into the courtyard of Malmaison Castle for inspection. His generals admired the magnificent thoroughbreds, and one of his favorite

---

mentioned here because his intention to introduce a uniform nomenclature is a very suitable one. I have not used this term as yet because of the fact that until now physicians have probably not been acquainted with it.

33. *Lehrbuch der Sprachheilkunde* (Vienna and Leipzig, 1913).

officers seemed to have his eye on one splendid black horse in particular. Bonaparte proposed to gamble one horse on the outcome of a game of billiards, and the general did not have to be told twice. Whether Napoleon was destined to lose or wanted to, his adversary won the match with ease. "I defeated thee," he exclaimed to the First Counsul, with whom he still was on informal terms as in earlier days, "and therefore I have the right to choose." And without waiting for permission, which, by the way, he did not even request, he ran down into the yard, looked for the black horse, the most beautiful animal of all, had a saddle put on it and mounted it.

"Farewell, Bonaparte!" he shouted "I'd rather get out of here than stay here for dinner, for thou art capable of winning thy horse back from me."

And before Napoleon had time to answer him, he had already gone a long way. In order to prevent a repetition of similar incidents, the all-too-bold officer received an embassy post in Portugal. However, the esteem and friendship of the First Consul for him was not in the least diminished.

The clutterer told the story in the following manner:

When Napoleon for the first time still was consul, he had beautiful horses brought to him in the courtyard of Malmaison. One of his favorite admired a horse **a horse** (*ein Pferd, ein Pferd*) which seemed to *ple*[34] [superfluous syllable anticipating the following word please—*ge* in the German text anticipating *gefallen*—Translator's comment.] Napoleon, who liked *e* [anticipating the ending of the following word *the*—in German *en* anticipating *den* (accusative masculine singular article)—Translator] the officer proposed a game of billiards to him and told him *he* [duplicated] he would give him the horse if he **if**

---

34. *Translator's note:* Incorrect morphological forms of declension or agreement are translated into English as closely as possible. Whenever there is no equivalent in English at all, a close analogy is sought in English for the incorrect form in German appearing in parentheses and underlined.

For the purposes of better comparison the original German text is given here. It reads as follows:

"*Als Napoleon* **für** [*superfluous*] *das erstemal noch Konsul war, liess er sich im Hofe von Malmaison schöne Pferde vorführen. Einer seiner Lieblingsoffiziere bewunderte ein Pferd* **ein Pferd**, [*superfluous*] *welches ihm* **ge** [*superfluous*] *besonders zu gefallen schien. Napoleon, der* **en** [*superfluous*] *den Offizier gerne hatte, schlug ihm eine Partie auf dem Billiard vor und sagte ihm,* **er** [*superfluous*] *er werde,* **wenn er** [*superfluous*] *wenn er beim Billiardspiel gewinne, ihm das Pferd schenken. Napoleon verlor und so* **somit somit** [*superfluous*] *bekam auch* **der** [*superfluous*] *der Offizier* **den** (*masculine accusative article*) **das** (*neuter accusative article*) [*both superfluous*] *das Pferd. Dieser* **dieser** [*superfluous*] *wartete überhaupt* **der** (*wrong case ending of wrong gender article*) [*superfluous*] *die Erlaubnis nicht ab* **nicht ab** [*superfluous*], *sondern* **sprengte** [*superfluous anticipation of the wrong verb*] *ging sofort in den Hof, liess das Pferd satteln und sprengte damit* **von** [*superfluous preposition*] *davon. Napoleon,* **der der** (*wrong case relative pronoun*) [*superfluous*] *den* **die die** [*superfluous*] *Kühnheit des Offiziers ärgerte,* **beschloss** [*superfluous*] *beschloss, ihn, den Offizier, um weiteren ähnlichen Szenen vorzubeugen,* **nach Por** [*superfluous*] *nach Portugal zu schicken, damit er dort eine Gesandtschaftsstelle bekleide.*"

he [duplicated] won at billiards. Napoleon lost, and thereby **thereby** [dup-licated] the *the* [duplicated] officer did obtain the **the the** [duplicated] horse. He **he did not** [duplicated] did not wait for the **the** [duplicated] permission altogether but raced [superfluous] went at once into the yard, had a saddle put on the horse and sped **on** [superfluous preposition] away on it. Napoleon **who who** [superfluous] whom the **the** [superfluous] boldness of the officer made angry **decided** [superfluous] decided to send him, the officer, **to Por** [superfluous] to Portugal to take over an embassy post there in order to prevent similar incidents.

Second Story: Young Destrem

On the occasion of the first award of the Grand Cross of the Legion of Honor in the Dôme des Invalides, a young man, almost still an adolescent, rushed up to the steps of the throne and exclaimed: "Mercy, mercy for my father!" Napoleon, moved by the young man's interesting appearance and his considerable state of emotion, approached him and wanted to make him rise. But the young man refused to change his position and, on bended knee and with his hands raised, repeated his plea. "What is your father's name?" asked the First Consul. "Sire," replied the youth in a voice choked by tears, "he distinguished himself greatly, but his enemies maligned him disgracefully before Your Majesty. But I swear to you, Sire, he is innocent! I am the son of Hugo Destrem." "Your father, Sir, compromised himself greatly by his con-nection with the most rabid factionists; nevertheless, I do not want to leave your request unfulfilled. M. Destrem may consider himself lucky to have such a son." Napoleon added a few more consoling words, and young Destrem left in the happy certitude of his father's impending pardon.

Unfortunately Napoleon's pardon came too late. Hugo Destrem, who had been sent to the island of Oleron after the bombing attempt—in which, inci-dentally, he had no part—died in exile before receiving the news of the par-don which his courageous son had obtained for him.

The clutterer told the story in the following fashion:

When the First Consul awarded the the honorary medals (**das die** *Ehren-kreuze* . . .) in the Dôme des Invalides, a young man fell to her knee (*auf* **den** *Knie* . . .) before him with the request to pardon his father. Napoleon whom liked (**wer** *gefiel* . . .) the emotion of the boy, and he asked him who he was. He answered he was his father was Hugo Destrem. It Napoleon answered, your father misbehaved himself him heinously (**dein Vater hat sich sie si sehr** *ver-gangen*) by compromising himself greatly through frequenting the most rabid factionists. And therefore he had to and therefore. (*Und somit musste er und somit...*) But who who you plead for him, (*Aber der der du für ihn bittest...*) I shall pardon pardon him. In the the pardon, however, came too late, for the the father had already been brought to the island of Oleron by ship, and there there he died died after long after long years.

A striking similarity between this type of diction and that of certain paraphasic aphasics is obvious at first sight. A more detailed psychological investigation of clutterers, as I was able to establish in agreement with Albert Liebmann[31] shows, in addition to a hasty temperament, gross attention defects in the acoustic domain. It would be tempting to assume a congenial anomaly of the temporal lobe, but up to the present no anatomical investigations of the brain of clutterers exist in the specialized literature. Nevertheless, in my description of cluttering, I do not believe that I am referring to something basically foreign to forms of aphasia.

The main thoughts illustrated by the last paragraphs are approximately the following: (1) There is no identity between thinking and speaking; (2) Various intermediary steps between thoughts and their utterance in speech—which possess a relationship of the preceding to the following, or, in other words, develop in the manner of layers—have indeed been brought to light; (3) An impetus of feeling "attitude" or "situation of consciousness" is inherent in the formulation of speech as well as in the interplay of thoughts; (4) Words are not at all the primary thing; on the contrary, they are rather preceded by other structural components of the sentence. According to Meyer-Lübke,[36] the individual word, to a certain degree, is an abstraction, since we do not speak in words, but in sentences. As to the choice of words, Pick assumes that the content words precede the function words "because they (the former) represent the essence of the formulation in general."

35. *Vorlesungen über Sprachstörungen* (Berlin, 1900), Heft 4, p. 41.
36. *Historische Grammatik der französischen Sprache*, p. 39.

Chapter 6

REFLECTIONS ON THE HISTORY OF EVOLUTION OF SPEECH AND THE FAULTS OF AN EVOLUTIONARY APPROACH

One of the most important methods in modern psychology is the evolutionary historical manner of observing psychological processes that proceeded on two different paths. The first one is a purely historical one, to wit: the study of the psyche of earlier people; and the second, the observation of primitive peoples and of the psyche of children. In order to characterize generally the great value of these orientations of research, it will suffice to refer to Wundt's epoch-making *Social Psychology*.[37] Its special value for aphasia research was probably anticipated by Kussmaul who, in his monograph *Die Störungen der Sprache*,[38] accords a great deal of space to the development of children's speech. I may, in my own right, point to various attempts to contribute to the understanding of aphasia research by using the findings of child psychology, and especially the development of children's speech and its impediments. The names of the modern speech doctors, Hermann, Gutzmann, Nadoleczny and, last but not least, the aphasia researcher Bastian, must be mentioned here as sharing these views. Once again we must refer to Arnold Pick, who in his monograph developed a step-by-step plan for using studies relevant to the understanding of aphasia.

In agreement with Pick, we were repeatedly able to point out, in the preceding paragraphs, how the development of thoughts themselves and their expression in speech proceeds, by storing one layer of functions upon another—functions that chronologically occur earlier or later. On the other hand, if the observation of the child's psyche, and the development of its speech also results in the emergence of the various,

37. *Völkerpsychologie* (Leipzig: Engelmann, 1900).
38. (Leipzig, 1910), 4th edition, ed. H. Gutzmann.

pertinent qualities in a gradual sequence, and if a certain parallelism between these two series can be noted, then a utilization of child psychology for the psychology of aphasia is indicated. This point of view becomes especially compelling where the clinical observation of aphasia patients shows many coincidences with speech disturbances that can be demonstrated physiologically, especially where they relate to developmental disorders of children.

I feel justified in reporting on this now in a broader frame of reference. On the other hand, I consider it necessary to point out once more that I am by no means of the opinion that every form of aphasia can be explained by an analogy to infantile stages of speech and speech impediments. For it is evident that any function taken by itself, no matter from what root it developed in term of evolutionary history, represents a newness and independence that must be taken into consideration to the same increased degree to which the function itself has developed. Indeed the theory of descendance, which explains later occurrences as being derived from preceding ones, shows how every step of the way we encounter phenomena offering in their whole makeup an impression of such isolation and originality as to threaten the overthrow of the entire theory. Undoubtedly, in this connection, it is in the realm of such methods of observation to refer, time and again, to the basic theory. Yet in questions like that of aphasia, which can be and are being served by so many orientations of research, the cause is being hindered rather than furthered, if we were to refer to all the far-fetched speculations. In this sense I will be content to quote only completely clearcut cases of analogy between infantile speech development and speech disturbances on the one hand, and aphasia on the other. In other cases I will merely point out the possibility of using these phenomena in children for aphasia research. After narrowing down the scope of the question like this, let us now examine the development of children's speech in greater detail.

Chapter 7

THE FIRST STAGE OF SPEECH

Crying

As we know, the first vocal activity of the newborn baby is crying. The first cry and also the crying activity of the first weeks of life are interpreted as pure reflexes: the former due to a sudden cooling-off process, a penetrating stimulus of light, and a flow of air into the lungs; the latter due to a feeling of hunger, pain, or other discomfort. It may be of interest to specifically point out that even this first activity of the speech apparatus coincides with that most artful action of the vocal cords which lead to vowel sounds. For it is well-known that crying is endowed with a vowel character,[39] and it is also known that vowels are caused by rhythmical vibrations of the vocal cords. If we treat a person with a severe case of motor aphasia (or even a deaf-mute, who has never heard or pronounced a vowel) by letting him feel the vibrations at the throat of the physician pronouncing a vowel, he will imitate the sound in accordance with this tactile impression by making his own vocal cords vibrate in a similar fashion. This completely instinctive act is possible in later life only on the basis of that innate reflex mechanism lending a vocal character to the cry of the newborn baby. What phonetically untrained individual knows anything about this peculiar activity of the vocal cords, and what person in general would be capable of activating his vocal cords if he were ***verbally requested*** to make them vibrate rhythmically unless he knew what the acoustic consequence would be? In the very first weeks the crying sounds are rather monotonous, so that even the most attentive mother cannot recognize the wishes of her child merely by hearing them. However, as early as the second month of life the cries begin to

39. C. and W. Stern, *Die Kindersprache*, p. 15, transcribe the first sound of their daughter as "ähä."

become more differentiated: they sound different when the child is hungry, and different when it is wet. It would not be incorrect to conceive of these various cries, at least in the beginning, as pure reflexes which differ from one another depending on the cause responsible for them. Gradually, however, they might be produced by the child because of the growing realization that he receives attention and care due to his crying. In that case they must already be considered a sort of language, if by language—in agreement with Wundt—we understand these actions by means of which communicating the contents of individual consciousness to others is effected.

The development of the muscular system of breathing favored during the crying stage is important for future speech, especially since the main characteristics of breathing during crying, that is, rapid short inhaling and slow and gradual exhaling completely resemble the type of breathing during articulate speech, as was pointed out by Flatau and Gutzmann.[40]

40. "Die Stimme des Säuglings," *Archiv für Laryngologie*, Vol. XVIII.

Chapter 8

BABBLING

The Emergence of Sensory Components of the Speech Mechanism

The so-called babbling activity occurs much earlier than was assumed by Kussmaul. It consists of an utterance of sound complexes that resemble our syllables to a certain degree. Kussmaul, in *Die Störungen der Sprache,* comments on them as follows:

> They are partly the known sounds of our alphabet, but not yet as rigidly and sharply pronounced as later on, and partly odd sounds that can be expressed in our characters only with difficulty or not at all, such as hissing, growling, clicking, and "pfuchz"-ing (blundering) sounds and others like them. . . . They are a result of the same muscular impetus which makes babies' hands fidget and their little legs kick, thereby preparing them for such activities as grasping objects and walking. They can be considered to be the original sounds given to man from the earliest beginnings, which during the course of innumerable generations developed into all those sounds contained in the alphabets of living languages [pp. 47–48].

Stern's daughter began to babble in her seventh week, his son in the tenth; and Gutzmann's youngest daughter as early as the fourth week.

The babbling period is important not only for the mobility and accuracy of the speech muscles, but also for a greater range of the mechanism which has the greatest influence on the entire subsequent speech development and speech. When a baby is in a comfortable mood—which seems to be the one most conducive to babbling—and has produced a sound complex for the first time, we may be certain that it will produce that sound over and over, and even that the baby is replacing sounds produced through earlier babbling by the new one. We shall not go wrong in assuming that the child perceives, by way of hearing, the sound complex produced in a purely motor-reflex manner, hears it over and over in case of repeated production, and that finally the auditory impression, or rather the pleasurable feeling connected with it, becomes the impetus for the renewed pronunciation of the babbled syllable.[41] It is not necessary to state in greater detail here the basic importance of the emergence of this function—through which, in a path from the hearing to the speech muscles, most future speech development proceeds.

The subsequent babbling period may already bring the first beginnings of imitation of sounds spoken by the mother, and this may bring additional proof of the fact that the process just described becomes possible during this period: Stern's little daughter, in her eleventh week, babbled the syllable *erre*. If somebody would say *erre, erre,* to the baby, when she was in a good mood, she would frequently react

> by uttering the syllables, which it normally produced automatically and effortlessly, only with an evident effort frequently lasting for seconds. The effort resulted in the baby's face getting red. We may exclude chance because the experiment was often successful without the baby uttering sounds by itself, either before or after. Her utterings definitely gave the impression of an intentional successful imitation. One week later, the same result was achieved with the syllable *kräh, kräh,* which for several weeks it had no longer been babbling.

Gheorgov[42] reports a similar fact about his 9-month-old son.

I myself would like to insert here some experiences from the pathological area.

CASE 2: ILONA N.

Twenty-three-month-old Ilona N., the only child of a 38-year-old father and a 36-year-old mother, weighed only 2½ kilograms (5 ½ pounds) at birth—which was an easy one—and she was very small. She was never seriously ill, and had her first teeth at 14 months. Her parents were not related to one another, and the family anamnesis is of no importance. The child could not walk then and was mute. She measured 80 centimeters (31½ inches), was well fed and very temperamental. Her crying sounded normal. There was a light case of inspiration stridor, and the hypodermis cellular tissue was of myxedemic consistency. Her face showed a mongoloid type, and there was a slight case of navel hernia and constipation. Internal examination showed nothing of a pathological nature, but the child always had a pulse of 100 to 130. The nasal cavity was

---

41. Reference is made here to Stransky's informative monograph (*Über Sprachverwirrtheit,* Halle, 1905, p. 37) in which he states that sometimes "a tendency for autoecholalia" exists even among adults.

42. *Le développement du langage chez l'enfant* (Ledeberg-Gant, 1912), p. 10.

unusually dry; the mouth organs normal. The hearing diagnosis showed intact eardrums and good hearing. Thyreoidin was being prescribed, and daily 20-minute speech-practice therapy sessions were held. The child was shown simple colored pictures of objects, human beings, and animals, each one on a quarto sheet, and the appropriate name was mentioned in connection with it. Red colors seemed to especially attract the child, whereas dark and green colors were rejected. After a few sessions, the child was instructed to observe the mouth when the pictures were designated by name. The sense of touch was also used in the above-mentioned fashion. It was apparent that the patient had some understanding of speech, since at the mention of the word *mama,* for instance, she indicated by a motion of her hand that her mother was sitting in the adjacent room. The treatment began January 1. On the 12th, the child suddenly pronounced an *u,* without a previous model pronunciation, whereas earlier she had not even repeated it. In this session and the following ones, she repeated the sound very frequently, accompanied by manifestations of pleasure. On the 29th of the same month, the syllables *ku* and *ko* emerged; also *fla;* and the author seized upon the opportunity to model the word *Kanne,* which the child repeated as *Kao.* On February 5 the syllable *scho* appeared all by itself, repeated by the child about 30 times. At the same time the syllables *ku* and *ko* disappeared; the child no longer wanted to repeat them. But they reappeared on February 18 and subsequently were promptly repeated. On the same day the child for the first time babbled the two connected syllables *hüta,* and during the entire session she could not be induced to say anything else. On March 13 she learned to repeat the pronunciation of a uvular *r* and repeated the word *Rose* as *Ro.* I must interject here that I tried to reinforce the newly acquired sounds, either by imitation of a model or, by inducing babbling, through frequent practice. It was interesting to observe how the child learned sounds—pronounced by me—in an optical–tactile manner and reproduced them in babbled syllables. The syllables *kakruka* which the child produced spontaneously 9 days after learning the *r* may serve as an example here. One more observation from this case history should be mentioned here. The quickest way of inducing the child to repeat a word was to slowly remove from her the picture in question immediately after it had been designated by its name. The child would then reach for it with her hands, bow her head in its direction and say the word more or less correctly. Thus it was the desire for the picture which especially motivated her towards speaking. The close connection of this observation with our introductory psychological statements is easily noticeable. However, there is an additional reason for stating this observation here: Through a similar maneuver, I repeatedly succeeded in recalling a missing word to the memory of amnesic aphasics. We may thus conclude that the same process can still be effective even with adults.

From the case just described and from similar cases, it develops that there is a possibility of stimulating the missing or delayed speech development by energetically using the patient's senses of sight and touch for the absorption of the spoken model. As Gutzmann[43] especially emphasizes, the eye, even in normal speech development, takes part to the extent that small children frequently observe the mouth of speakers. However, the sense of touch outside of the speech organs proper is no physiological component of normal speech development. We know that the eye and the sense of touch are now being used for artificial speech development in the so-called *German deaf-mute method* invented by the Swiss physician Amman.[44] It is therefore important to ask whether there exists an essential parallel between deaf-muteness and muteness with good hearing, since the method of treatment is the same. Although in this monograph I will illustrate through individual examples the most important types of muteness accompanied by good hearing, a systematic study of the bibliography is nevertheless advisable to understand of this group of speech impediments. Reference is made therefore to Gutzmann's *work,* and to the third volume of Liebmann's *Vorlesungen;* also to Coën, *Die Hörstummheit und ihre Behandlung,* Vienna, 1888; H. Stern, *Die verschiedenen Formen der Stummheit,* Vienna, *Med. Woch. (Medical Weekly)* 1910, and Fröschel's *Vorlesungen über Taubstumme und Hörstumme,* Vienna and Berlin, 1911.

43. *Vorlesungen über Sprachstörungen,* 2nd edition (Berlin, 1912).
44. *Surdus loquens, seu methodus, qua, qui surdus natus est, loqui discere possit* (Amsterdam, 1692).

Chapter 9

THOUGHTS ON THE AUDITORY PART OF THE BRAIN AND ITS INFLUENCE ON SPEAKING

No matter how many fundamental questions in aphasia research are still undecided, of one thing there is no doubt. A hearing stimulus penetrating the brain is necessary for providing the first impetus for movement of the speech organs in terms of articulate speech. A child that is born deaf, or becomes deaf at an early age, remains mute without any exception. Therefore, we are probably justified in believing that there has to be a connection between the hearing part of the brain and the one servicing speech movements if repetition is to be achieved, which without any doubt is the precursor of spontaneous speech. It is necessary, even at this point, to discuss more closely a problem which I have already discussed extensively in two publications.[45] In order to state in a few brief words the point of view discussed there in detail, let us begin with the following remarks: Inasmuch as hearing, on the one hand, and the speech organs, on the other, play a part at least in learning speech, it is permissible to assume from the start that the lack of speech development—not to mention understanding of speech—may have its cause in either the hearing, the speech organs, or in the connection between them. The fact that the central hearing mechanism, as well as the central speech-movement mechanism and the connection between the two, must in some causes be held responsible for muteness is only part of what has just been said. But now more light must be shed on the functioning of these individual central parts.

45. " 'Über die Behandlung der Aphasien," in *Arch. f. Psych. und Nervenkrankheiten*, Vol. 53, and "Zur Behandlung der motorischen Aphasie," *Arch. f. Psych. und Nervenkrankheiten*, Vol. 56.

No matter how paradoxical it may sound, it is not senseless to ask why children are not born with the ability to repeat speech. As an answer to that question, the circumstances in each of the three domains must be taken into consideration. We may assume that children are born with the essential parts of their sensory organs capable of functioning. This wording is meant to be a very careful one, so that even the opinion of those authors who claim that newborn babies are born deaf[46] may be taken into consideration.

Canestrini[47] singles out hearing as the function most important to our purpose, which is hearing. He quotes scholars who believe children to be deaf for the first few days or weeks and establishes as certain the fact that even very young children show a change of brain pressure in connection with hearing impulses. Canestrini's methodology is extremely accurate, and therefore its results are unassailable. It consists in his placing the rubber membrane of a registering capsule on a fontanel, and graphically recording, in the usual manner, the fluctuation of air pressure in the capsule produced by the respective increase or decrease of brain pressure. Many other authors were able to observe reflex movements, especially reactions of sudden fright in very young children who were subjected to more or less loud auditory stimuli and O. Kuttwirt has proved that three-quarters of the newborn babies observed reacted to the tuning fork sounds $c1$, $c2$, $c3$ within the first 24 hours. However, if there are infants who do not react to hearing stimuli, that does not always mean they do not hear. It could still be a question of a reflex arch insufficiently developed from the motor point of view. Canestrini's experiments, it seems to me, are especially important, particularly when checked against a great wealth of material; which in all cases supports Canestrini's findings. This is because the experiments prove that increased brain pressure connected with functional sequence in the brain, which many people today accept as the physiological basis of brain activity, is already characteristic for each newborn baby. Here at least one common base

46. Thus among 50 newborn babies examined with the "Cricri" toy Moldenauer found one that did not yet react at 3 days of age. Preyer (*Die Seele des Kindes,* Leipzig, 1912, 8th ed., p. 49) reports on an especially well-developed child who did not react to any kind of sound 1 hour after birth. He ascribes the deafness of children so young to two facts: First: The jelly-like fluid filling the middle ear before birth has not yet been replaced by air. Secondly: The walls of the inner ear may be completely adjacent to one another, as ascertained by Urbantschitsch. However, as I in principle discuss elsewhere (Fröschels, "Über Hör- und Sprachstörungen bei Kretinismus," *Monatsschr. f. Ohrenh,* 1911) only a more or less severe hearing defect can originate from such factors, whereas complete deafness must be ascribed to central factors. Villiger (*Sprachentwicklung und Sprachstörungen beim Kinde,* Leipzig, 1911, p. 9) takes the position that newborn babies are deaf, without however quoting any proof for this belief.

47. *Über das Sinnesleben des Neugeborenen* (Berlin, 1913).

would be established; a physiological prototype condition[48]—if we may
use this term—on which various facts differing from one another for
various newborn babies could then be structured; because the above-
mentioned differences of behavior in newborn babies thus far examined
for acoustical reactions or nonreactions to auditory stimuli, derive, as
stated before, from a greater reflex arch in which the faulty functioning
of various localized parts may cause the nonoccurrence of the reaction.
If we now venture into the field of consciousness, for which the question
under discussion provides the most immediate background, then the
unsolved problems become so numerous that we shall not readily be able
to deduce anything common to all newborn human beings. And if we
consider the difference in agreement among a number of modern
biological researchers, then from the number of reflex arches simultaneously stimulated, the value of establishing at least one common original reflex arch as the basis for a function, such as hearing, of which we
are certainly conscious in later life, becomes clear—especially in view of
the fact that in various babies the most variegated reflex arches will be
induced in a primary manner according to disposition and circumstances in each individual case.

If we then assume that sounds produced, within sufficient proximity,
create a change of brain pressure in all newborn babies, we would then
have established the fact that the sound-transmitting organs function
more or less adequately. We could even assume, with particular regard
to the variation of brain pressure, that the brain also is already receiving
the sound. Whether this happens with a glimmer of consciousness or not
cannot be answered today. But certainly in the earliest months of life,
however, awareness of acoustic experiences occurs. In any case we can
assume that this part of the brain although competent, originally cannot
distinguish among all the different acoustic stimuli. Let us just mention
in passing, that here, too, at least two problems are present. We must not
overlook the fact that the experienced listener understands each sound,
as it is heard, as if he had been told that the sound was coming from one
source or another. Such correlation of perception to its cause (which,
according to Schopenhauer's *Über den Satz vom Grunde,* is a primary
activity of reason) can without any doubt be brought about only by
experience, in which the newborn baby is certainly lacking. This alone
might already mean that the competent part of the brain originally
would not be able to distinguish among the various acoustic impressions.
But it is also possible that the hearing part of the brain does not yet
differentiate sounds as being acoustically altogether different. An anal-

48. Kassowitz, *Allgem. Biol.,* Vol. 4 (Vienna, 1906).

ogy with sensory aphasia can be perceived here. For, in the case of sensory aphasia, too, we have to think of two possibilities: that the patient has lost the ability to correlate sound to source, and that he is no longer capable of receiving and distinguishing on a purely acoustical level. Psychological studies show what gradations are possible even in this second case. Wolfgang Köhler, for instance, states (*loc. cit.,*):

> In other cases, however, it might well be that we cannot speak of tone-deafness, but really only of melody-deafness. That means that possibly the relative pitch of individual sounds is being heard, but what we call melody no longer objectively corresponds to consecutive tones, and the natural bond has been lost. Tonal sensations without a fixed organization among them appear where formerly there were rigidly formed sequences. This interpretation of sensory amusia is particularly appropriate in those cases with preserved hearing—apparently the majority—where, in addition to melody deafness, there exists sensory aphasia of a type where the spoken matter itself is heard, but the words and sentences are not being absorbed as the customary rigidly organized sequences, and therefore are not being understood [p. 67].

It seems to me that there is even more to this phenomenon; however, in the interest of coherence I do not wish to enter into this discussion for the time being (see Case No. 7, which follows).

Undoubtedly then, the newborn baby cannot differentiate among the various sounds. If we keep the introductory psychological statements in mind, we must not completely forget the factors of "mental attitude" and "positioning," respectively. If in the ordinary course of events we say of a man that he is not interested in music, and if we now hear from Wolfgang Köhler that human beings in whom pitch discernment does not develop in a normal fashion find no pleasure in tones, then perhaps in the case of the newborn baby with still defective functioning of the hearing center of his brain—*sit venia verbo*—a lack of interest, which is an emotional component, might be held partially responsible for the defective hearing. In the case of the sensory aphasic also, we would have to expect such an emotional lack much more readily under similar circumstances. To illustrate the peculiar states of slumber or twilight in the hearing part of the newly born brain, we would like to put forward some pathological cases.

CASE 3: A 2-YEAR-OLD-GIRL

Case 3 concerns a 2-year old girl brought to Privy Councillor Urbantschitsch's outpatient ear clinic by her mother for examination of her hearing. The anamnesis showed that the child had been born easily and on schedule, received breast feeding for 6 months, and was up to that time no different from any other healthy baby. Later on the mother observed that she rubbed her head on the pillow a great deal and did not stand up or sit up. Teething occurred as late as age 14 months. The child was spared any acute illnesses, but the older she became, the more the mother noticed that she did not hear. People could call her or make noise behind her back without her turning around. When an organ grinder played in the courtyard, it made no impression at all on the girl. All this and a hundred other observations made by the worried mother convinced her that her child was deaf. But once in a while, she doubted that conviction, for she saw the little girl suddenly turn around when the alarm clock rang or when her father whistled a tune. The circumstance, however, that much louder noises made no impression on the girl caused the mother to believe that the turning around was merely accidental. The child evinced pleasure in looking at pictures, and spent a very long time on each of them. She *uttered no sound,* but she did not otherwise give the impression of being stupid and did not wet or get herself dirty. She did not play with the other children. Her walking ability had improved; she was able to stand and walk. Occasionally she snored at night. There were no startlereactions.

The family case history was negative—no speech defects or nervous diseases anywhere at all. The mother, a woman 26 years of age, had never aborted. The patient was her parents' only child.

The child would sit quietly in her mother's lap and look the examiner in the face. If a hand was extended towards her, she hid her head against her mother. She was anemic and perhaps somewhat smaller than she ought to be. The head was rather large and both fontanels were open. She was bow-legged, and there was a suspicion of her being chicken-breasted. The baby therefore suffered from rickets. Nothing of an abnormal nature was found somatically other than small adenoid growths, which could easily be observed in the child and which covered approximately the upper third of the nasal cavities; with particular reference to the ears, the eardrums were normal, and there was an extremely lively tickling reflex starting from the outer ear passage.

This last symptom was the only clue that induced me to arrive at a diagnosis of muteness with hearing.[49]

At that time, I was unable to furnish clearcut proof for the correctness of my diagnosis to various colleagues who were interested in it. I tried, by all kinds of facilitating devices at my disposal, to act upon the child's sense of hearing, but in vain. There was no reaction to loud trumpets and whistles. Urbantschitsch's harmonica and strongly vibrating tuning forks were unable to capture the child's attention. Only once did it ap-

---

49. Cf. *Fröschels,* "Zur Differentialdiagnose zwischen Taubstummheit und Hörstummheit," *Med. Klin.,* 1910.

pear as if the patient were turning around precisely at the moment when the *c*-fork was struck. (All these hearing tests were carried out *behind* the little girl, and great care was taken that there would be no source of error.) Clapping one's hands proved just as unsuccessful as stamping one's feet.

In the course of all this, I succeeded in finding an instrument to which the child reacted regularly. This was a so-called "autophone," an automatic music box which, after slight pressure on a button, begins to play a soft, tinkling sound. Each time this music started, the child began to listen and turned around to find the source of the sound. During this time her mother also, whom I advised to buy some different-sounding music boxes, found some bells that attracted the child's attention.

At this new stage the child showed a quite unusual reaction to noises loud enough to make ordinary people jump. For instance, when a glass was broken behind her, or a cap pistol fired, she turned around immediately—without, however, becoming frightened.

In contrast with her acoustic underexcitability, the child showed an unusual amount of pleasure in interesting optical events. She looked at each picture put in front of her immediately and, as the mother correctly indicated, did so for an unusually long time. This may be called a state of remaining "stuck" to opitcal impressions, and whenever it happened, it would no longer be possible afterward to stimulate the child with the autophone.

We might now ask ourselves whether hearing existed only for certain individual pitches, and whether it was for just those pitches which the autophone and the bells were producing. This was not the case. Whenever tuning forks corresponding to the bells were struck, the child did not react. This means that it was not the pitch of the tone but the remainder of its components—its timbre—which was of primary importance.

The following is a second example taken from my private practice.

CASE 4: A 4-YEAR-OLD-BOY

A small 4-year-old boy was referred to me for speech therapy as a deaf-mute. The case history showed nothing worth mentioning outside of the belated beginning of standing and walking. Likewise the somatic findings were negative. The eardrums were normal, there were no growths in the nose, and the tickling reflex from the outer ear could readily be accomplished. Otherwise the patient offered a picture of complete deafness. He reacted to no sound stimuli whatsoever. In contrast with the previous case, it was also difficult to captivate his interest visually. He did see a colored design put in front of him at once, but his attention stayed with it only briefly before he immediately looked at something else, again for a short time only. Thus he was the picture of utter distraction, and even toys placed in his hands were unable to interest him for any length of time. He was accepted by the Sanatorium for Speech Disorders, where he was subjected mainly to two types of influences. He was put into a room as bare as possible, so that not too many objects could make optical demands on him. This was designed to counteract his optical restlessness. Several days later the nurse assigned to him began to show him a few pictures—always the same ones—one after the other, for a period of 5 minutes each, several times a day. Secondly, attempts were made with numerous instruments; trumpets, whistles, Urbantschitsch's harmonica, a gramophone, drums, human voices. Bells were suddenly made to ring behind him in order to "stimulate" him acoustically. For 3 weeks everything of this sort seemed to be in vain, and the impression of his deafness was so complete that all residents of the sanatorium, including my scientific assistants, doubted the accuracy of the diagnosis of "auditory amnesia." On the twenty-first day of the patient's stay in the sanatorium, during the joint noon meal, I left the dining-room through one door only to reenter it by way of another door situated about 10 feet behind the patient. All present had been instructed not to betray my reappearance by any glance or sound. The moment I opened the second door I sounded a newly purchased delicate little bell, and as quick as lightning the patient turned around in his chair and looked at me. From this moment on, the boy reacted frequently, though not always, to the little bell. However, care was taken not to tire him, or—if we may use the term—not to diminish his interest by using the same stimulus too frequently. Gradually, as other similar little bells, and later tuning forks, trumpets, and the human voice were tried on him, his "attentiveness" began to stretch further and further, so that after one additional month a consultant pediatrician no longer had any doubts concerning the patient's hearing ability. At that time it was also already possible to awaken him from his sleep by acoustic means, something which had been impossible at the time treatment started. After 3 additional weeks, on November 1, 1912, an entry in the case history reads as follows: "The more the restlessness of the child decreases, the more he pays attention to his surroundings." Success was probably due to both the measures mentioned, but especially to that of "optical starvation." On November 20 he began to babble clicking sounds. Subsequently the babbling increased in frequency and volume, and on December 17 he pronounced an [r] sound modeled by me while closely watching my mouth. The entry of January 13, 1913 reads: "Pictures are viewed with great pleasure. Patient repeats individual syllables of words pronounced in connection with the pictures." Entry of January 22: "Patient imitates pronunciation of *a, o, i, u, m,* correctly." Item of February 1: "He imitates all syllables, also *Uhr* and *Baum,* however, he says either *Uhr* or *Baum* for either picture whenever he is not first cued with the appropriate word." At this point the patient was released in the care of his parents, who had him tutored further by a nursery school teacher according to my instructions.

A third analogous case (Case 5) from the logopedic outpatient hospital of the Imperial University Ear Clinic (Privy Councillor Dr. Urbantschitsch) may be quoted as proof that in due time auditory amnesia can gradually change into hearing under the influence of the ever-present acoustic stimuli of everyday life. I shall quote here the report of the house doctor, whose name, unfortunately, I cannot recall, and of the governess who took charge of the patient's further training—according to my instructions—after he had been treated in the above-mentioned outpatient hospital for 6 months by means of systematic hearing exercises and optical–tactile speech practice. The exact report of the governess is also suitable for informing the reader of the progress and the difficulty of the pedagogical speech-practice therapy.

CASE 5: A 7-YEAR-OLD BOY

The child, born in Vienna, was a treasury official's 6¾-year-old son—case of forceps birth during which the head had been rather severely "squashed." Up to age 5½ he did not speak one word or syllable, nor did he understand a single word. Only a very scant degree of communication was possible with him by various gestures or pantomimic signs. He had almost no reaction to exclamations, shouting, clapping of hands, or music behind his back, so that the suspicion of deafness, which, however, was rejected by ear specialists, seemed justified. Nevertheless, all efforts to teach him any syllable whatsoever, or to make him understand any words, remained futile. His uncomprehending expression, together with his forehead and skull formation, indicated a diagnosis of cretinism. With all that, since the fourth year of his life, the child showed a strikingly systematic, orderly disposition—although otherwise he was not even interested in toys, and picture books were the only thing that seemed to interest him somewhat. The previous year he had been operated on for polyps of the nose.

At age 2½ he suffered from a severe attack of whooping cough; one year later from a light case of scarlet fever without serious aftereffects. Two years ago he had a normal light case of measles. For the last two years he has been prescribed thyreoidin tablets of 0.3 grams each at the rate of one a day. Almost simultaneously, however, as yet hardly affected by the use of the medicine, he began to repeat the word *mama*. It was also possible to teach him other single, easily pronounceable words of one or two syllables, although he did not understand their meaning. On the other hand, it became easier and easier to make oneself understandable to him through signs and gestures. It became apparent that he gradually learned to think and figure things out to some extent. If, for instance, he saw somebody pick up a cigar—his father did not smoke—he immediately went to get a lighter and ashtray. In the course of 18 months, his intelligence developed rapidly, so that today he understands almost as much as an intellectually normal deaf-mute. This occurred mostly after he was taken out of his domestic environment. Older brothers, although normal, were not especially gifted, and a younger 4-year-old brother is now exactly as he was at that age. Also in the last 8 weeks the patient has learned to understand much of what was said to him. He carries out various instructions promptly, although in the beginning he had to be helped along to some extent by gestures. He now possesses a frequently astonishing gift of correctly figuring things out, and a remarkable memory and power of orientation. The most difficult thing is the repetition of sounds, words, etc. Physically he is completely normal.

With regard to a hereditary taint, the following facts must be mentioned:

The boy was the child of a marriage between close relatives, who were the children of first cousins. There was nothing special to be reported about his grandparents, except that the grandmother on the mother's side had been suffering for many years from a migraine caused by anemia that resisted all treatment. This grandmother was also afflicted with chronic gout. There had been no case of cretinism in the family otherwise, nor had there been any other mental disorders, alcoholism, or syphilis.

However, after her forty-second year, that is, after all her four children had already been born, the common great-grandmother started suffering from untraceable cramplike headaches which occurred so often and violently and resisted all treatment to such an extent that she was forced to resort to morphine. For almost 40 years she was a heavy morphine user and was able to absorb such large doses that she astonished the medical experts.

At the time the child started his treatment by the specialist, he was 7 years old, and his hearing ability could be easily demonstrated at a distance of 3 meters (10 feet), even for only moderately loud speech. And now to the report of the educator (Mrs. Wolfram):

"When Marian came to me in October, 1911, he knew how to name a number of objects, and he also knew the letters of the alphabet.

But whenever a new word was pronounced before him loudly, clearly, and repeatedly, he did not understand it correctly, and he also confused the words.

I began to teach him reading, which required great effort and tenacity.

When he finally was able to read, learning came much easier to him. I would write a word down for him, and after he read it, it stayed in his mind clearly. He also found, with great ease, every word he had already read once in the book.

I taught him the reading process itself through writing. I pronounced each word very distinctly and slowly, strongly emphasizing each letter, until he wrote it correctly. There was no other way to teach him how to read.

Then we learned the correct use of the words: *der, die, das* (the). Concepts such as *gehen* (to go), *tanzen* (to dance), *stolpern* (to stumble), etc., had to be acted out before him in order to make them understandable to him, and subsequently he himself had to practice them by repetition. Colors he learned easily.

I taught him the concept of a plural, for instance, at Christmastime, 1911, in the following manner. Everywhere there were many trees. Pointing to an individual tree, I said, *Baum, Baum, Baum* ('tree, tree, tree'), and pointing to a greater number: *Viele, viele, heisst—Bäume* ('many, many is called—trees'). I did the same for lanterns and other objects. He was soon able to count to 100. Later on he learned the meaning of the words *mein* and *dein* ('my' and 'your'). That was very difficult for him to grasp. I took an object away from him and held it in front of him. I took his hand and, pointing to him, I said, "Das ist dein Soldat" ('That is your soldier'), and did similar things for objects belonging to me. In spite of the incessant practice he had trouble retaining the words. In pronouncing a sentence, he has to think for some time even to this day in order not to confuse *mein* and *dein*.

Dr. Fröschels gave us a picture book with balls, horses, cows, hay wagons drawn by a team of oxen, and other pictures. At first we learned: That is a dog, a cow, a butterfly, etc.; then: The butterfly is multicolored, the grass is green, the ball is round. And now I taught him the correct use of the words: *Ich habe einen, ich habe eine* ('I have one'—masculine form, 'I have one'—feminine form), by writing it in the following way:

> *der—ein,*   ('the'—'a', masculine)
>
> *die—eine,* ('the'—'a', feminine)
>
> *das—ein.* ('the'—'a', neuter)

For all pictures in the primer I wrote the articles *der, die* or *das* (the masculine, feminine, or neuter article 'the'). If, for example, he was supposed to say *Das ist ein Baum* ('That is a tree'—masculine), he first read the caption associated with the picture, and only then answered correctly. He could not learn it any other way. Then he learned, from the same book, *Das ist eine Kuh* ('That is a cow'—feminine), *das sind Kühe* ('Those are cows—plural), and learned in the same way for all the pictures and all his toys. From the previous picture, he learned *Die Kühe ziehen den Wagen* ('The cows pull the cart'), and then later *Der Bauer hält die Peitsche in der Hand* ('The peasant holds the whip in his hand').

For the pronouns *er, sie, es* ('he', 'she', 'it'), he learned the example *Der Knabe läuft, er läuft* ('The boy runs, he runs'); *Das Mädchen spielt, es spielt* ('The girl plays, she plays'), etc.; and the same way for the plural. Soon he was able to form similar simple sentences alone. When the occasion presented itself, he used the acquired knowledge all on his own.

At this point I taught him the usage of *er, sie, es* ('he', 'she', 'it') in connection with adjectives. For instance: *Der Pfau ist schön, er ist schön, sie sind schön* ('the peacock is beautiful, it (he)—masculine pronoun—is beautiful, they are beautiful'). At the same time, he learned from his three primers easily understood words, then later on more difficult ones.

He also learned many abstract concepts.

He understood compound nouns easily. The greatest difficulty was found in connecting words, even in the simplest of sentences.

He was already able to do small calculations, and learned the days of the week from a sheet calendar I gave him. On Sundays he got his bath, and he remembered that. On Tuesday and Thursday we used to go to Grandpa, and in this fashion he mastered the notions of tomorrow and the day after tomorrow.

If something is asked of him, one word is sufficient for him to draw logical conclusions, even if he does not understand the sentence. However, he does not comprehend even the simplest sentence if a word appears in it which he has not learned, or if the sentence structure deviates from a simple, ordinary sentence.

Tenses were taught in the following manner: I kept one of his wooden animal toys behind my back and said, *Ein Hase wird kommen, er kommt schon* ('A rabbit will come, it is arriving'). Then, slowly bringing it closer, I said, *Er ist schon da* ('It is here already'). Everything had to be done with great animation. He continued to make short statements, but everything only from pictures. One had to show him these pictures and tell him the sentences innumerable times until he was able to form the sentence by himself; for example: *Das Mädchen sitzt auf dem Sessel* ('the girl sits on the chair'); *Der Pfau hat einen schönen Schweif* ('the peacock has a beautiful tail'); *Das ist ein schönes Haus* ('that is a beautiful house'); *Das ist ein schöner Vogel* ('that is a beautiful bird'). There were never any surprises with him; he had to be taught everything the hard painstaking way.

In October, 1912 the child came down with pleurisy accompanied by exudation. For a long period of time he could receive no instruction. When I was able to begin again, I had to start some things from scratch. He had greatly lost the habit of speaking in short sentences.

He knew how to use comparison of adjectives and combinations of sentences by way of *und* and *auch* ('and' and 'also'); however, he was never able to answer in a connected form and on his own.

While on summer vacation, he saw a great many new things. Everything stimulated his curiosity, and during those 2½ months he made tremendous progress. Besides repetition we mainly practiced sentence formation. He now made up short sentences about a great variety of things, but always only about topics for which he had been coached.

In the morning he wrote sentences on the blackboard, and in the afternoon into his notebook so that they might be more thoroughly impressed in his memory. Most of the time, however, these were only about what he saw and about what had happened to him. When he received a postcard from his parents, he already was able to answer the question, *Was hast du heute von deinen Eltern bekommen?* ('What did you get from your parents today?') by saying *Ich habe heute von meinen Eltern eine Postkarte bekommen* ('Today I received a postcard from my parents').

In the beginning he had difficulty in understanding arithmetic, but he made comparatively rapid progress. At present he performs calculations such as, for instance: 1×1 up to $3 \times 5 =$ _____, $70 + 30 =$, $70 + 35 =$, etc., $9 + 7 + 5 =$, $8 + 5 - 6 =$, $8 - 4 + 7 =$, $1 \times 15 =$, $15 \times 1 =$, $19 - 10 - 8 =$, $24 + 16 =$, $82 + 10 =$, $75 + 15 =$, $70 = 30 + \ldots$, $30 = 15 + \ldots$ In the recent past he began to show more interest in questions addressed to him. but for the most part he answers in slogans. In dictation he rarely makes mistakes in spelling, and he places periods and commas correctly. He shows great diligence and intellectual curiosity, learns with eagerness and tenacity, and is good-natured and tidy."

November 30, 1913: A hearing test with Edelmann's tuning fork series yielded the following results:

Right side		Left side
moderately shortened	C	moderately shortened
12 seconds shortened		12 seconds shortened
moderately shortened	G	moderately shortened
moderately shortened	c	moderately shortened
very little shortened	g	very little shortened
very little shortened	h^1	very little shortened
very little shortened	c^1	very little shortened
very little shortened	d^1	very little shortened
very little shortened	g^1	very little shortened
very little shortened	a^1	very little shortened
very little shortened	c^2	very little shortened
very little shortened	d^2	very little shortened
very little shortened	f^2	very little shortened
very little shortened	g^2	very little shortened
little shortened	c^3	little shortened
little shortened	g^3	little shortened
(14 sec) rather shortened	c^4	rather shortened (12 sec)

Since then the patient has made great progress in every respect, and at present he is learning the subject matter of the fifth class in public school.

A more compelling reason for attempting to explain psychological deafness[50] is to be seen in the fact that we expect to derive from it a better insight into the normal central hearing process. Which part of the hearing function is liable to furnish the cause for the above-mentioned disturbance? The peripheral ear and the auditory nerve must probably

50. Villiger (*loc. cit.*, p. 78) applies this term only to complete lack of understanding of speech. However, I recommend its use for cases such as the one I quoted. I would like to call the congenital problem of linguistic comprehension either "sensory infantile muteness" or "sensory auditory muteness."

be excluded, since experience shows that in case of illness of these parts, completely normal hearing cannot be achieved without local therapy. The remaining areas then are the central auditory field or the reflex arch connecting with the motor sphere. Is it conceivable that a severe organic deformity exists here? This is unlikely in view of the satisfactory results of the practice therapy. We are therefore reduced to the area of the "functional," the area which in everyday life causes the differences in the mental talents of normal individuals. The beginning student of painting sees and paints a leaf uniformly green, whereas one year later he perceives a great many gradations of color. A person without musical training does not notice when the singer is one tone lower than the accompanying orchestra. Through practice he will acquire the ability to spot false singing involving only fractions of a tone. However, there also exist persons without any ear for music at all. The types lumped together under this category represent a number of individual problems. Let us mention here only those people who have no interest in music at all, and whose attention, according to Stumpf (Köhler, *loc, cit.,* p. 61), is comparatively little directed toward the tones. In other words, they are not "tone-oriented." That, however, the author would ascribe above all to a defective excitability of the brain centers involved. Indeed A. Liebmann was the first one to point out that auditory mutes, similar to artists, often manifest a "hypertrophy" of one sensory area. While they are hard to stimulate acoustically, without being hard of hearing, they keep clinging[51] to optical impressions. The author even saw two children, who were neither blind nor even nearsighted, groping at everything with their hands. This seems to be caused by a disturbance of equilibrium among the various sense spheres, which is most likely the basic prerequisite for a normal development. (Let us mention only briefly in passing that this "state of equilibrium" is probably not based on the equivalence of the various sense spheres. What would happen, for instance, if we became conscious of each step we took, or each glance we cast?) It will probably have to be assumed that "the defective excitability on the part of the brain involved" somehow is organically caused; and there might be numerous transitions ranging from broadly organic to microorganic, which we might be able to observe externally with a degree of success in a practice therapy. Such a microorganic constitutional disturbance must now be assumed to cause psychological deafness, as I among others stated in my monograph on hearing and speech disturbances in case of cretinism.[52] And this condition, which we identify with defective excitability, can be recognized externally as a lack of interest and personal attitude.

51. Cf. Fröschels, *Vorlesungen über Taubstumme und Hörstumme.*
52. *Ibid.*

Similar cases of psychological deafness in the literature[53] are mentioned by V. Urbantschitsch in his book *Über Hörübungen*, Vienna,
1895, p. 78.

As Urbantschitsch describes it in detail, the behavior of people who
are hard of hearing toward hearing exercises contains a multitude of
recognition possibilities at the outset. For we may perhaps claim that the
lack, or, alternatively, the gradual emergence of those individual components of the hearing complex that are peculiar to the various forms of
defective hearing, but which generally surface only during the
therapeutical hearing exercises, can be helpful in analyzing the complex.
I am aware that I have not said anything new: Indeed, psychologists and
physicians had in individual cases been benefitting from this knowledge
for a long time. Once more let us remember Köhler, as well as Alt[54] and
Revezs.[55] However, a general and comprehensive analysis of Urbantschitsch's vast body of observations, especially for the understanding
of forms of aphasia, has not been undertaken up to this date. Let us
refer here to the slow emergence of "hearing images," and especially to
the delayed sudden flare-up of an acoustic impression that had indeed
developed, not by a combination of individually perceived parts of a
word or a sentence, but spontaneously without any thinking involved.
This points to the question of the speed of stimulus transmission and to
the delayed tempo in grasping and understanding the spoken word,
which is indeed a known symptom of sensory aphasics. However, since
the incidence of delayed flare-up in persons who are hard of hearing
frequently is greatly reduced by therapeutic exercises, we can see in that
fact an indication of the relationship between experience (*id est* practice)
and the speed of central cortical functioning. For instance, in a case of
"transcortical" sensory aphasia we may have to consider that a functional
decrease of the cortex, which does not yet have to manifest itself as a
central case of auditory deficiency, may possibly cause a cortical slowing
up of the functional process. This may then result in a delaying of the
associative process in a natural way without the necessity of disturbing
the association as such.[56]

The two cases of psychological deafness permit a more tranquil insight
into the development of the hearing in children, or of some of its indi-

---

53. Krügelstein, *Badische Annalen der Gerichtsarzneikunde*, 1890, 8. p. 4; Heller, *Natur-
forschervers.;* Benedikt, *Nervenpathol. u. Elektrother.*, 1874, p. 449.

54. *Über Melodientaubheit und musikalisches Falschhören* (Leipzig and Vienna, 1906).

55. *Zur Grundlegung der Tonpsychologie* (Leipzig, 1913).

56. According to these exposés, certain cases of transcortical sensory aphasia go only
one step further, as, for instance, the patient of Bischoff ("Zur Lehre von den sensorischen
Aphasien", *Arch. f. Psych.*, Vol. 32) who repeated well and was able to read, however,
without understanding speech. Indeed, Bischoff explains his observations entirely in the
sense outlined above.

vidual steps. I would venture to compare the study of such impediments of speech development to the viewing of a photograph lying on a table, whereas the observation of normal speech development in this comparison corresponds to a film as seen in a movie theatre.

Functional relationships in newborn babies might be similar to those in our two patients. Patients appearing to good observers to be deaf after birth presumably were psychologically deaf. On the other hand, newborn babies with definite hearing ability may be different in this respect from older people. For, in their case, the reaction to acoustic stimuli does not take place with at all the same regularity, nor do they respond to such weak stimuli as in the case of older children. However, experience to date shows that there are newborn babies appearing to be deaf, and that frequently reactions to acoustic stimuli of sizable intensity occur regularly. Transitional cases, where hearing can be proved only here and there, have also been written up. We might be justified in assuming for the single individual a gradual transition from the stage of an isolated reaction to more frequent and, ultimately, regular reactions.

It is obvious that the reaction, if we may use the term, may take place internally, and that it does not have to be visible from the outside. Nevertheless, this process seems worth mentioning, for, if we think of sensory aphasics, we may recall some who will react to each acoustic stimulus with a sound complex, usually of the paraphasic type, and others for whom this is not the case. If we now consider that the first type possesses a specifically delineated subtype in the case of "echolalia," whereas the second, or "cortical–sensory aphasia" contrasts to the former or "transcortical" type, the question arises in the context of the previous sentence as to whether the reason for the different behavior of the two types mentioned above must really be seen here in terms of an anatomical localizing difference, as is almost universally assumed. It is necessary here to go further afield and to mention a new stage of the speech development of children.

Chapter 10

CHILD ECHOLALIA

Attitude and Obstruction. Echolalia

By echolalia, the repeating of nonunderstood words, we mean the echolalia of children, which is not recognized by all authors as something physiological. Meumann[57] and Sully[58] take the view that it generally occurs in a physiological way. Preyer[59] opposes this view, whereas C. and W. Stern (*Die Kindersprache*) accept it, but to a much lesser degree than Meumann. They state that

Contrary to Preyer it is a fact that sounds and sound complexes are being imitated long before an awakening of understanding occurs for what is heard. On the other hand, this act of imitation does not in the least play the independent role of preparation attributed to it by others. At least in the cases of our three child patients, we found that the imitating instinct did become quite lively at the age of 9 months but applied very heavily to gestures (such as hand-clapping), to unarticulated sounds (clicking, squealing, etc.), and to the intonation of the voice. The repeating of individual articulated sound complexes, however, receded far into the background and made tremendous progress only in the third year of life when numerous words were already understood and a very few of them were spoken meaningfully. That peculiar period of echolalia, in which the child with untiring tenacity repeats all kinds of heard words and sentences, either in their entirety or in their final parts only, falls right into the middle period of acquiring speech [p. 153].

My comments on that question are as follows:[60]

In the individual case it will depend on the relationship between motor speech urge and speech understanding. Children with little urge for speaking, which undoubtedly may still fall into the domain of the physiological, or children who understand quite early what they hear, will prattle less than others, yet still repeat mechanically.

57. *Die Entstehung der ersten Wortbedeutung beim Kinde* (Leipzig, 1902).
58. *Untersuchungen über die Kindheit* (Leipzig, 1897).
59. *Die Seele des Kindes*, 8th edition by Schäfer (Leipzig, 1912).
60. *Ges. der Ärzte in Wien* (Vienna Medical Society), December 7, 1916.

Here, too, the deplorable lack of observation in speech development, especially observation which takes the remainder of the physical and psychical behavior into consideration, impedes further understanding. Stern states elsewhere (*Die Kindersprache,* p. 143) that we must refrain from distinctly setting the stages of imitation and understanding off from each other, and both of them again from the stage of actual speech, as was done for the purpose of analysis. Nevertheless, further research may here again result in many individual differences.

As to child echolalia, it undoubtedly exists in many of the observed cases.[61]

If we base further discussion on my position as previously described, the question remains as to how to imagine "motor speech urge" and its relationship to the understanding of speech. The former belongs to the domain of individual disposition and to the realm of types of senses. As long as simple babbling is involved here, we may think of simple, especcially well-developed reflex arches. It is true that here, too, a triggering cause, or stimulus, is needed, but at the moment we cannot indicate as yet where this sensitive component is located. Acoustically induced babbling, or self-imitation, however, is caused by a function well known to us, namely the acoustic one. It must be assumed that when the child hears its own babbling and listens to it with pleasure, the latent motor reflex process initially runs parallel to that of hearing, and also that the pleasure of this auditory impression forms a secondary stimulus that accompanies the primary stimulus for babbling and reinforces it to some extent. Due to this fact, however, the original reflex arch is nevertheless being completed. The more often the auditory stimulus contributes to activating the reflex, the more we might assume that the auditory stimulus itself induces a reflex. The primary cause of the development of the reflex would fade into the background to the same extent that a new reflex arch became capable of functioning and then actually functioning. Its first station would be in the hearing brain section itself (or the process taking place there with the accompanying sensation of pleasure), and its terminal station would be situated in the speech organs put to use. This event is echolalia, since babbling has nothing to do with the understanding of speech. If a child now begins to imitate sounds articulated by people around him, we no longer have to assume any additional new mechanism at all, assuming the theory just quoted is correct. Here, too, the acoustic stimulus induces the release of speech movements. Whether this event may be connected with reflex arches, or whether we interpret it as an act of will is inherently a rather significant

61. Liepmann, "Ein Fall von Echolalie," *Neurologisches Zeitblatt,* 1906, calls echolalia the oldest and simplest speech function.

biological–psychological question. It rather disappears, however, if confronted by the theory quoted above. For this theory states that a reflex mechanism may become a path for an act of will or emotional occurences under the influence of frequent use, possibly resulting in a change of the triggering impulse. The impetus for this in our case is the substitution of an acoustic stimulus for the primary one unknown to us. Naturally, in any given case, the transition from a spontaneous repetition to an act of conscious will must be considered an intermediary link in this change. This is the point which has already led me to discuss this additional stage of development of children's speech in this context.

Is there such a thing as spontaneous repetition of speech? In order to answer this question, we must first define the term "will" more carefully. There is good reason for such a definition, since the word is used with so many different meanings as to make a qualification absolutely necessary in order to impart an orderly sequence to our observations. The question of the essence of "will" has been treated so often and so variously by other people that the continuity, or at least the clarity, of this monograph would suffer if I tried to explain here the pros and cons of their different answers. At the outset, then, let me only refer to Kassowitz,[62] a medical researcher, who states:

> If we now ask ourselves in what way we believe that voluntary movements differ from involuntary ones, our first answer must be that we become conscious of the former for the same reasons we generally attribute to the process of becoming conscious of reflex chains set off within ourselves. For we have reached the conclusion that we become conscious only of those reflex chains or parts thereof in which a sizable part of the organism's reflex apparatus is being affected. On the other hand, reflexes set off locally, and also more complex chains of movement, if well practiced and proceeding without impediments—and especially when they do not encroach on the sympathetic system and the domain of speech movements—will become removed from our consciousness either entirely, or nearly so. But becoming aware of a reflex chain or of any part of it is not at all completely interchangeable with its qualification as an act of will. In order to receive the feeling of an act of will, this act must be preceded either by its image without immediate execution or by an act of reflection, no matter how brief, that is to say by some hesitation between execution and impediment.

In accordance with that line of reasoning, the daily act of getting dressed, for instance, would no longer be an act of will. On the other hand, the narrowing of the pupil under the influence of light must be classified as a voluntary movement, insofar as an educated person is aware of this

62. Kassowitz, *Allgemeine Biologie*, Vol. 4 (Vienna, 1906). Kassowitz's theory of the will belongs to the group characterized by Wundt (*Grundzüge der physiologischen Psychologie*) as having a *sensualistic* orientation (Spencer, Meynert, Münsterberg).

peculiarity. The objection that we are dealing here with a movement and not an action could be countered by saying that this antithesis is a case of *petitio principii* (begging the question). For then, by "action" we would mean act of will, by which fact the entire proof of Kassowitz just quoted would be moving along lines of circular reasoning. The image of a movement is thus probably necessary for it to be intentional, but the image of a movement does not yet necessarily make it an intentional one. In my opinion, the degree of consciousness is equally as little relevant. The act of getting dressed, for instance, cannot very well be excluded from voluntary intentional movements.[63] I feel that Kassowitz's theory previously quoted, which agrees with that of many other researchers, is weak to the extent that it is based too heavily on thinking operations. I, in accordance with modern psychology, would like to postulate the following: Acts of will are actions that always need a certain specific psychological attitude and run their course with such a disposition. That, of course, does not prove very much, but presumably this definition will become clearer as the nature of "attitude" is increasingly understood. In any event, it is usable for practical and clinical purposes. When compared with Kassowitz's definition in examples to be quoted later on, its serviceability will be clearly demonstrated.[64]

Within this framework there now exists involuntary repetition, a form

63. In his masterful *Entwurf zu einer physiologischen Erklärung der psychischen Erscheinungen* (Leipzig and Vienna, 1894) pp. 139–140, Sigmund Exner comments on the question of the various types of movements in a way that I believe agrees with my own definition:

I sum up: the movements of the animal body are influenced by sensory impulses to a high degree. This influence is achieved through processes in the central nervous system which are centered partially subcortically and partially cortically.

The lowest stage is represented by pure reflexes (for instance in the intestinal tract), of which neither the centripetal phase nor the effect of the centrifugal phase sends information to the organ of consciousness; or else the centripetal stimulus (pupil reaction), or this stimulus together with the accomplished movement (blinking) reaches the cortex. In the latter case this subcortical mutual effect is supplemented by a cortical influence (impeding the blinking) due to the fact that this subcortical control can be arbitrarily modified. A set impulse of will may be modified by subcortical controls and adjusted to the prevailing circumstances (steps with tendon reflex).

Subcortical control loses the independence of a pure reflex and becomes dependent on the action of attentiveness. Intention control of instinctive movements based on sensory cortical impressions (such as staring, eating motions of horses, etc.) occurs in which the intentional impulse is unable to replace the subcortical process of regulation. Attention brings about the temporary installation of a subcortical reflex apparatus serving the intended purpose.

The conscious movement causes conscious sensations. The latter are indispensable for the correct execution of the former and thus serve as a cortical regulation (speech).

64. According to Wundt (*Folk Psychology*, Vol. 3, p. 828) an act of will as well as reflexes arise from instinctive movements which again develop from external stimuli. Their external success and the sensation activating the movement fuse into an inseparable complication; and "by soon gaining a dominating degree of importance in this combination, it appears to the conscious mind to be the main reason for the action."

of repetition towards which the individual is not attitudinally oriented. Simultaneously with the continuation of this thought, a way of concieving the related material process shall be analyzed here. We assume that small children, individually differing in age, have sufficiently exercised the auditory part of their brain through perception, since changes produced by each acoustic stimulus have been diffusing through the brain since birth. In agreement with Niessl[65] we shall assume that the changes are of a chemical nature. Thus, subsequent stimuli will enter a terrain already prepared in advance, which will react with more certainty. We may picture this particularly as a certainty in grasping weak and short stimuli and as a certainty of differentiation, previously explained in greater detail. We could also suppose that the central effect of each acoustic stimulus proceeds along preformed—but as yet unused—tracks over the auditory circuit, and that such charging of the motor parts of the brain occurs simultaneously with that of the acoustic parts. Or we could suppose that extra forces are liberated with a certain development of the brain's hearing center, as new stimuli which act upon the motorial

---

Reference is made here to James's statement of principle (*Principles of Psychology*):

The other day I was at a railroad station with a small child when an express train pulled in with a great deal of noise. The child, standing near the edge of the platform, jumped back in fright, closed his eyes, gasped for breath, and burst out crying. He ran towards me, mad with fear, and hid his face. I do not doubt the fact that this boy was almost as surprised by his own behavior as by the train, and that his actions astounded him more greatly than they did me, who was merely an onlooker. Naturally, after such a reaction has taken place frequently, we learn what we have to expect from ourselves; and then we can anticipate our behavior, although it remains just as spontaneous and uncontrollable as before. However, if a movement in those actions specifically referred to as arbitrary ones must be foreseen, then the conclusion must be drawn that no individual unendowed with prophetic powers will be able to execute any movement in an arbitrary manner for the first time.

Griesinger (*Pathologie und Therapie der psychischen Krankheiten*), who is known to look for reflexes as the basic principle of organization of the central nervous system, generally accepts the transformation of centripetal states of stimulation into motor impulses as the base for assuming that the tendency towards utterance is inherent in intellectual happenings. In a recently published monograph by Pick (*Die agrammatischen Sprachstörungen*), which he was kind enough to present to me only after this part of the present book had been completed, Pick reaches a similar conclusion by comparing echolalia of children with that of aphasics. He conceives of child echolalia in its development as a kind of conditioned reflex (Pavlov). He states that a case of Behier and one of his own (involving the occurrence of echolalia exclusively or predominantly in one language in the case of a polyglot) were proving the fact that an adjustment of the receiving apparatus stimulated by a specific acoustic stimulus constitutes the basic condition for echolalia. The corresponding reaction is thereby triggered, in analogy with the attuned reflexes.

The precision of pathological echos can only be explained by the existence of a receiving apparatus so finely attuned and of a transmitting apparatus evidently quite similarly constituted which we acquired and developed in childhood and retained ever since.

The process of learning how to speak by the child in the echolalia stage is nothing but the ongoing development of the speech apparatus according to the type of a conditional reflex. This goes hand in hand with a perfection of the receiving apparatus which, of course, proceeds rather gradually in its adjustment to acoustic stimuli.

65. *Das Geheimnis der menschlichen Sprache* (Wiesbaden, 1914).

sphere are received. In any case, one can suppose that with children the first stimulus to mimic speech results from the capacity of the acoustic part of the brain to be charged to a high degree, and that it occurs without motorial adjustment. Stated negatively, this hypothesis would mean that there are no obstructions at work to hinder the movement of the acoustical overflow into the motorial sphere.

One can attribute a similar condition to the echolalia of some sensory aphasics. This agrees with Pick's[66] view that under normal conditions a stoppage function could be attributed to the temporal lobe. Whereas other authors, such as Goldstein, in agreement with Quensel,[67] and also in a certain sense with Flechsig, place such a blockage center in the prefrontal brain, I do not consider that as a contradiction to Pick. Rather, it is my opinion that each center has the duty to prevent the further flow of its content to certain areas.[68] Accordingly, the prefrontal brain would have to prevent the further flow of the motorial–idea stimuli into the motor performance areas. If, however, we agree with the opinion that a too highly charged condition of the hearing area of the brain results in speech movements—and one may assume such a condition in a child who does not speak or understand very much as yet; hence, a child in whom the output also does not proceed to the "transcortical" side—we might be able to assume a relief of the inhibiting function in the more or less regular flow of these stimuli to the motorial and above all to the transcortical side, as occurs with a person who speaks. It is a very noticeable phenomenon that mute children who can hear are usually very wild. They hit everyone and everything; and to the inexperienced they give the impression of being mentally disturbed. On the other hand, persons who are deaf mutes are usually very well-behaved and friendly. This difference is so reliable a sign that the specialist is often able to make the sad diagnosis of deaf-muteness before he has examined the hearing ability of the child who has been brought to him on account of muteness. Could we not construe the wild behavior of persons who are mute but can hear as the outflow of the charge of the hearing area of the brain into its nonspeech motorial part, whereas we might attribute the calmness of deaf children to a lack of such a charge? Where there is an absence of partial discharge of the hearing area of the brain in a speaking person through rerouting of the transcortical cir-

66. "Zur Frage nach der Natur der Echolalie," in *Fortschritte der Psychologie*, Vol. 4, Fol. 1.
67. Quensel "Über die transkortikale motorische Aphasie," *Monatschr. f. Psych. u. Neur.* Vol. 26, p. 285: "The essential difference between the view suggested here and that of Hartmann is that we are inclined to rank the prefrontal area not equal to Broca's area but superior to it, according to the situation of our case."
68. Anything seen, heard, etc., will flow off in the transcortical direction. Supposedly this is the case for the thinking individual, not for the mere chatterbox.

cuits, echolalia will be the result.[69] It may likewise be produced cortically by deficiencies of the inhibiting function itself. The last statement, more recently, should be viewed in its relation to "attitude." As a rule people are geared to thinking rather than to chattering. (Too much wine makes many people talkative and loosens their tongues.)

For clarity's sake let us now return to the passage from which our last considerations started. We had assumed that a newborn gradually develops reactions to acoustic impressions, and that these reactions may "internalize" under certain circumstances. This internalizing means either a drift of the acoustic stimuli into a sphere other than the motorial one, or an inhibition. In the case of a young child it could merely consist of the drift in another direction. In any event, an analogy was found to exist between young children and adults, although the inhibitory function of a cortical nature might already be present in the adult. Such a drift will take place in a direction other than the motorial one. This analogy or its negative, repectively, may thus be utilized to explain echolalia. However, the missing cortical inhibition, also could rightfully be used as an explanation for other aphasia cases which have been assigned this same designation (echolalia). In this category fall those cases of echolalia which can be explained by a desire to speak spontaneously, and those in which the patient's words are either not found or are not found quickly enough. Case No. 6 will be shown as an example of the foregoing.

Returning again to attitudes, we tried to interpret them as a degree of excitability of a central sensory area. We might now add that inhibition also is an attitude, psychologically speaking. One may suppose that from a physiological point of view both attitude and inhibition essentially move on one line in two opposite directions, or one might visualize a rectangle divided into two triangles by a diagonal line, and this rectangle being filled with vertical lines at equal distance from each other and intersecting the diagonal line. The area between two verticals and the diagonal would measure the relative importance of attitude and inhibition respectively (see Fig. 1). However, with the two types of attitude and inhibition, the discussion of everything going under that name is a long way from being exhausted. (From a psychological standpoint, inhibition may be included in the concept of attitude.)

The present explanation is being greatly enlarged, to be sure, if one assumes, as one would probably have good reason to do, that there also exist reciprocal influences of specific attitudes of the various central

69. This is the type of problem which the literature in the field up to now has primarily recognized. (Goldstein, *Die transkortikalen Aphasien*, Jena, 1915, pp. 456 ff.)

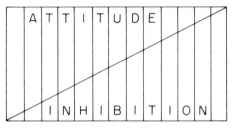

Figure 1.

regions. This assumption particularly seems to open up to me a perspective on the general relationship of attitude to inhibition. If someone wants to say something, but fails to do so because his eye catches sight of something interesting, then the optical attitude has become a speech inhibitor.[70] But beyond this we must consider if there is not something purely psychological (concerning both attitude and inhibition) that is not connected to any known centers, but is perhaps in itself localized into a center, exerting an influence on all the others. Partially in this sense, Goldstein states the following (*loc. cit.*, pp. 380 ff.): "A specific excitation of will is necessary for further speech [after the choice of words—Fröschels]. Here, too, we are not dealing with simple, but highly complex situations." Likewise he is citing a comparison with the speech development of children:

> The language of a child is being put into operation by psychological stimuli. At first it is because of certain feelings of pleasure which accompany the movements that the child activates its speech muscles. Later, after associations among specific words and specific experiences have been formed, emotional stimuli will cause the child to speak. In this stage the sensory–motorial, in general, and thus also the speech processes, possess such great independence from their "sense" and "meaning" that the processes of imitation occur with particular promptness. So does repetition which occurs uncontrollably [in an echolalic manner], insofar as the child has learned now to speak altogether. We find . . . that children almost always accompany their concepts with speaking, and, on the other hand, that they try to repeat everything they hear. Gradually spontaneous speaking recedes; . . . in particular, repetition lessens, it gradually loses its echolalic, automatic and compulsory character and turns more and more into a conscious and intentional occurrence. . . . Children must learn to be silent, and they do learn it. This inhibition gains such power over our speaking that

---

70. We know from Verworn and Fröhlich (Verworn: "Die zellularphysiologischen Grundlagen des Abstraktionsprozesses," *Ztschr. f. allgem. Physiol.*, (vol. 14); Fröhlich: "Die Analyse der an der Krebsschere auftretenden Hemmungen," *loc. cit.* (vol. 7), that even weak stimuli are able to impede excitation. Based on this phenomenon Verworn also explains the physiological observation that every newly occurring conceptual complex in the realm of consciousness erases any previously present one. If the excitation of a freshly stimulated group of neurons hits an associated neuron-group in a state of prior excitation, then the more recent stimulation will block the earlier impulse.

with the adult, finally, release from the inhibition requires a special effort to bring about his speaking. . . . The inhibition [in general—Fröschels] may be brought about either through a simple loss of a function, or it may consist of an impediment caused by a simultaneous counteraction: hence, it may either be a passive or an active occurrence.

Thus it is Goldstein's opinion that inhibition does not only develop passively—through the nonoccurrence of one performance because of focusing on another—but that active occurrences, too, play a role here. With the adult, therefore, it is circumstances of lowered intellectual activity and lessened volition which bring about the loss of inhibition, as opposed to the child, in whom the reason for the nonoccurrence of inhibition is a lack of intellectual relationships.

Concerning the localization of inhibition and intention, Goldstein believes that these functions are to be located in the prefrontal area of the frontal lobes, especially quoting Quensel in support of this. He further bases his belief on cases by Stransky, Pick, Liepmann, Nöthe, and others, where a reduction of spontaneous speaking became apparent since they, too, showed that the frontal lobes were affected. Prior to this we already established our position concerning his quarrel with Pick. Let us only add that clinical observation of motor aphasics seems to point to the assumption of an attitudinal or inhibitory function—I am thinking specifically of a lack of inhibition—which is to be looked for in the affected part itself. If systematic therapeutical treatment succeeded in bringing the cortically based motor aphasic to the point of repetition, and if the patient already possesses a certain fund of vocabulary, however limited, which he can use for questioning, then one frequently observes that he also repeats the question, or the last part of it. To illustrate let us quote the following example.[71]

CASE 6: THE FIRST LIEUTENANT

First Lieutenant H. L. (patient in the clinic of Privy Councillor Freiherr von Eiselsberg), head bullet wound on the left side, operated for a brain abcess in the temporal crown region. Paralysis of the right extremities, of the right facialis (facies) and of the right half of the tongue. Began treatment 2 months after the operation on December 10, 1914, with the reading of single letters. (Railroad Antiaircraft Corporal K. C. Rothe, who was assigned to me in his capacity as a military consultant physician, helped me with the treatment.)

71. Already published in part in Fröschels's "Zur Behandlung der motorischen Aphasie," *Arch. f. Psychiatrie u. Nervenkrankh.*, Vol. 56, Folio 1.

With each *m* he says "Margit," his wife's name, which he suddenly began to pronounce during the past few days and which he has frequently repeated since. He enunciates some syllables correctly, others not, in which case there appear mostly similar syllables or words. For example, he cannot say *k*, but he does say *Acker* ('field'). He is also unable to repeat the sounds *l, p, d, t, r, f, l, sh,* (German *sch*), as such, but rather he says *be, pe,* (the sounds of bee, pee), etc. On January 4, there is a condition of echolalia, that is to say, when asked a question, he repeats the last words without answering the question, even though he certainly understands much and means to answer. Frequent confusion of *r* and *l*. He reads the numeral 27 as 20, 35 as 30; yet he knows that this is incorrect. He sings the Hungarian anthem almost flawlessly. On January 8, he is unable to speak at all for 4 hours, following a great emotional upset. On January 11, strong perseverance in repetition and reading, also of individual letters. On January 14, he is asked to choose one of two letters presented to him on command. He can not comply, and, moreover, he does not understand what is expected of him. On January 27, the following notation was entered in his medical record: "Reading of syllables is substantially better than the reading of individual sounds." Nevertheless, he is usually unable to correct himself when he reads a syllable incorrectly, even though he is being intensively helped with the individual sounds that occur in that syllable. That is due to the fact that he does not put the syllable together from its letters, but rather that he reads the syllable pictorially, in toto. Also, it happens that he pronounces a whole polysyllabic word instead of only the one syllable and here, too, he is incapable of correcting himself. For example, he reads the word *schade* for *sch* [*sh*]. If he is to read *i*, he says mostly "infantry regiment," laughs, and knows evidently that the same letter symbol occurs at the beginning of the word, an idea he might possibly wish to convey with this word, without being capable of pronouncing the *i* alone. February 15: He already says some words spontaneously, for example: *Frau Influenza* ('Mrs. Influenza'), *amputiert* ('amputated'— referring to a comrade). For some time now we have him repeat simple sentences in which it frequently happens that he only says the last word. He also pronounces syllables belonging to a later word too early, and he perseveres on the other hand in using words that are similar in sound or meaning. We are also writing words with one incorrect letter, for example: *Wasserglaf,* 'waterglaf,' (instead of *Wasserglass,* 'waterglass'), and he immediately points to the incorrect letter, but the association between the correct part of the word and the completely correct word nevertheless is so strong that he always reads *Wasserglass* ('Waterglass'). Then he is told incomplete sentences and he is to say out loud the missing part. We also use picture books.

In this manner therapy was continued three to four times a week. It was interrupted on occasion by epileptic fits, a surgical correction of the scar, and a prolonged stay in the country at the Rosenhügel Sanitorium for mental disorders. Now the patient has progressed to the extent that he has very good speech comprehension and already speaks a great deal spontaneously, although frequently only in telegram style. Nevertheless, it still happens frequently that he repeats the last part of a question directed at him before he answers it. He does not do this, however, when a doctor makes a declarative statement. It becomes clear from this that when he is ready to answer, that is, to speak, he does not have sufficient control over himself to speak only when he begins his answer. The readiness to speak is so strong that the power to check the impulse of not repeating the question is missing.

I realize that, in view of the absence of an autopsy report and particularly in view of the initially existing, although minimal, signs of unsatisfactory speech comprehension, this case might be included among the sensory-type cases, or possibly among what I called cases of "expressive sensory aphasia" in the article "Über die Behandlung der Aphasie" (*Arch. f. Psych.*, vol. 53). An excuse might be found in Goldstein's medical case histories, gathered both from the bibliography and from his own experience, to the effect that in this respect Goldstein's cases are no different from the case mentioned here.

In conclusion we may say that our earlier statements have automatically led us to a localization of the functions of attitude and inhibition, since we identified it, at least partially, with the degree of excitability of a sensory sphere. In part, we have indeed recognized the phenomenon externally appearing as inhibition as a dispersal of stimuli to motor, or rather, nonkinetic areas of acting, in order to avoid contradicting the recent, now widely popular view (Kassowitz, Müller-Freienfels, etc.), according to which every psychical action goes hand in hand with muscular activity. And now the question arises whether this so highly praised "attitude" is really anything new. Now, we have already known for a long time that someone with a damaged speech center in the brain is unable to speak well; or else, that someone with a more developed speech center is able to speak better than someone with a poorly developed one. Thus we may reply by saying that the consideration of this result of modern psychological research leads directly to new points of view. These are, among others, the transcortical forms of aphasia. If, for example, it was previously said that transcortical sensory aphasia stemmed from an intact condition of the cortical regions, and that nonrepetition was proof of their being diseased, we now still have to think of the possibility that in individual cases this malfunctioning might be simulated by a true functioning of inhibition. It cannot be predicted, however, of what value all this will be in the future, when the importance of the application of the attitude problem will have proved itself, even if only in connection with a partial problem, such as transcortical sensory aphasia.

Chapter 11

THE HEARING OF SEVERAL
SIMULTANEOUS SOUNDS

Now, however, we must consider the specific question of the physiological capacities that we believe are localized in the temporal lobes. This presents the problem of how we are able to experience sound combinations as represented by speech sounds.

In the passage on tone deafness, we have already seen that there is an acoustic factor, which may be present or absent, independent of hearing single tones: namely, the hearing of a succession of objective tones—a phenomenon we call melody.[72] A second capability normally coordinated with hearing single sounds is the comprehension of several simultaneously occurring sounds or noises.[73] This assumption needs no detailed proof. One only has to consider that not everyone who recognizes a note on the piano is also able to analyze the parts of a chord. To be sure, a diagnosis is something larger, something substantially more difficult than mere perception. In the long run, however, we are dependent

---

72. I have reason to suppose that further research will show possible accord with James's theory of "transitive consciousness content" or with his "fringe theory." Perhaps it is just this gliding from one tone to the other in a psychological sense which some tone-deaf persons do not experience, and the lack of which causes tone deafness. (Stumpf, *Tonpsychologie*, 2, p. 139, speaks of a successive blending of octave sounds).

73. Barth, *Einführung in die Physiologie, Pathologie und Hygiene der menschlichen Stimme* (Leipzig, 1911), pp. 3–9, defines the difference between sound and noise as follows:
The difference between sound and noise consists generally in the fact that in the course of the occurrence of a noise a rapid change of various kinds of sound perceptions takes place; whereas, a musical tone appears to the ear as a sound of regular and unchanged duration for as long as it lasts, and in which no change of various different components is discernible. Sound, therefore, corresponds to a simple and regular kind of perception, whereas noise includes many varied types of sound perceptions that intermingle in an irregular and confused fashion. Thus one can compose noise from musical sounds by throwing them together in an irregular manner; for example, when one touches all the piano keys within a range of one or two octaves at the same time.

upon recognition of individual pitch levels in order to establish the nature of correct hearing of simultaneous sounds. Révész (*loc. cit.*) explains the difference as follows:

> The impression of tonal distance (that is, of the difference of two notes according to pitch), perceived as intervals, is lacking or much diminished. We can speak of a spatial symbolism, which illustrates the reciprocal position of the two notes of the interval, manifesting itself in spatial terms such as higher, lower, nearer, more distant, only in the case of intervals [p. 102].

Speech sounds also represent the simultaneous sounding of several tones or noises, or the sounding of tones and noises of the same type in succession.

When Wernicke made his pioneering discovery of the localization of sound–tone images, it was based on the assumption that the function occurring in the first left-side temporal convolution consisted mainly in comprehending and storing the tones contained in words. This hypothesis is practicable to this day, in° spite of the results of experimental phonetics. Only a few researchers have modified it. Sachs,[74] for instance, is one of them, and he states:

> We perceive as simple sense impressions tones that are different from each other in quality; that is to say, in pitch and intensity, or tone volume. A larger number of simultaneously sounding notes first produce in us the impression of confused noise. Besides this, however, we perceive something additional, quite different from the tones themselves; namely, the relationship of the single tones to each other. This relationship is independent of the volume and pitch of the tones. A melody, considered as melody, does not sound differently in the bass or soprano ranges, and no differently in C major, C sharp or in any other key. Likewise, a spoken word remains the same, whether it has been spoken in a bass or a soprano voice. Once it has been perceived and absorbed by us at any pitch, we would again recognize it regardless of the range.... We probably have to use several areas of the cortex also for impressions coming from the hearing organ, one for the tones themselves and one for sorting them out into noises, sound shadings, melody, and words. In this second center, it is the intervals between the various tones that come to cognition, rather than the pitch and volume of the tones.

We must give full consideration to these words from Sachs's significant work. For experimental phonetics do show that only one particular tone, within certain limits, is characteristic even for the single sound. Otherwise, however, it is the relationship between the respective pitch of single tones which is characteristic. Sound analyses, the most fundamental one of which is associated with the great name of Helmholtz, have

---

74. *Gehirn und Sprache* (Wiesbaden, 1905), p. 45.

recently been continued with ceaseless endeavor by Hermann.[75] The principal question as to whether the characteristic tone of a vowel is absolute or relative in nature has been decided by him in favor of the former. "As far as characteristic tones are concerned, analysis corroborates beautifully that they have an *approximatively fixed* [emphasis added] position, and therefore move up the numerical ladder with increasing vowel pitch." Let us cite the vowel *A* as an example. Its characteristic tone lies between *c2* and *e2*. But others have two characteristic tones: the *U* has a deeper one between *e* and *f* and a higher one between *d* and *c*. Otto Weiss[76] holds that whispered vowels acquire noise character. The characteristic tones for whispered vowels range within the following frequencies:

> for U between   400 and   600
>   O between   500 and   710
>   A between   700 and   840
>   E between 2200 and 2600
>   I between 2500 and 3100 vibrations.

"Whereas the curve of an *A,* sung loudly, contains none of the vibrations of the basic tone, the basic tone vibration becomes quite apparent when the vowel is sung in a low voice."

Benjamins,[77] differing from Hermann, concurs with Auerbach:

> The sound depends only upon the law of relative distribution; a change in pitch changes this law and with it the sound of the vowel. Indeed no one can claim that there exists a vowel tone that is completely independent of tone pitch; in some the change becomes so strong that it reaches the realm of the sound differences of two different vowels.

These opposite views have nevertheless something in common which is most important to us; namely, that within one and the same sound there exists an infinite variety of changes in pitch or in the distance of the tone partials from each other; so that for the recognition of a vowel as a pattern familiar to us we must look for a function that recognizes and relates the qualities of pitch, volume and tone length of the tone partials to one another. This recognition is an isolated one, at least within broad limits, and within these broad limits there are many separate functions that we in a certain sense experience as identical. Here the reader is again referred to the earlier discussion of accents. Goldstein's

---

75. "Phonophotographische Untersuchungen," *Pflügers Arch.* from Vol. 45 to the last years.
76. "Die Kurven der geflüsterten und leise gesungenen Vokale," *Pflügers Arch.*, Vol. 142.
77. "Über den Hauptton des gesungenen oder laut gesproche-nen Vokales," *Pflügers Arch.*, Vol. 154, 155.

remarks (*loc. cit.*) complement our views best of all: "What do we have to imagine as being localized in the sense-perception areas? Not the complete memory-images, but only their sense-qualities [p. 371]."

The function of grasping the importance of several simultaneous skills for normal speech development and normal speech will be illustrated by a recent example from the pathology of infantile speech development.

CASE 7: A 10-YEAR-OLD BOY FROM GALICIA

A 10-year-old boy from Galicia, of normal size and well nourished, was brought to me because of a serious speech difficulty. He is the brother of three normal siblings, aged 8, 5, and 1 year. The parents are not blood relations. Likewise, the rest of the family anamnesis is negative. The birth of the boy was an easy one; he was breast fed for 1 year, had pneumonia in his third year, and repeatedly suffered from gastrointestinal catarrh until his fourth year. He began to walk at age 1 ½. His first teeth came in during the sixth month. He already showed some speech comprehension at an early age; however, now he still understands only common, simpler sentences. His internal organs are healthy, reflexes at the extremities very lively, bilateral Chvostek's phenomenon is present on the upper lip. The genitals, as well as the fundus, mouth, throat, and nose are normal. The eardrums also show no pathological changes. The patient gives an impression of being intelligent. He handles all sorts of objects quickly and intelligently, and promptly recognizes all colors and shapes. Each movement of the lips, of the tongue, and of the mimic muscular system is correctly imitated. Now to the hearing examination. It was carried out with the Edelmann tuning fork series and Urbantschitsch's harmonica at intervals of 1 week each, partially in order not to tire the patient through lengthy examinations, and partially in order not to overlook some existing variations in the sharpness of the patient's hearing. Mr. Stein, a colleague at the Urbanschitsch Clinic, was kind enough to assist me. The patient heard each tuning fork for a shorter period than the examiners, and the numbers alongside the notes indicate how many seconds shorter that period was.

Right		Left	Right		Left	Right		Left
5	A′	8	3	g	2	5	e″	5
3	C	4	4	a	3	8	f″	5
3	F	3	2	h′	4	5	a″	3
8	A	3	5	c′	5	8	c‴	8
6	c	4	0	d′	5	6	g‴	6
3	d	3	3	e′	3	18	c⁗	18
5	e	2	2	f′	2	10	g⁗	15
3	f	4	3	a′	4			

Subsequent examinations resulted only in very minor differences, so that those findings may be omitted here. There exists therefore a minor lessening of hearing acuteness in the major and in the first three minor octaves, a more significant lessening in the fourth octave. With just light blowing, tones in the range of the two-stroked major octave to the two-stroked minor octave produced on the Urbantschitsch harmonica (which has the advantage, among other things, of resembling the pipe tones made by the human voice more closely than those of the tuning fork), were regularly heard through two rooms (8 meters). The 3rd and 4th minor octaves, upon light blowing, were only heard at a distance of 4 meters. Since, according to Gutzmann[78], human speech sounds range from A and d', (male voices A—d, female voices a—d'), tests for hearing single tones offered no clue to the almost complete muteness shown by the patient. For, when he was introduced to me, he was still in the first stage of speech imitation, that is to say, he imitated a word now and then more or less correctly, but without speaking spontaneously. He was a wild boy otherwise, hitting his siblings and also his mother, a fact mentioned here only because, in my opinion, it belongs to the speech diagnosis. (Indeed wild behavior is characteristic of almost all children who are mute but can hear, and could be explained, as mentioned, by the fact that they do not have a sufficient motor discharge to result in speech. In fact, wild behavior diminishes almost without exception with the progress of speech development during therapy.)

A striking result showed up in the hearing diagnosis of speech sounds. The boy said k for p; b or m or n for t; k for l; u for n; n for i; o for u; b for f. The remaining sounds were correctly imitated, either individually or in syllables. Whenever he pronounced one of the above sounds incorrectly, he could not be dissuaded from it even through repeated correct models, and it became clear that he absolutely did not know that the sound that he produced was not the same as the one he was supposed to repeat. In other words, he did not acoustically apprehend the spoken sound. The tests were conducted in such a way that the patient could not look at the doctor's mouth. Treatment, on the other hand, consisted in allowing him to lip-read, enabling errors to be quickly corrected. After a visual demonstration, the sound was always pronounced again, while the patient had to turn his face away from the speaker. After several months of daily exercise it was thus possible to establish a functioning connection between the visual impression, or the patient's conscious speech movement, and the acoustical sound.

It is perhaps permissible, in view of the striking difference between the hearing of individual sounds and that of speech sounds, to attribute the patient's defect to his inability of grasping several sounds, or noises, at one time. I would like to state, however, that such a defect cannot be held responsible for the entire severe speech disorder. If one considers

78. *Stimmbildung und Stimmpflege* (Wiesbaden, 1912).

what decisive significance the purely passive "charging" of the central hearing region of the brain has for motor speech, one may allow the supposition that the stimulus so essentially different from the physiological one is insufficient in this respect. For although the boy spoke many sounds correctly, it would not be amiss, in interpreting these data, to assume that this, too, was but a consequence of much practice in which the sight of the speaker's mouth played a considerable part, and that only very few stimuli were physiologically grasped from the outset by the central acoustic speech apparatus.

If the reader is willing to be guided by this latter interpretation of mine, then he will probably not reject the assumption that a cortical sensory aphasia may develop from a synonymous dissolution of the central sound mechanism through illness.

Certain forms of stammering might also belong to the same group of central speech disorders. H. Gutzmann (*Die dysarthrischen Sprachstörungen*, Vienna and Leipzig, 1911) emphasizes quite rightly that faulty sounds, insofar as they are not based on malformation of speech organs, are centrally caused. In discussing the forms motor aphasia may take, we will also have to consider stammering. But there are also speech defects, congenital in nature, extending to several sounds, which seem to find their explanation in the hearing area of the brain. There are, for example, sigmatics[79] who, without looking at the mouth, are incapable of selecting a correct S sound when one pronounces both a correct and incorrect S for them. Their inability goes so far that during several successive tests following each other without interruption, they select sometimes one sound as correct, sometimes another. One cannot escape the assumption that these people never hear the S correctly, but that they hear it rather in the changed form in which they pronounce it. If,

---

79. Sigmatism means the lack of S sounds or their mispronunciation. Physiologically the S is formed in such a way that the tongue lies straight in the mouth and that the tip of the tongue rests near the incisors; along the midline of the tongue a groove is formed through which the air is moving in order to leave the mouth, concentrated in the middle of the line of teeth. The sharp S sounds (for example in the words *es, was, Fuss, nass*) are voiceless, that is, the air comes from the larynx without causing the vocal cords to vibrate rhythmically. The opposite is true for the soft S ("*Nase,*" "*besonders*"), where the vocal cords vibrate strongly. If one places one's hand on the larynx while pronouncing the sharp S, one feels nothing; however, when pronouncing the soft S, a strong vibration is felt.

If one presses the tip of the tongue against the teeth while saying S, the part of the tongue behind it rises, making the groove formation impossible. Air then moves over the entire breadth of the fore part of the tongue, and the sound rings false. It is more disturbing still when the tongue is pushed between the teeth. The first is a case of *Sigmatismus addentalis*, the second of *Sigmatismus interdentalis*. If the groove is too deep, it is called *Sigmatismus stridens* because the S sounds unpleasantly strident. If the tongue does not lie flat in the mouth, but is raised on one side, and air leaves the supraglottal vocal tract through the corresponding corner of the mouth, we have a case of *Sigmatismus lateralis dexter* or *sinister*. If the soft palate is slack while pronouncing an S sound, and air does not move through the mouth but through the nose, a snoring sound is produced, *Sigmatismus nasalis*.

on the other hand, one ascertains a completely normal hearing for all tuning fork tones, as I was able to do repeatedly, one will have to look for a defect in the function of simultaneous perception of several tones.

There are among sigmatics still other patients—one can find these, incidentally, in all groups of stammerers—who are quite capable, when offered both choices, of differentiating between correct and false sounds. However, even after having been taught the correct sound in an optical–tactile manner, they immediately mispronounce it again if they are asked to repeat it acoustically. Gutzmann (*loc. cit.*) comments on this as follows:

> It becomes clear, especially by this experiment, that sound impression bears the same relationship to sound production as stimulus to reflex. If we pronounce the normal *S*, it is an adequate stimulus for the *S* production of our patients, whether it be an interdental, lateral, or nasal *S*. Perception of the correct *S* and production of an incorrect one are tightly ancored to each another [p. 178].

Such cases seem to deal with a defect of a purely motor nature, although centrally triggered, and these patients know of their speech defect in contrast to those we were discussing before, who had to be told of their speech defect by others. Also, in the case of sigmatics who recognize the incorrect *S* acoustically, it is often noted that they try to hide their *S*-defect with additional auxiliary lip movements; mostly they pull down their upper lip to a considerable extent, especially in cases of interdental sigmatism. J. Fein[80] has pointed this out. This type of stammering therefore belongs to the group of motor central speech disorders, and has been mentioned at this point only because its reaction to an acoustically modeled *S*, in contrast to one that was shown visually, might suggest the postulation of an acoustic deficiency. As we realize, such an assumption would not really be able to explain the symptoms.

Let us point out at the conclusion of these observations on the hearing of tone combinations that in this connection Urbantschitsch's hearing exercises for the hard of hearing have also brought some clarification and promise to bring more.

80. "Über ein neues Symptom bei *S*-Fehlern," Vienna, *Med. Woch.*, 1912.

Chapter 12

THE INFLUENCE OF THE AUDITORY CENTER OF
THE BRAIN ON SPONTANEOUS SPEECH

Motor Aphasia

After this analysis of the hearing function—still far too little detailed in comparison with actual circumstances—let us proceed to its overall importance for speech.

I have a certain personal interest in this question because my views on the influence of disorders in the sound-tone image mechanism (L-K-M) on speech, as given in my monographs *Über die Behandlung der Aphasien* and *Zur Behandlung der motorischen Aphasie*, were not accepted by two such eminent aphasia researchers as Liepmann and Pappenheim. I believed then and still believe now, that whenever spontaneous speech passes through the sound-image center, the latter feeds this speech movement, and therefore an impairment of speech may result from damage to one of the following areas: the L-K-M, the connection to the motor speech region, and the motor speech region itself. As proof for this assumption I cite the well-known phenomenon in pathology of children up to 10 or even 12 years of age with completely normal speech development, who, upon becoming deaf, always became mute as well. In some cases a child who is ill with fever will awaken from a state of unconsciousness deaf as well as mute; in other cases, only deaf while his speech slowly deteriorates. Just as we shall find out later for cases of transcortical motor aphasia whose speech disappears while repeating syllables before the eyes of the listener, the speech of a child who has become deaf disappears in precisely this fashion in front of his horrified parents, only over a longer period of time. We may very well call these patients motor aphasics, if we choose so to classify people with good speech comprehension who do not speak. Unfortunately, this fact is difficult to ascertain as far as our deaf children are concerned, although no one will doubt it. In their case what change ever occurred in the motor part of their speech apparatus? Probably none, anatomically speaking! Only the feeding mechanism is lacking; the sound images are not yet firm enough—they dissipate. Gutzmann tells in one of his books of such a child who, after staying in an institution for deaf mutes for many years, suddenly, in an emotional state, made an unprintable utterance which he had never seen in the institution (one must say *seen,* for the child could not hear), but had retained inside himself from the time he was still healthy. The emotional state had carried him over the threshold. How can the strange dissipation of the sound-tone image be explained? Of all the words used by the healthy child, he might hear each single one again in short intervals, and that represents a new stimulus, a new reinforcement of the central remaining impression. Only through this does the sound-tone image mechanism (L-K-M) obtain the strength for giving off energy itself—for the purpose of triggering speech movement. One might possibly say that the child is an imitative creature that ceases to speak because, apart from individual sound images, he no longer hears. However, I do not deem such an assertion about 7-, 8-, and 10-year-old children to correspond to facts.[81]

The form I designated as expressive–sensory aphasia, and which today I would prefer to call expressive–auditory aphasia, would be the analogous speech impairment caused by a certain damage of the sound–tone image mechanism (L-K-M), without impairment of speech comprehension. Contrary to this, Liepmann and Pappenheim[82] are of the opinion that in cases of damage to acoustic word residues, comprehension as well as speech are probably affected. Pick[83] endorsed my theory in one article, and in another one[84] spoke out against the Liepmann–Pappenheim opinion. He emphasized in particular

that impairment of word comprehension involves an automated function, completely lacking in voluntary movements, which accordingly reconstitutes itself more quickly; whereas for the speech function (apart from echolalia), a certain voluntary impulse is always needed. The difference in voluntary participation because of this fact means that the speech function is the more difficult of the two; a circumstance that serves as a point of reference for the understanding of Fröschels' previously mentioned theory.

81. See the debate in the *K. K. Ges. der Ärzte in Wien (Imperial Society of Physicians in Vienna),* June, 1917.
82. *Ztschr, f. d. ges. Neur. u. Psych.,* Vol. 41., p. 27.
83. "Über das Verhältnis zwischen motorischer und sensorischer Sprachregion. Bemerkungen zu dem Aufsatz von Fröschels," *Arch. f. Psych. u. Nervenkrankh.,* Vol. 56, Fol. 3.
84. "Kleine Beiträge zur Pathologie der Sprachzentr.," *Ztschr. f. d. ges. Neur. u. Psych.,* Vol. 30, Fol. 2/3.

Since apparently we have a debatable point here, and since in my opinion the irrefutable proof furnished by the development of muteness in young people who have become deaf apparently does not support Pick's views sufficiently, I will gladly attempt a second proof, which I consider particularly useful in illustrating attitude, the main idea of this paper.

CASE 8: A 14-YEAR-OLD BOY

An intelligent 14-year-old boy in the ninth grade, born with a cleft palate, received an obturator from a dentist a short time ago. His nasalized speech improved, but the patient could not pronounce the palatals G and K. Up to that point he had not learned them because he had had no palate. He substituted for them a so-called "coup de glotte," an explosive noise, brought about by strongly pressing the vocal cords together and through a sudden opening of the closed passage by the air stream. In writing one could represent such a word by the Latin term *spiritus lenis,* which was supposed to have corresponded to a somewhat weaker glottal stroke. Instead of "Karl" and "Gabel" he therefore said "Arl" and "Abel." For this reason he came to the logopedic out-patient department of the Vienna Ear Clinic (Privy Councillor Prof. Urbantschitsch) where I started to treat him. Through frequent systematic exercises, he was able to pronounce both sounds in syllables and words after a few weeks. Then he suddenly interrupted his treatment for 3 weeks. When he returned, I asked him the reason for his absence, and he said: *"Meine Mutter ist 'estorben"* (My mother died). I purposely did not want to understand him and asked him to pay careful attention to what he was saying, since one of the newly learned sounds was missing somewhere. Nevertheless, the boy repeated the same mistake eight times, even though it was pointed out to him again and again. Finally, I said to him, "Listen carefully. *Meine Mutter ist 'estorben."* The boy immediately stopped short and correctly said, *"gestorben."*

It becomes very apparent from this that among other motor ones. Although there is much similarity here with Bastian's well-known theory on various deficiencies with variously severe damage to the regions, there is a difference of opinion on one essential point: The evaluation of orientation towards hearing or speaking relative to the functioning of the central sound–tone image mechanism. Here, too, a situation similar to the proverbial one seems to exist: We cannot see the mote in our own eye, but we always see the splinter in the eye of our neighbor.[85] Both

85. As previously mentioned, I am not alone in my views about the significance of the temporal lobe in spontaneous speech; Nrène is only the small merit of the burden of proof. Lately, for example, Kleist has expressed a view that approaches in certain respects the

things there is a great difference in whether someone is oriented toward speaking or toward listening. The sound–tone image which another person evokes is immediately recognized as being correct or incorrect. As long as the boy was speaking, he was focused on something entirely different and failed to recognize the sound that he himself produced as incorrect. The tone image that "flashed" inside of him was not actually strong enough to trigger correct speech. The validity of Pick's and Gutzmann's theory on the reflex-like process of speech stems from this observation. It also follows, however, how much higher one must assess the stimulus value of a word penetrating from the outside compared to one that "resounds" from the inside. In other words, an acoustic stimulus coming from the exterior may produce a strong effect even in a normal brain, which stimulate corresponding cells and tracks with an

---

view presented in this monograph. "(Über Leitungsaphasie und grammatische Störungen," *Monatsschr. f. Psych. u. Neur.*, Vol. 40).

He explains transcortical aphasia as a mixture of impairment of sound discrimination and slight word deafness, which is caused by impairment of a certain level of comprehension of word sounds. Anatomically speaking, he situates it in the temporal lobes, the insula, the arch group and the gyrus supramarginalis. He stresses the fact that sound discrimination impairment may probably be a milder form of a regressive stage, respectively, of sensory aphasia. He locates agrammatism, which he divides into impairment of grammatical comprehension and grammatical speech, in the posterior temporal lobe. He furnishes no proof for the assumption that agrammatism might also be the result of a lesion of the motor speech region. In a very valuable article with a title, in my opinion, too extensive in scope, i.e., "Über den gegenwärtigen Stand unserer Kenntnis der Aphasielehre" (On the present state of knowledge in the study of aphasia) (*Monatsschr. f. Psych. u. Neur.*, 1914), Mingazzini likewise cites facts that seem to support my contention. The results of studying three cases of complete sensory aphasia, which he undertook together with Giannuli, confirm Bastian's theory, according to which an injury to both verbal–acoustic regions results not only in sensory aphasia but also in a high degree of limitation to vocabulary. The patient only utters paraphasic words of one, two or three syllables. In my opinion, if we contrast this result with Pick's famous case where the patient spoke well despite his inability to comprehend numerous words, only the importance of a determination of sensory types, however difficult it might sometimes turn out to be, may be concluded from it for the time being. Mingazzini also cites cases of Liepmann and Beduschi that show the picture of total aphasia where Wernicke's left zone and the lobulus parietalis inferior have been destroyed. Mingazzini states that:

in order to explain this syndrome, it is sufficient to remember that an injury to the temporoparietal region means damage not to the fibers carrying verbal–acoustical stimuli, but to fibers of association which link optical images (perhaps also tactile and visual (?) images) of the object with the medulla, or posterior part of the (left) lobulus parietalis inferior. Most likely, this is where the optic fibers coming from the right posterior lobe after passing through the corpus callosum cerebri come together. In this case the patient's (optical) store of images will suffer a considerable loss. Almost all of the no longer stimulated verbal–acoustic images become incapacitated in turn, including the foci of the left Broca's area, whereas the sparse verbal–acoustic stimuli from the right Wernicke area can only awaken the syllable images of the intact right Broca's area through the corpus callosum cerebri.

It seems open to question whether this complicated explanation is necessary, or whether we could not make do with mere faults of verbal–acoustic components. In any case and apart from that, the words "and consequently also the foci of the left Broca's area" may be considered as supporting my previously mentioned theory.

intensity that does not exist in case of internal "resounding." This can only be explained by the physiologically lesser intensity of the internal stimulus, coming, for example, from the transcortex, as compared to that of an external one. We may therefore conclude that in case of impaired sound–tone image mechanism (L–K–M) the external stimulus may still be effective (*comprehension*) when the internal one is already breaking down (*speech*). This, incidentally, might explain the frequent occurrence, in cases of so-called total aphasia, of sensory symptoms subsiding much more rapidly than parts of the central speech path analyzed above; namely, the connection of the sound–tone image mechanism (L–K–M) with the motor area and the motor area itself, will be examined later in more detail.

Chapter 13

THE OCCURRENCE OF SPONTANEOUS SPEECH IN A CHILD

(Memory for Names)

In tracing the speech development of children we have now reached the stage of echolalia. We already know that the repetition of words which are comprehended appears at the same time. As to understanding them, Preyer (*loc. sit.*, p. 266) points out that some concept of understanding must by its very nature exist in the child's brain even before comprehension occurs. We want to note the place of this historic stage in the evolution of the separation between thought and speech, and again confirm the fact that infantile speech characteristics also exist later on. (By the way, we already inferred this from Gomperz's "hypological thinking.") Preyer points out that in onomatopoetic descriptions, the word and image appear almost simultaneously. There the connection sometimes seems to be of a lasting and particularly close nature, as I would like to conclude from a case of sensory aphasia that I treated. On bad days, when the patient had difficulty finding the right word for rooster, he would promptly remember the rather onomotopoetic word *kura* (he was Ruthenian), [86] whereas it was more difficult for him to remember *Kohut.*

Shortly after the beginning of meaningful imitative speech, the first beginnings of spontaneous speech occur. Exact and generally valid data cannot be established, nor can they be expected if we consider the many individual differences that come into play here. Most researchers uniformly state, however, that there is a long interval between the very first beginnings of spontaneous speech and any further development. Gheorgov's oldest son spoke his second word 3 weeks after the first one;

86. The Ruthenian language is essentially Ukranian. "Ruthenian" was the term applied to ethnic Ukranians living within the Austrian Empire [—editor].

it took his second son 2 months; and it took the Stern children 2 ½ and 2 months, respectively. In this phenomenon Stern recognizes a common property of speech development and even of psychological development in general, namely that of rhythmic undulation (W. Stern, "Tatsachen and Ursachen der seelischen Entwicklung," *Ztschr. f. angew. Psych.*, Vol. 1):

> It consists in the alternation of periods of rapid and slow progress; the amount of energy that a child has at its disposal is limited and therefore cannot be applied simultaneously and evenly to all functions necessary for his development. A kind of alternation between the main phases of development of these functions can therefore be observed. The stagnation of spontaneous speech noted just now usually coincides both with a strong increase in speech comprehension and, above all, with intensive progress in physical abilities.

I do not completely agree. Many experiences in the pathology of children's speech and of aphasia show that a similar, prolonged standstill repeatedly occurs with the first acquired speech components, and that progress is made more quickly after this period. I would rather assume a process of drilling and breaking in of a central region here, similar to the long repetitions of a babbling complex before the emergence of others. After all, we find similar situations at all stages of life when we acquire any new skill, and we express this by the proverb, "All beginnings are difficult." Even if a person's speech development is influenced by systematic instruction and systematic practice therapy, and consequently by a certain amount of force as opposed to a purely automatic and normal progression, his earliest store of learning will not be followed as rapidly by new acquisitions as the latter will be by subsequent ones. As far as treatment through exercises is concerned, it is valid for motor as well as sensory speech defects. I pointed this out especially in my lectures on deaf-mutes and mutes with hearing. Specifically, when teaching congenital transcortical sensory aphasics terms and designations by naming two or three pictures over and over again in the beginning, the thought occurred to me that it would be a sad thing indeed to have to teach the patient all the terms in the same painstaking way as in the beginning. However, this is not necessary. It is only a question of breaking in the brain passages in question, which will make it easier and easier and finally quite automatic. It would indeed be unusual if such a "rhythmic undulation movement" (Stern) would always manifest itself precisely after the first word.[87]

87. Gheorgov probably had the same thing in mind as I did when he said: "From that time on [the patient's] objective designations increased, above all through imitating the speech of his older brother. It is perhaps here that we may state that the Rubicon has

Among all the individual word categories it is the nouns that appear in greatest number at the earliest point. Verbs also soon make their appearance, whereas adverbs, adjectives, and pronouns appear later on in time. In their book the Sterns offer a table (p. 133) of the "threshold or liminal value" of individual word categories. By "threshold" they mean any condition of stimulus that just begins to become psychically effective. Accordingly then, there are also upper and lower threshold values. The advantage of such a presentation over a mere chronological record of words as they exist at various age-groups is that it illuminates the stratification of all speech components. It is very important for them to emphasize the fact that though children at first tend to favor words that are easier to pronounce, they soon select those which are adequate for their particular stage of development.

> The subconscious selection of imitation will proceed according to the urge to enter into an active reciprocal relationship with the environment, according to the direction of interests, and according to the development of intellectual maturity. This will lead to a great difference between the quantitative and qualitative speech structures.

The term "unconscious selection" seems to warrant a closer investigation of a phenomenon encountered not too infrequently in both physiology and pathology, and from which we may hope to derive further insights into the psychological bases and the psychological supports of speech. I recall a patient who manifested a strong tendency to forget family names and occasionally also first names. This was due to progressive amnesic aphasia brought about by incipient slowly progressive weakening. To be sure, a poor memory for names is commonplace, and it is therefore all the more necessary to look for an explanation of this phenemonon. Everyone can recall some people who continually confuse the first names of members of their own family, although such persons often have a generally poor memory for words. Aside from a poor memory for names, however, a loss of words in their ordinary everyday conversations is not noticeable. When a child learns to call things by names, it does so by gradually associating, recognizing and then remembering an expression that is used by the environment over and over again for an object or an activity. A prerequisite for this is the fact that the word is used in a truly uniform fashion or at least with reference to objects of the same kind. The word "window" will always be heard by the child in connection with the same or similar objects. Let us suppose, however, that Carl is the name of a member of the family, as well as that

---

definitely been crossed, because from that moment on language development progressed much more rapidly and easily." [Translated from the French.]

of a distant relative and of a friend,[88] so that the same name is used for different people. This could cause a certain confusion in the child and could lessen his interest in names; his unconscious selection would reach out for them with diminished force, and his orientation would be weakened. This could explain a looser degree of retention. In other instances where there is confusion of first names in the immediate family, especially of one's own children, we could theorize that a deficient attitude towards one individual child might favor a less precise connection between the names and their bearers because interest and care are evenly distributed among all. A particular stimulus is really necessary for children to use proper names, which means that the internal process of association between a person and a name does not occur in such an automatic manner as perhaps that between objects and their designation. This is clarified by a remark by Laura Bridgmans quoting Jerusalem[89], that at first she used names of persons only when she "thought lovingly of the person" (quoted in *Ziehen,* Leitfaden der physiologischen Psychologie, Jena, 1902, p. 247).[90]

Assuming that the reader accepts this attempt at explanation, he will find in it a new indication as to the role which attitude plays during speech development, but he will also recognize that such influences as existed at the start of speech learning may under certain circumstances be significant throughout life.

88. In *Umriss einer Theorie der Namen* (Vienna, 1899), Stöhr says that "proper names are universal names, i.e., names of extensive logical scope as long as no closer designation is added."

89. Laura Bridgman, *Eine psychologische Studie* (Vienna, 1891).

90. Freud directed his attention to the field of faulty memory for names in his *Psychopathologie des Alltagslebens* (Berlin, 1912) and tried to explain it through subconscious processes. He closes the chapter by stating that besides the simple forgetting of names there is also a forgetting through repression. I am far from denying this possibility; however, I believe I have found a basis in my investigation to explain why proper names are generally so easily forgotten and confused, whether or not subconscious repression may attack at this point of minor resistance in any given case.

Chapter 14

AGRAMMATISM IN THE CHILD AND THE ADULT

In the opinion of all authors, individual word groups emerge in children according to their needs for expression and comprehension at a given time; and, therefore, nouns and verbs take precedence. This will automatically remind us of certain aphasics who speak in a so-called telegram style. This thought association becomes more vivid yet if we consider that in the beginning children use verbs almost exclusively in the infinitive form. Moreover, in order to express the past tense they use only the past participle for a long time. The Sterns coined the striking term "need for speech" (*Sprachnot*) which describes a deficiency making itself felt, in conjunction with a growing store of experiences on the one hand, and on the other, forcing us to original learning. This same term could be used for aphasics with respect to their lack of words as compared to their need for expression. In such cases a patient will, of course, first search within himself for the word which is the most important one for understanding. This may gradually function as an exercise so that later on these word categories or grammatical–syntactical formations already possess a functional precedence over other less important ones.

CASE 9: A 36-YEAR-OLD ENGINEER

Mr. A. St., a 36-year-old engineer, suffered an apoplectic seizure 5 years ago which left him with a paralysis of the right half of his body and total motor aphasia. The latter improved to such a degree during the following years that the patient possessed a fairly large vocabulary, which he used spontaneously but highly agrammatically. All verbs were employed in the infinitive only, and frequently one one word was used instead of a whole sentence. He said, for example: "I yesterday go park" or answered the question, "How did you get from Munich to Vienna?" by simply saying the single word "railroad." He never spoke in orderly, regular sentences. The sequential speaking of words went very well. However, for *a, e, i, o, u* he said: *a, o, u,* and when asked to say the vowel sequence in reverse, he said: *u, a, e, i, u.* His behavior during dictation was most interesting. Generally, he did better with long words than with short ones. Words which he did not use, such as *I, you, he, she, it, there, here, from, for, in order to,* etc., he also could not write. Echolalia was contained within the same limits as his spontaneous speech. He immediately changed a correctly spoken sentence model into an agrammatical structure. When nonsense syllables were pronounced resembling a word, he would repeat that specific word. For example, instead of *heissa* (nonsense) he would say *heisse* ('my name is'); instead of *Waffa* (nonsense) he would say *Waffe* ('weapon'). It also became apparent that he could not spell while writing. Orthographic errors occurred frequently for that reason. Indeed, he did not write any (single) letter or any nonsense syllable during dictation, but he did write many words. While reading, he seemed to have an ample inner grasp of words and sometimes pronounced one of them; yet almost never was he able to read syllables or even single letters out loud. His speech comprehension was very good. During his entire 2-month stay in the sanatorium there was never any evidence that he did not understand something. In the course of a 2-month treatment it was possible to make him speak grammatically by making him describe each individual scene on picture sheets shown him in short simple sentences. However, he always preferred to speak only in single words. One had to force him to speak in organized sentences.[91] At first he had to be given a correct speech model, but not for long. Repetition of nonsense syllables was diligently practiced, which only gradually became half-way correct. This was done with the aid of a mirror.

Reading and writing exercises began with single latters. My method (cf. *Über die Behandlung der Aphasien*) of using colored letters was very helpful in this respect. The patient's reading ability improved remarkably quickly, so that he could read complete sentences out loud. On the other hand, his writing ability went never beyond writing syllables. He succeeded in spelling words correctly only when they were dictated syllable by syllable. Nevertheless, the results were quite satisfactory for this short period of time. Unfortunately, when the patient visited his sister in the fall, he suffered a new seizure which manifested itself somatically in dizziness and feelings of weakness. His speech progress, however, was significantly impaired, so that during a new examination he again spoke highly agrammatically and had lost his reading ability.

91. When we asked him repeatedly why he would not talk in whole sentences, he himself used to say: "Isn't necessary." This is very similar to Case 6 (First Lieutenant L.). On good days he forms many correct sentences; however, on bad days, when he has considerable difficulty finding words, he speaks very agrammatically and asyntactically.

Agrammatism, however, may also arise from other causes. Delayed speech development especially is not an infrequent reason for a disproportionately long duration of agrammatism, as shown in the following example.

CASE 10: AN 11-YEAR-OLD BOY

Eleven-year-old Leo W. successfully attended a fifth-year elementary school class, and was supposed to take the entrance examination for a gymnasium (High School). His birth had been easy, he was breast-fed, began to walk at 2 years of age and to speak at 4. He had suffered no serious disease. For the first 2 years after speech had begun (that is, until the completion of his sixth year), his speech was limited to individual words. At that time he began treatment with a speech therapy physician, which lasted 1 year. The positive result achieved consisted in a larger vocabulary and in the fact that now and then he showed beginnings of sentence structuring. He then entered school, but had always had tutoring at home from the beginning. The fact that he regularly advanced despite his most severe speech difficulties, as will be shown, is probably due to the understanding of his teachers. Since the boy diligently acquired all necessary knowledge, except speech, they concluded that he suffered from a pathological disorder of the speech apparatus. He has been stuttering for 1½ years. The physical state of the patient was normal, aside from a presence of Chvostek's phenomenon and of an increase in tendon reflexes. In testing his ability to name objects and actions a slight delay is evidenced. Articles, however, are frequently confused. The conjugation of verbs is full of errors. He says, for example: *I go, I went, I am gone* [wrong auxiliary].[92] In order to determine his ability to form simple sentences spontaneously, he was required to build sentences around single words. Here are some of the results: In each case, a stop watch accurately measured the time he needed for reflection, and it is given here.) Pocket watch: *The pocket watch one one carries the pocket watch in the pocket* (15 seconds). Pencil: *The pencil is being written by the children* (4²/₅ sec). Balloon: *The balloon is round* (3³/₅ sec). Clothes hook: *The clothes hook is being used by the coats and the coats* (5¹/₅ sec)" Chain: *One wears the chain with watches.* Christmas tree: *The Christmas tree occurs on Christmas* (7 sec). Spontaneous narration: *Today I am been in school in the morning; it was style 8 to 9; 9 to 10 geography; 10 to 11 writing; 11 to 12 singing. In geography we about Budapest learned* [wrong word order]. *That Budapest is a very large city and that it is on the Danube.* Description of pictures: *Here is a spinning wheel to which* [wrong case of declension][93] *belongs to the peasant woman and from which belongs*

92. The German text reads reads: *Ich gehe, ich ging, ich habe gegangen* instead of *ich bin gegangen* [translator's note].
93. The German text reads as follows: *Hier ist ein Spinnrad, welchem* [instead of *welches*] *der Bauernfrau gehört. Oben um* [instead of *auf*] *dem Ofen steht ein Topf. Oben der* [instead of *über dem*] *Topf hängen Strümpfe* [translator's note].

to the peasant woman. **On top** [wrong preposition] **around** *the stove stands a pot.
Above the* [wrong article] *pot stockings are hanging.* Another day, when discussing the same picture—although it had already been described to him in short sentences at his first examination—*a spinning wheel*[94] *which belongs to the peasant woman in* [superfluous *in*, wrong case of declension] *which belongs to the peasant woman, that* [wrong relative pronoun gender] *belongs to the peasant woman.* [Various incorrect uses of genders, word classes, and grammatical structure—untranslatable into English.]

Aside from his poor speech, tests for color and shape perception, for keenness of hearing, for ability in drawing, arithmetic, natural sciences, etc., show no pathological problems.

94. The German text reads as follows: *ein Spinnrad, welches der Bauernfrau gehört,* **in** [superfluous] *welcher* [instead of **welches**], **der** [instead of **das**], **die** [instead of **das**] *der Bauernfrau gehört* [translator's note].

Chapter 15

SO-CALLED TRANSCORTICAL MOTOR APHASIA

We must add a further observation to the stage of speech development of children last described by us. This stage is characterized in part by spontaneous repetition, whereas there is another part which is merely repetitive (although comprehension is already partially present).

It is known that there are aphasics with good speech comprehension who are incapable of expressing their thoughts, although they can repeat correctly. In accordance with Wernicke and Lichtheim, these cases have been labeled transcortical motor aphasia. As is well known, it was just this type of aphasia that made Wernicke adhere to the speech-path theory involving the *transcortex and Broca's* region for spontaneous speech. Considering also that this type of aphasia was explained by Wernicke and Lichtheim as a blockage of the path between the conceptual center and Broca's region, it becomes conceivable why the postulation of a transcortex–Broca path seemed indispensable to these researchers. Other authors have interpreted transcortical motor aphasia as a less severe stage of cortical motor aphasia. The quarrel is an old one. Already Bastian[95] who, as is well known, postulated three kinds of functional impairments of a center, explained transcortical motor aphasia as a regressive stage of the cortical type. (The aforementioned three kinds of functional impairments are as follows: either a center may no longer be stimulated voluntarily, but rather must be stimulated through another center or by means of a powerful stimulus; or a powerful stimulus will be successful; or, finally, this stimulus, too, remains ineffective.) Freud[96] agrees with Bastian and, based on the well-known Heubner case ("Über Aphasie," *Schmidt's Jahrb.*, 1889) attempted to prove that a functional

95. "On Different Kinds of Aphasia," *Brit. Med. Journ.*, 1887.
96. *Zur Auffassung des Aphasien* (Vienna, 1891).

impairment of the sound–tone image center (L–K–M) may lead to the complex of symptoms under discussion. This doctrine must be stressed here all the more, since it already acknowledges the importance of the role of the L–K–M for spontaneous speech—a position with which the I agree—but which other investigators only recognized later. Brosch,[97] Pick,[98] Jacobsohn,[99] Quensel,[100] Bischoff,[101] and others agreed with Bastian's theory. A patient of Bonhöffer[102] is especially interesting. He showed aphasia as a result of a post-operative hematoma. After resorption of the hematoma, the aphasia regressed in such a manner that, at first, repetition became possible, but not followed by spontaneous speech until later on. One of Strohmayer's[103] cases is also significant. Here total motor aphasia changed into a typical transcortical aphasia which remained stationary for a long time. The liveliest opposition to this theory came from Heilbronner,[104] who referred, above all, to the fact that not enough proof was available to establish that it was basically even possible for cortical motor aphasia symptoms to regress, either spontaneously or through treatment. In my essay on the treatment of aphasia, I have produced proof that it is indeed possible, and simply refer to it here.

I also proved that transcortical motor aphasia may actually be a regression stage of the cortical type. I would like to restate the proof advanced there, for two reasons: First of all, this proof was not sufficiently appreciated, even though it was the first real proof; and second, it contains new points of reference with respect to speech development in children, and thus also with respect to our main theme. Let us reinforce this proof again through recent case histories not yet published.

CASE 11: PATIENT WITH GUNSHOT WOUND

This was a patient in the convent on Hartmann Lane (Vienna), in the section of Chief Surgeon Alesius. He was admitted there in October. A gun-

97. Über einen Fall von transkortikaler motorischer Aphasie (Berlin, 1892).
98. "Zur Lehre von der sogenannten transkortikalen motorischen Aphasie," *Arch. f. Psych.*, Vol. 32.
99. "Zur Frage von der sogenannten transkortikalen motorischen Aphasie," *Ztschr. f. exper. Pathol.*, 1909.
100. "Der Symptomenkomplex der sogenannten transkortikalen motorischen Aphasie," *Monatsschr. f. Psych. u. Neur.*, 1909.
101. "Zur Lehre von den amnestischen Sprachstörungen," *Jahrb. f. Psych.*, 1897.
102. "Zur Kenntnis der Rückbildung der motorischen Aphasie," *Mitt. a. d. Grenzgeb. d. Med. u. Chir.*, Vol. 10, Folios 1 and 2.
103. "Zur Kasuistik der transkortikalen motorischen Aphasie," *Dtsch. Ztschr. f. Nervenheilkunde*, Vol. 24, Folios 5 and 6.
104. "Über transkortikale motorische Aphasie," *Arch. f. Psych.*, Vol. 34.

shot had passed through his left forehead, or rather the left parietal bone, and he was completely unconscious. A severe decubitus complicated his condition. The patient lay completely unconscious for 5 weeks; he took nourishment, but otherwise did not react to any stimuli at all. He had no control of his bowels or bladder. At first, no operation was contemplated, since his temperature was subfebrile. Within 5 weeks, however, his temperature rose. Chief Surgeon Alesius therefore performed a trepanning operation and removed numerous bone splinters. There appeared to be no abcess, and the meninges were not incised. A brain prolapse that appeared after the operation partially receded spontaneously and partially regressed, whereupon the wound gradually closed. The healing process proceeded without interruption, and after about 2 months the wound had healed. New bone structure was formed starting from the edges, so that plastic surgery, which was at first considered, was not performed. After the trepanning, consciousness slowly returned, yet there still was complete paralysis of the right extremities and of the right side of the face. In this respect too, there had been slow improvement, so that the patient was now able to walk fairly well. Only his speech would not return. Other patients in the hospital also made every effort for a while, but they were not able to make the patient repeat even sounds. For this reason, on February 17, I was called in for consultation. In order to test speech comprehension it had to be established, first of all, which language the patient had spoken before his injury. German, Czech, Polish, Ruthenian, Russian were tried—not a sign of speech comprehension was to be noted. The only clue offered was the fact that he leafed through a Ruthenian Bible with interest while putting others aside. One could have drawn certain conclusions from the patient's name—but his name was not known. The physicians at the hospital were even of the opinion that he had forgotten his name, for when all the baptismal names of the Greek calendar as well as our own were read to him, he did not acknowledge any of them. Liepmann points out how careful we must be in the examination of aphasics before drawing conclusions as to their speech comprehension from their answers, or even from their mimic behavior. For a patient might lack the correct word when answering, or the right gesture might no longer be in his power. His answer then might suggest a lack of speech comprehension, whereas in fact his deficiency might only lie in the expressive sphere. It was not possible to determine the situation in this particular case—at any rate, we could not determine his first name. The military authorities, as mentioned previously, had assigned two assistants to me, both teachers: a Mr. K. C. Rothe, a remedial speech therapist, and a Mr. Hans Mülleutner, a teacher who was beyond the age for Home Guard duty and who had volunteered his help to me. After the patient was already able to read, one of my assistants succeeded in tracking down his name in the following manner: His regiment was known, and Mr. Mülleutner compiled a list of all its wounded men from the casualty records. He put each name on a separate card and noted thereon also the various increases of rank. The patient always wept while pointing to the same card. The date of the casualty list coincided more or less with the date of his injury. He was then photographed, and we had him identified through his regiment. (One may assume that he could identify his name because he had the written image before his eyes for a longer time span, whereas the sound-image disappeared quickly when his first name was pronounced.)

At his first examination the patient spoke nothing but the syllable "na" (also refer to table immediately following).

Date	Sound Formation	Remarks	Repetition of Speech
2/17	*m, a, o*	optical–tactile assistance	
2/18	*p, t; u*	mirror; manual assistance	
	f	raising of upper lip	
2/23	*l*		
	r	vibration of the floor of the oral cavity	
	n	finger on the nose	
2/25	*g*	pushing back of the tongue with a spoon, etc.	
3/2	*h*	hands on chest, thrusts of exhalation while depressing the tongue in the back	*Ma, mo pa, pe, etc.*
3/4	*r = l; k*		
	servus[a]		*servus*
	s		*sa, so, . . .*

[a] Translator's note: In Austrian dialect, *servus* is a greeting meaning hello or goodbye.

March 11:	Completely without practice, all sounds and syllables acoustically, even the *h*.
April 14:	Patient learns *I* [German] in connection with *ija*, then *i* alone. Patient learns *r* derived from *Servus*.
April 19:	Consonants are mostly combined with a vowel *E (a)*, etc.
April 22:	Reading, pointing to sounds that were read (small letters also are on the blackboard) works quite well; he recognizes letters that belong together. Capital *A* and small *h* create difficulties. He writes capital *A, B, C* by himself, but very unsteadily.
April 23:	While repeating syllables (without script) he suddenly says *bla* instead of German *Lampe* (lamp) [lampɛ].[105] However, he does not seem to have any understanding of the concept; upon repetition and upon being shown a sketch of a *lamp = bam*.

105. *Translator's note:* Phonetic transcriptions in English are added. Of course, they are not necessary in German. The + sign obviously stands for a check mark representing correct repetition.

April 26:   Repetition of the syllables (*dabo* = *di*) [dabo = di] creates
              difficulties. Reading is difficult for the first few minutes but
              then comes along pretty well, for example: *M* + e = *me* [m
              + e = me].

May 3:   Repetition: *Kappe* (English 'cap') = *Pan Gappe* [kapɛ = pan
              gapɛ]. Re-repetition *Ka O. Klappe* 'flap', 'trap') = *Lampe
              Glampe* [klapɛ = lampɛ glampɛ], *Glas* ('glass'), *Gla* creates
              difficulties. *Tisch* ('table') = *sitn, tins, trin* [tɪ = sɪtn, tɪns, trɪn].
              Tasche = *Tasche* ('pocket') [taɪɛ].

May 5:   *Klappe* = *K—lappe* [klapɛ = k—lapɛ]. Repetition: *Kap.
              Lampe—La—m—pe* [lampɛ—la—m—pɛ].

May 7:   *Lampe* +. At re-repetition: *Lampe* [La]. *Blume* ('flower') =
              (*Be Bl*) [Blumɛ = be bl]; he cannot say it yet.

May 13:   Newly acquired letters *sch* [ɪ], *tsch* [tɪ]. Mimic: *sabu, sab, se
              tale, deso* = *sida, disa.*

May 20:   Reading of letters, after all of them have been put out, goes
              along moderately well; frequently motor difficulties can
              clearly be noted.

May 21:   Reads letters very well.

June 7:   Pictures good; letters, except a few, good. Says *Da—ni—al
              Sa—do—wy* [da-ni-al za-do-vi].

June 9:   Says *Daniel* [daniɛl] well.

June 16:   Sang along the melody of the national anthem, with the
              syllable *la, la*. Tattoo (military retreat bugle call) with *tra, tra*.

June 18:   Syllables create great difficulties.

August 4:   Repetition *lido* = *ligo* = *lige* = *licher*. *ligo* = *li—gu—ter* =
              ligo. At *re-repetition: ligo, liga, ligo.*

September: *Re-repetition gets better and better.*

September 31: He answered the question (by way of a Ruthenian[106] in-
              terpreter) whether he used to be able to read, with *yes;* do
              you write?: *yes;* profession?: *peasant;* family: *single;* did
              mother or father speak German?: *no.*

December 9:   Designated without coaching: *Mann* + ('man'). *Baum* +
              ('tree'). *Frau* ('woman') = *fan*. *Kind* + ('child'). *Hund* ('dog')
              = *un*. *Bett* ('bed') = *bä* [bɛt = bɛː].

January 15, 1916: Acoustic repetition: *glogloda* = *glafien* = *blosogo; glafi* = *blosi;
              glafi* = *glafi–blofi;* optical: *glasi* +.

January 24:   Reading: *o* +; he recognizes *U* from the spoken model as
              such, but his lips are too rounded when repeating (similarly
              oen is read as *oeo*).

              U is spoken or read correctly without an optical *U* picture,
              when one points to the lips.

              M and *N* create great difficulties and produce slight stut-
              tering.

106. See footnote 86, p. 176.

February, 1916: Optical repetition goes easily, acoustic repetition often occurs with difficulty.

March 7: Reading exercises from a Ruthenian primer—very slow—after he had pronounced each letter out loud. He also copies syllables.

March 11: Patient recognizes and designates after lengthy reflection *lamp, cushion, stove, cat, doll, box, window* in the Ruthenian language. Fairly good execution of writing exercises.

March 22: Reading improves daily and patient can give short answers to questions: *Gdeie pytra rybra?* ('Where does the fish swim?') Patient: *W rika* ('In the river').

March 24: Talks quite intelligible about yesterday's concert, with great interest especially about the monkeys,—using nouns without connecting words. Nonsense syllables (acoustic):

$$sekvere = sekveveve$$
$$sekvere = +$$
$$vasatuge = vasoga$$
$$vasatuge = vasaloro$$
$$vasatuge = +$$

March 28: *Optical repetition. Mefrea* = me, mo, me—wosa, *faso* +, *mefrea—me me sole; General = Genelas (R = L!); Korporal = korpoporal; Telegramm = tegaram* (cluttering!); *Admiral = amimiral.*

April 5: Patient recognizes and also names the pictures in a picture book and does writing exercises beautifully.

May 4: Additional trepanation (operated upon by Prof. Finsterer) because of epileptic fits of the Jacksonian type.

May 21: Reading improves daily, and the patient gives short, intelligible answers to questions. Arithmetic is not yet grasped.

May 29: When asked to describe a horse, patient says: *The horse has three, no four feet, head, two ears, two eyes, one mane.*

June 5: Today patient started to count up to 10. He also calculates, but very slowly: $3 + 2 = 5, 2 + 5 = 7, 2 + 1 = 3.$

August 11: Patient describes the room in nouns only, but quite correctly. Optical and acoustical nonsense syllables almost without error, at the most up to three syllables only.

September: Little progress in the month of September.

October 21: The patient begins to repeat short sentences. He calculates quite well with two-digit numbers.

October 28: Nonsense syllables:

$$blodarepo = blogovelso$$
$$blodarpeo = +$$
$$dorfapero = dorfageno$$
$$dorfapero = +$$

October 31:   Patient studies German with great pleasure. Reading from
                   the primer almost without error.
November 24:   Speaks German sentences (two words) quite well.
December 5:   Patient tells with great difficulty about his day off from the
                   hospital and what he ate.
December 9:   Sentences with three words good. Nonsense syllables acous-
                   tically:

> *lamidoli* +
> *falegato* +
> *repligure* = *replimure*
> *kalabero* = *kabaleto*

December 12:   Reading very well already, only syllables ending in *pt* are
                   difficult for him to pronounce.
January 5, 1917:   After his Christmas vacation the patient read with more
                   difficulty and calculated very slowly. Nonsense syllables
                   acoustically:

> *dabi gute* = *dabi—dabi*
> *dabi gute* = *labi gute*
> *dabi* +
> *gute* +

January 17:   Patient describes his day off. *I was District 5. Sister Hortulana,*
                   me given one crown (krone), me given coffee and bread.
February 1:   Patient repeated a complete reading selection, when two or
                   at the most four words were pronounced together for him.
February 16:   Patient recounts, without error, the kind of useful animals
                   we have. Nonsense syllables:

> *tschulana* = +
> *brontofe* = *brontalo*

Particularly significant for our proof is the stage at which the patient is
already able to repeat correctly, but with re-repetition still very faulty.
For example, he twice repeated *golowa* correctly, without additional
prompting by the teacher. The third time, however, the word became
golom, the fourth time *ga*, and at this point re-repetition of the word
ceased altogether. However probable the assumption that the memory
picture itself disappears here, one could nevertheless maintain that the
word, initially only mechanically repeated, related at first to the concept,
and that upon re-repetition it was stimulated by this concept precisely up
to the point at which this stimulation ceased due to an impairment of the
path from the transcortex to the word. Here we might have to consider
that the initial re-repetition was aided by the chargeability—stemming
from the sensory stimulus—of the sound–image center. From this it

would follow that there is at least a certain influence of the cortex and its condition upon the symptomatic picture of transcortical motor aphasia. If one observes the patient's behavior towards nonsense syllables, this influence becomes all the more evident; and the role of the path from transcortex to cortex in this case will be recognized as nil. The patient's behavior towards nonsense syllables is exactly the same as towards words. He repeats the nonsense combination of syllables *radiwosa* just as well as the word *golowa;* re-repeats it correctly the first time, but subsequently more and more incorrectly, until the combination starts crumbling and finally disappears completely. This really has nothing to do with the transcortex! And therein lies the first part of the proof. Nonsense syllables, too, can only be repeated, but not re-repeated.

As long as the patient is not capable of re-repeating for as long as he wishes, he is also not capable of spontaneously using a specific word. Had we not, through Wernicke's and Lichtheim's theory, gotten so far away from this obvious interpretation, nothing would have seemed more self-evident than the fact that someone affected by a decrease in coritcal memory does not have cortical memory possession at his disposal! Herein lies the second part of the proof.

I claim for myself the modest merit of having been the first one to prove that transcoritcal motor aphasia is a state of retrogression or, as we might add here, a lighter state of cortical aphasia. I base my claim on the following consideration: The mere observation that cortical motor aphasia can transform itself into a transcortical one, or as in Pfeiffer's case, (Annual Meeting of the Society of German Psychiatrists, Berlin, 1910) that a case of initially transcortical aphasia changed to the symptomatic picture of cortical aphasia, can be explained by a double localization in which we find regression of one center of imapriment and the appearance of another. Now one of these centers may imply cortical aphasia; a second one, a transcortical case. Naturally, the latter was masked by the cortical type.

Nor do I at all wish to completely dismiss this possibility. In such a case, however, re-repetition should take place just as well as repetition. That alone would be proof that it is not the loss of cortical memory or memory, respectively, that provides the basis for the symptomatic picture of the case!

By the way, I do not wish to state in any way that the type discussed here in detail is the only possible one.[107]

107. In his monograph (p. 460 ff.) Goldstein deals with the various ways in which aphasia of this type originates. He acknowledges the type I discuss here, following Sachs. Goldstein believes, however, that the strong presence of spontaneous writing is a prerequisite for this type. In contrast to this, he explains the symptomatic picture as follows: All

Sometimes an interruption of the paths between "concept area" and sound-tone image mechanism (L-K-M) possibly could also bring about symptoms of transcortical motor aphasia. Indeed, Lichtheim believes that forms of transcortical aphasia show signs of both sensory and motor disorders.[108]

However, I rightfully feel entitled to require that in each individual case from now on we must search for symptoms of faulty re-repetition before a decision is made as to the type of aphasia we are dealing with.

---

other speech functions are completely or almost completely intact only in the case of serious isolated defects of spontaneous speech and spontaneous writing, caused by (partial) interruption of the connection of the speech apparatus with the center of intention, the frontal brain. Of particular interest here are the previously mentioned patients of Kleist who failed to answer questions about their illness, for example, and especially about their speech impediments, at a time when they were already able to answer casual questions. The third type, according to Goldstein, stems from an impairment of the ability to choose words. This process is dependent upon the comprehension and speech centers, as well as the connective apparatus, remaining intact. This process will be affected by a defect in any of the three areas mentioned. The disorders in case of a defect in the concept center will be connected with sensory disorders, "since it is the same apparatus which transmits spontaneous speech as well as speech comprehension."

108. Liepmann, too, holds a similar view, and Lewandowsky wrote about such a case in detail ("Über eine transkortikal sensorisch gedeutete aphatische Störung," Ztschr. f. klin. Med., 1914).

Chapter 16

THE SENTENCE FORMATION OF
THE BEGINNING SPEAKER

The sentence formation of a child at an early age has not interested researchers as much as word formation. Numerous publications end with determining the quality and amount of vocabulary at a specific time, without ever investigating sentences. Meumann[109] especially deserves great credit for having ascertained that a child's first spontaneous words are words of desire and that they have the characteristics of a sentence. It is not that the child wishes to explain or convey in any way that it now knows the expression for the specific object. The basis for initial spontaneous speech[110] lies in whether it does or does not want the object. In my textbook of speech therapy I made the following qualification: Based on the observation of my nephew, certain babbled words are to be excepted from the general rule and are to be ascribed to a "higher lalling" activity. Aside from that, however, Meumann's doctrine is correct; especially the part stating that the first spontaneous words have sentence value is of considerable importance for the problem of aphasia. After all, in the physio-psychological part we did discover the primacy of the sentence, which appears to us here in a new light, in that it is also being conditioned by its developmental history. C. and W. Stern state correctly that the very nature of the first words also constitute the am-

---

109. *Die Entstehung der ersten Wortbildung beim Kinde* (Leipzig, 1902).

110. This emphasizes nothing more than the existence of a relationship of these words with the main characteristics of subsequent speech. Stöhr (*Logik,* p. 42) writes: "Most of the time the sentence serves the purpose of communicating the content of consciousness through the relationships of situations in the areas of comprehension. The sentence communicates an event, expresses a command, or a wish, a question, a fear, or a hope ... but not the relationship of situations in areas of comprehension for their own sake." Much more rarely does it serve this latter purpose.

biguity which earlier confused the observer. (I suggest the designation "word comprehension" for the content of words spoken by someone else and the designation "word meaning" for the content of one's own words.) *Mama* means *Mother, come here; Mother, give me; Mother, put me on the chair; Mother, help me;* etc. Since first spontaneous speech utterances are purely expressions of feelings and particularly of wishes, Meumann called this the "emotional–volitional" period. We might contradict Meumann by stating that these one-word sentences not only express emotional states but also contain objective items, for a purely emotional state would not use a conventional designation. When we learn about intellectualization (Meumann) as the next stage, we shall find many things of an exclusive or perponderantly denotative nature, since everywhere in life there are only smooth transitions, particularly at a time when the emotional factors in speech are emphasized. According to C. Stern and W. Stern, the first words are "symbols denoting familiarity on a purely associative basis." Here logic is not the directing, classifying element which would require the knowledge that each word has permanent specific meaning. For this, however, we would need a comparison of earlier applications with later ones, an impossible activity for beginning speakers. The child designates something because it reacts to a specific experience at the moment.

> Earlier experiences which caused the same word to be released have only an underlying effect. We have here a general psychogenetic fact; the first "re-recognition" of the child, therefore, is not a "re-recognition" of something previously existing. It is only a feeling of familiarity with the immediately perceivable; this familiarity factor, as this shade of feeling has been called, chronologically always precedes conscious recollection.... While the child keeps hearing a specific sound sequence over and over through the repetition of a certain experience that becomes more and more familiar to him, an association between this sound sequence and the familiar experience is established which results in the appearance of the word with the re-emergence of the familiar experience.

In connection with this, one or more characteristics which are quite often very far from an adult's concept are singled out from the respective experience. These characteristics, then, become the link—the factors distinguished by their quality of familiarity. I collected numerous examples in which the use of a sound complex (word) for different things provides evidence of these factors. A woman named Emma once threw a spool to my nephew and accompanied this gesture by the expression *Oh!* For a while the nephew called each woman who remotely resembled Emma, as well as each spool and each small ball *Emma oh.* This type of manifestation is called "change of meaning."

Chapter 17

SPEECH COMPREHENSION OF
THE BEGINNING SPEAKER

Sensory Aphasia

During this period and the following one, speech comprehension is markedly different from fully developed speech. My nephew Fritz was asked *Do you want the toy soldier?*, and in the same questioning inflection he was told *Give me the toy soldier*. In both instances he looked at the toy figure in the same way. However, when the word *give* was loudly emphasized, and the entire sentence was uttered as a command, he did not visibly react at first, and only after several repetitions did he again look at the toy. It is clear from all this that he really only understood the word *toy soldier*. The loud emphasis of the word *give,* which he obviously did not understand, drowned out the only word in the whole sentence that was familiar to him. Out of the torrent of words that the small beginning speaker hears, he understands only a few. Thus it could be said that for this function, although not generally speaking, the sentence has merely word value for him as far as comprehension is concerned. Such a comparison of "word comprehension" and "word meaning" will not be without influence on our main theme. It will rather point to certain fundamental differences between speech comprehension and spontaneous speech. Now if, as we shall soon discuss in detail, the essentially affective character of first spontaneous speech is gradually reduced up to a certain degree by one of a more distinctive nature, causing a closer relationship between "word comprehension" and "word meaning," we then would still have to consider the possibility of a strong difference between the respective attitudes toward hearing and speaking. Outside of external influences, the child's initial comprehension certainly also depends again on a certain affective selection process by the inner person, whereby the need for expression may take charge. As a rule, however, the affective basis will be considerably greater in speaking than in listening.

Since the sentence veils words already familiar to the listening speech beginner, the resulting comprehension difficulties it causes are a manifestation analogous to that in sensory aphasia. Our Case 12[111] reacted much more promptly to requests given in isolated words than those given in sentences. He did not always carry out the requests to completion because he had either forgotten the second word in the meantime or had never clearly comprehended it in the first place. The most important criterion for our patient must have been the amount of time he had at his disposal in which to grasp the meaning of a word, quite similar to Case 11, who recognized his name only in written form, since a stimulus here could recur any number of times, and a specific one last for any length of time. This could not happen to the same extent with acoustic stimulation (speech modeling.) For, even where frequent repetition of the name is possible, individual stimuli cannot be prolonged with any degree of certainty in accordance with the momentary need of the patient. And the prolongation of the word beyond his momentary need, or insufficient for this purpose, will only have a disturbing effect. Lately we begin to realize what sublime occurrences take place in the totality of processes we call speech. These occurrences, however, may come to light only in pathological cases; given the adaptability of the normal cerebrum, they will largely remain in the background.

Is there really an analogous reason for assuming that the speech beginner does not understand a word within a complete sentence as well as in isolation? Or is the brief mention of the word within the sentence sufficient in itself, with faulty comprehension due to the distraction caused by other words? One should really consider both factors, because it is a sufficiently documented psychological phenomenon that the "routing" (Exner) becomes the more complete, at least within certain limits, the more frequently the same stimulus occurs, and that the central stimulation process initially depends to a greater degree than subsequently on the strength of the stimulus (to be understood as strength as well as duration). There is nervous tissue, to be sure, that follows the "all or nothing law," thus reacting to a certain stimulus and without undergoing any change in reaction, even under the influence of a stronger stimulus. Verworn calls such neurons isobolic systems, whereas he calls various reactions to stimuli of varying strength, or consecutive stimuli, heterobolic systems. However it has not yet been sufficiently established which part of the central nervous system belongs to either

111. Fröschels described Case 12 more thoroughly in the appendix, which is not included in this translation—editor's note.

system, aside from the known fact that under certain conditions there are overlaps. Distraction through the other words of the sentence does the rest. The sensory aphasic will be affected by these distractions as well, even though he may conceivably focus more exactly than a baby on a hearing selection of the most important words—so far as this ability to focus is not pathologically impaired.

An analogy between beginning speakers and aphasics, therefore, may exist in the last case, as well as in all others where analogy has been claimed. It particularly exists in the outward behavior towards certain kinds of stimuli, or in hesitation; that is, in a delay or in a partial or complete deficiency of the hypothetical central process.

Chapter 18

THE SENTENCE

According to Preyer and Stern, the ability to comprehend sentences precedes the use of several connected words. However, in the earliest period only parts of sentences, although more than one in number, are being understood. The use of several words connected with each other begins around the middle of the second year of life, judging from available observations. But this connection is more an internal than an external one. The words are being uttered one by one, and the notable difference of these embryonic sentences from fully formed ones can be detected, especially in a pneumogram. Whereas the speech of an adult (as shown in Figure 2 and as already explained previously) goes with a completely different type of breathing from that of breathing in a state of rest, the child hardly shows this difference in the initial stages of speaking. Instead he often draws a new breath after each word, which frequently is spent entirely in producing the next word.

Figure 3 shows the pneumogram of a second-grade school girl during her reading. The child had much difficulty in this, since she was still so much preoccupied with spelling that she did not grasp the meaning of the sentence and perhaps not even that of any of the words. Thus she paid no attention to the totality of the sentence, but only read word for word. When arriving at a period she used a falling intonation, as she had been taught, but this period probably was the only sign by which she recognized the end of a sentence or rather the fact that everything after the last period represented a whole. Accordingly, we can see her inhaling anew after each word, although in some spots we can clearly recognize that the amount of air previously inhaled was not yet used up, since the descending part of the graph had not yet returned to the zero position.

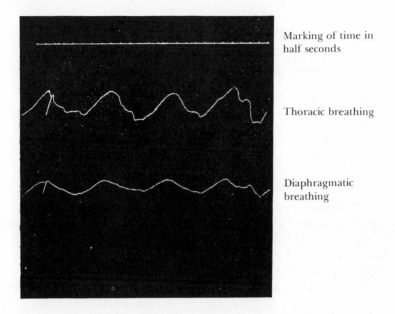

Marking of time in
half seconds

Thoracic breathing

Diaphragmatic
breathing

Figure 2a.   Normal breath graph.

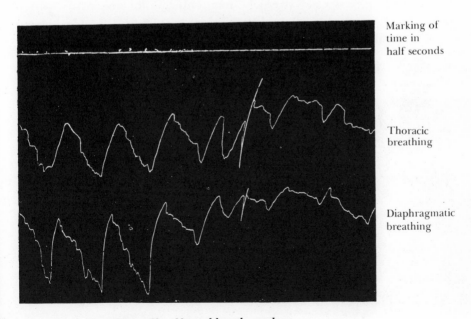

Marking of
time in
half seconds

Thoracic
breathing

Diaphragmatic
breathing

Figure 2b.   Normal breath graph.

Thoracic
breathing

Figure 3.   Reading breath graph of a second-grade schoolgirl.

Inhaling during the speaking process is a completely automatic activity unless the children are instructed by special breathing exercises to inhale copiously before each sentence. Yet, such exercises, most commendable from the phonetic–hygienic point of view, are in use only in a very few schools. As a rule therefore, breathing for speech goes on unconsciously. Now if a trained speaker at the beginning of a sentence inhales sufficiently to be able to reach the end of a sentence or at least a continuous part of it without being interrupted by additional inhaling, this may be considered proof of the fact that the feeling for the total sentence structure precedes the precise choice of words. This feeling is lacking in the beginning speaker. At best he will utter several words based on an emotional state which can not sufficiently be expressed by a single word. C. and W. Stern correctly state that in this stage every individual word taken by itself has the value of a sentence.

Very similar pneumographic pictures are furnished by aphasics who at the same time speak extremely nongrammatically and in so-called telegram style, and for whom difficulties in finding words constitute a condition for their agrammatism. Figure 4 shows the pneumogram of a

Breathing for speech: *Gestern mit der Schwester Erna lernen. Lernen und gehen und dann Mittagsmahl essen und dann Ausgang, Master Master gehen und dann Kino!*

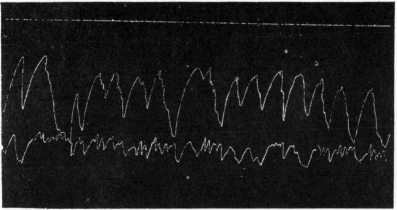

Marking of
time in
half seconds

Thoracic
breathing

Diaphragmatic
breathing

Figure 4.   Patient Karl L. inhaled 16 times during 23 words.

soldier, with a head injury, in a branch of the Imperial Garrison Hospital No. 2 (Commandant: Staff-Surgeon-Major First Class Dr. B. Drastich). The soldier, with normal respiration in repose, inhaled 16 times during a span of 23 words. The recording of time elapsed indicates that he needed 34 seconds for these 23 words. We shall come back to the pathological incongruence between throacic and diaphragmatic breathing only later on.

Quite different from this graph is the one given in Figure 5. It comes from Case 12 [N.B.: in Fröschels' appendix, which is not included in this translation], for which we were able to prove a distinctive feeling for sentence structure. Indeed, his breathing is hardly distinguishable from normal respiration.

We must now come to grips with the question whether it is justifiable, as we thought in agreement with Wundt, Gomperz, Pick, and others, to talk about a primacy of the sentence, even where, in cases of difficulties in finding words, the sentence fades into the background in such a definite manner. Outside of the fact that findings in pathological cases must not unconditionally be cited in opposition to physiological phenomena, we must distinguish here between psychic conditionality and outward appearance, and their reciprocal influences on one another. Psychic conditionality has become sufficiently apparent from our introductory chapters, and our interpretation of the beginning of sentence formation in children confirms what was proven there. We can recognize the striving for a sentence even when word amnesia brings about a picture similar to that just described: These patients, far from merely pronouncing one word after the other without internal formal connection, as if they were reading a dictionary, actually document the fact that the words do belong to a sentence, precisely by their very agrammatism, paradoxical as this may sound. For indeed, they do not speak without grammar; they only speak incorrectly from the point of view of syntactical grammar. Just as we could hardly deduce from a painting with mistakes in its perspective that the painter had not meant to paint a coherent picture, but rather a number of disconnected objects, it does not follow from the nongrammatical, nonsyntactical manner of speaking, that we are not in the presence of precisely that which develops from grammar and syntax—namely the sentence. Thus it might be better to generally introduce the term "paragrammatism" for "agrammatism."

Concerning the grammatical structure of the first multi-word sentences, the Sterns state that "in the very earliest period sentences predominate in which one component consists of a vocative or an interjection, whereas the other component represents the true center of reference of the communication." Soon, however, subject and object appear on the scene,

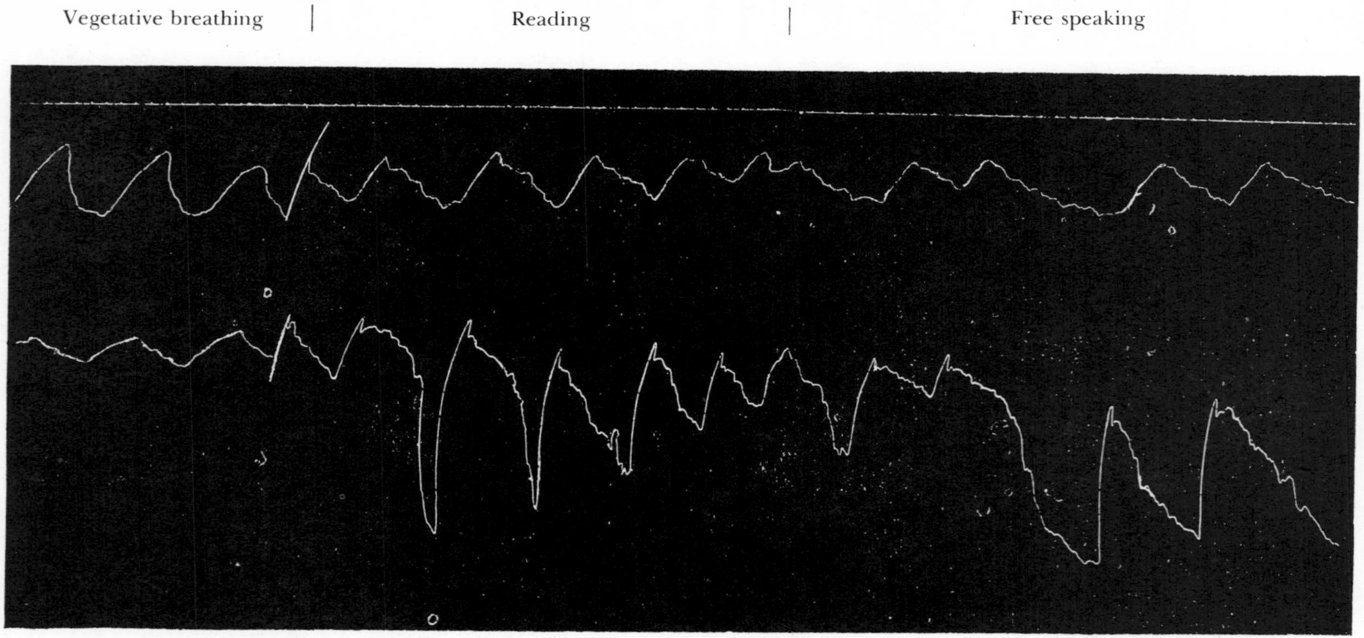

Vegetative breathing | Reading | Free speaking

Figure 5. Patient F. v. W.

202

verbal and adverbial determination, subject and predicate nouns, and above all, verbs and objects. If then a third or fourth word is added, according to C. Stern and W. Stern, something resembling the transition from the one-word to the two-word sentence seems to reoccur: namely, not the initial incorporation of the new component into the grammatical correlation of the sentence but, its addition as an independent word in the sentence.

The subordinate-clause stage usually occurs at the end of the third year of life. Among other things the Sterns quote are these examples: *Look Hilde has made; The doll always laughs when Hilde comes; I cut, looks funny* (=what I cut out, looks funny.)[112] With interrogative clauses, those which ask for the object and those which ask for the place occur rather simultaneously; however, interrogative structures are sometimes formed very late (at the end of the third year). Occasionally the interrogative expression is not present yet, but intonation, word order, and context are sufficient for characterizing the question. Based on their own observations the Sterns assume a second age of questioning, where dependent clauses appear in a formal way. From the psychological–logical point of view, questions will be asked directed towards a *when* and *why*. The *why* questions again are of an emotional nature at first and pursue the objective of receiving reasons for certain commands.

C. Stern and W. Stern devote a whole chapter to word order, a subject of great importance to our study. Sometimes we find correct conventional sentences; on other occasions, structure with completely arbitrary word order. My 29-month-old nephew pronounced the following sentence: *Mama birdie away tree* ('Mother, the bird flew out of the tree'). The chances of success are rather small for establishing the reason for such unconventional word order. The Sterns single out a few possibilities, such as: (*a*) pre-position of any element which stresses feeling; (*b*) preposition of that which is intuitively evident—in agreement with Wundt, who sees a condition for perceptual clarity in his statement that "we find the concept that can be thought up without any other positioned first, and that another concept follows it when the first requires the presence of the other in the given combination of thoughts [Wundt, I, p. 217]." According to C. Stern and W. Stern, the post-positioned negations so frequently used also belong here.

In this very context again, the Sterns complain of the lack of numerous observations, and I can only concur. For if a precise analysis of infantile speech phenomena helps us to understand many a question of aphasia and to come closer to the nature of many types of aphasia, we

---

112. Somewhat in baby talk in the German original version—translator's note.

also would certainly succeed in shedding light on some forms of para-grammatism if only they could be sufficiently studied in early childhood. For every aphasia researcher probably has heard sentences from his patients which possess manifold similarities to childish sentences. Yet, the emphasis on one or the other example as being analogous to chil-dren's speech will remain an idle undertaking as long as children's speech itself has not yet been thoroughly explored in this respect; and, indeed, an ample body of pertinent observations does not exist.

It can be seen from the preceding statements that the emotional–volitional stage is followed by that of intellectualization (Meumann). Naturally the two stages cannot be sharply differentiated from one another, either in time or in content. In this period the words are more closely connected to the objects, actions, etc., corresponding to them in a conventional manner, and the child begins to use them for the purpose of designation and no longer for mere emotional relief. The Sterns emphasize the transition from the concrete to the abstract as a main characteristic of this stage. Whereas in the intellectualization stage (also named the *associative–reproductive* stage by Meumann), it is not the most important characteristic, but rather the most striking features at the moment of perception, which become associated with the word; now the process of connecting the most important elements of perception slowly crystallizes into conception, and the process of conception, along with the conventional term, ripens into a concept. Meumann calls this the logical–conceptual period.

Chapter 19

SOUND FORMATION

Let us now turn to the formation of individual sounds as performed by the beginning speaker. Some of them will be pronounced correctly right from the beginning. Others are replaced by different ones or are completely omitted. The sequence in which they occur can probably be determined for each individual case. Agreement in many respects can be found among certain children, but rigid general rules do not exist. The G and K sounds most of the time occur later than B, P, D, and T, but here too, there are numerous exceptions.

In accordance with this, speech specialists also have been unable to establish whether there are any sounds that always emerge spontaneously in spite of delayed speech development. I refer to the absence or faulty pronunciation of sounds as stammering. Indeed, there is no sound that could not be included in this group of speech defects. Some children do not even pronounce vowels correctly, if at all. It is true that in this respect the sounds of G and K, Sch and S, frontal Ch, and R take precedence over all others. Yet there are children who replace every D and T by G and K. Stammering can be caused either centrally or peripherally by malformations, injuries, etc. A central cause again may have a cortical or subcortical seat. In the first case we are dealing with disturbances related to cortical dysphasias; in the second case to those pertaining to subcortical disphasias or related to dysarthrias.

One type of stammering merits special interest here. Gheorgov (loc. cit., p. 5) and Sikorsky[113] emphasize that Slav children are accustomed to replace an R by an L, or simply to omit it when it is adjacent to a front or

113. "Du développement du langage chez les enfants," *Arch. de Neur.*, 1883.

back consonant. However, the opposite could also be noted, namely the replacement of an *L* by an *R*. This speech defect occurs far more seldom in other languages, and practically never in German. Gheorgov is inclined to explain this type of stammering by the fact that the Slav *R* has an alveolar formation, thus it is in the area of articulation of the *L*. I agree with this explanation, with the reservation that other factors in addition to the proximity of the articulation area may play a supporting role here. In my paper, "Über die Behandlung der Aphasien" (On the Treatment of Aphasia), I indicated a symptom that frequently struck me *in aphasics*, that is, the confusion of *R* and *L*. The previous observations can now be confirmed by a great amount of data in full agreement, and it may well be said that the *R–L* symptom is one of the most frequent aphasic symptoms. As already stated in the quoted article, it often remains as the last clear sign of a form of aphasia. If, on the other hand, we consider that the confusion of the two sounds in words such as "parallel" is known as a sign of neurasthenia, the question under study here becomes even more interesting. May we also add that the interchangeability of *R* and *L* is an almost regular phenomenon even in the case of aphasics who pronounce not an alveolar, but a uvular *R*, and who always had been accustomed to speak it that way in their language.

It is a known fact that there are peoples who do not recognize any difference between *L* and *R* at all. They rather pronounce a sort of *Rl*, and even that not in a regular fashion but in the same word in the same place sometimes an *R*, another time an *L*, and a third time an *Rl*. I have proved[114] that the Japanese belong among these peoples, also certain Negro tribes, according to information provided by Professor Stigler.

The *R–L* symptom probably signifies a setback in cases of aphasia, which contradicts Delbrück's view, quoted in Pick's monograph (p. 70). Delbrück answers the question as to how a setback from disease might be explained by reasoning from the point of view of the theory of heredity that quite possibly a loss of neuron groups could disturb a function not as yet completely settled. Similar attempts at explanation (such as the one by Gierlich,[115] who attempts a very well-documented proof of the theory that a residual hemiplegic paralysis is indicative of a setback) can be found ascribed to other neurological areas.

Now, is the *R–L* symptom aphasic or dysphasic in nature, or is it dysarthric?

---

114. "Untersuchung über einen eigenartigen japanischen Sprachlaut," *Sitzungsberichte der Kaiserlichen Akademie der Wissenschaften in Wien. Mathematisch-naturwissenschaftliche Klaase*, Vol. 72, Section 3, December, 1913.

115. *Über Symptomatologie, Wesen und Therapie der hemiplegischen,* Lähmung (Wiesbaden, 1913).

It is very difficult to answer this question. As far as completely defective articulation, retardation of speech tempo, or hesitation as a result of aphasia is concerned, this question has already been posed by numerous researchers such as Monakow, Pick, Liepmann, and others. H. Gutzmann[116] wrote an excellent, detailed paper containing among other things several valuable studies such as the case of Räckes—a case by O. Maas merely showing articulation disturbances which, however, may very well be interpreted as being disphasic in nature. Gutzmann sums up the state of our understanding of the relationship between anarthria and aphasia in these words:

> It may be assumed that the supposed center of higher order from which inner language, or diction, depends, dominates a number of centers of a lower order. These, in turn, are forcing other centers still further below them to joint or isolated action. Thus, a voluntary act of inhaling, interrupting the automatic breathing in the state of rest, must be interpreted as depending from a center in the frontal cortex. Consequently, there has to be a center for voice production which obviously does not simply govern the adduction and abduction of the vocal cords, (since this alone does not lead to voice production), but also at the same time forces the cortical breathing center to cooperate. A center of still higher order will finally have to set the articulation movements in motion, starting from the individual focal points of the speech nerves, sometimes with and sometimes without the utilization of voice. . . . Each complete cortical motor aphasia therefore consists of two components, a dysphasic and a dysarthric one.

These statements are no doubt very worthy of consideration. However, we must not lose sight of the fact that Gutzmann here introduces the word dysarthric in an unusual meaning, namely for cortical deficiencies, whereas otherwise it had been used only for more deep-seated subcortical ones.

Adopting Gutzmann's nomenclature, therefore, we can designate the R-L symptom as dysarthric in nature. On the other hand, we may quite rightly assume that it can result from cortical deficiencies.

Again and again we have occasion to observe other phenomena belonging to the group of dysarthrias in the previously mentioned sense, (even without classifying them as being of a cortical or high or low subcortical nature), especially when we use experimental–phonetic methods. Already while discussing Figure 4, we were able to point out the strong incongruence between the respective graphs of chest and abdominal breathing. At that time we postponed answering the question of whether this symptom should be explained as a dysphasic or dysarthric phenomenon. Now it is at least established that it can develop

116. "Über Aphasie und Anarthrie," *Deutsche medizinische Wochenschrift*, 1911.

dysphasically, cortically, or high subcortically, since if we must assume the existence of a center in the cortex promoting voluntary breathing, we probably must also accept focal points which are connected with either thoracic or abdominal breathing. For instance, some singers are trained to strongly suppress or even completely eliminate chest movements while singing, so that only diaphragmatic breathing remains. Thus there exists a voluntary splitting of the two components of breathing.

Other dysarthric symptoms become manifest if we test the degree to which the lips or the tongue become tired, when repeatedly pronouncing individual sounds, by way of a Rousselot balloon or, even better, by a small rubber balloon put on a little glass tube, something like an eye dropper. If we hold the balloon, which is connected to an Edelmann or Marey writing capsule through a hose put on the other open end of the glass tube, between the lips of a patient saying *b b b,* etc., we can come to

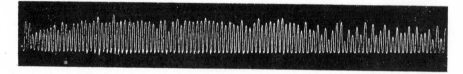

Figure 6.

Figure 7.

Figure 8.

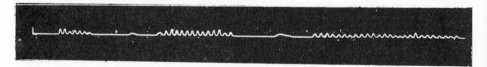

Figure 9.

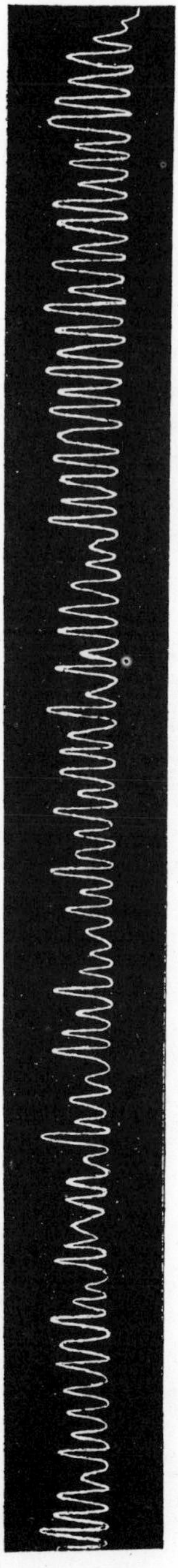

Figure 10.

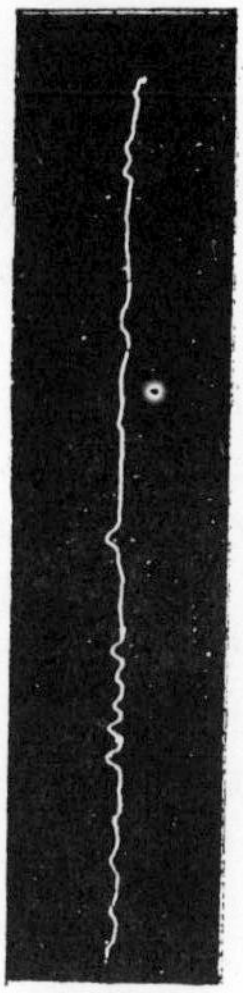

Figure 14.

Figure 11.

Figure 13.

Figure 12.

conclusions as to the force of the lip closure from the degree of deviation of the writing device or the elevation of the kymograph respectively, or as to the frequency of lip closure from the greater or smaller distances of the individual impulses or graph elevations. Simiarly we can test the tip of the tongue, while pronouncing *D, T, N* or *L* by holding the balloon behind the upper middle incisors. For testing the back of the tongue, we hold the balloon to the middle line of the mouth at the borderline between the hard palate and the velum. In this fashion I and my assistant, K. C. Rothe, obtained graphs which seem to be quite noteworthy.

Figures No. 6 and 7 show graphs of a normally spoken *bababa*, etc., and a *dadada*, etc., respectively. In each individual graph we can see elevations of almost always equal height and distance. In the case of the *ba*, signs of lasting fatigue only appear after repeating it some 70 times. The peak elevations in graph become lower and more irregular. *Da* was being pronounced with uniform force and speed during the entire recording (75 repetitions).

If this is compared to the *dadada* of patient S. (Case 11, Figure 8), we note the extremely small force, and within the graph the very frequent and (considering the low peak elevations of the graph) very important differences in the force of the impulse. The *papa*, etc. (Figure 9) of the same patient is interrupted by long pauses and, as a whole, very much lacking in strength and unequal in force.

Figure 10 shows the tongue tip articulation of a case of so-called motor aphasia that was very far advanced in therapy, but this case too, reveals very important irregularities in the force of the individual articulations, and perhaps even in the time elapsed between the occurrence of the individual tongue movements. This becomes even more apparent in patient V. (of Figure 11), a case of initially serious motor aphasia which, however, could be considered practically cured at the time of recording the graph. He was able to converse fluently and in a grammatically correct manner.

Similar progress was shown by patient H., who made the graph of Figure 12. Whereas abnormal irregularities still can be detected here, they are not so serious by far as those of the previous graph. Yet the previous patient is speaking rather better or certainly no worse than the latter. From this we may conclude that such experimental phonetic analyses are capable of creating new insights, since they bring symptoms to light that escape our sense organs in free observation. Figures 13 and 14 are taken from two cases of amnesic aphasia. The second case shows strongly paragrammatical speech.

Chapter 20

STUTTERING IN CHILDREN AND IN APHASICS

A phenomenon of the developments of infantile speech, which is not infrequent and can hardly be considered pathological, is the repetition of syllables. By this we do not mean the peculiarity of reduplication stressed by Wundt as existing among primitive peoples, and among children by C. Stern and W. Stern, which consists in repeating syllables more than once and which probably goes hand in hand with a certain economy of energy,[117] but that type of repetition of syllables usually described as stuttering. Although this term has already been incorporated into the language to such an extent that it would now be very difficult to eliminate it or at least to limit its use, I would like to insist, however, on calling this infantile speech defect "initial stuttering." As I stated in many papers, including a most recent one,[118] nothing proved more confusing and impeded research in the group of speech defects called "stuttering" more than the thoughtless application of this term to any speech defect manifesting itself in an unintentional interruption of speech. Thereby all symptoms accompanying such interruptions were thrown together into one pot and were considered equivalent to one another. More precise research and anamnesic data, however, resulted in the conclusion that, at least in the greatest majority of cases, repeating syllables is the first external symptom. Furthermore, precise observation proved that a temporary lack of words, parts of words, or thoughts could be responsible

117. It is an interesting fact that children who have difficulties in learning how to speak find it much harder to repeat individual syllables than the repeated model of these syllables, for instance *lalala*. I cannot make a decision as to whether there exists a connection between this phenomenon and the one mentioned above.

118. "Über den derzeitigen Stand der Frage des Stotterns," *Zeitschrift für die ges. Neurologie und Psychiatrie*, 1916.

for this fact. These data did not merely make it possible to come closer to a solution of the heretofore completely unsolved enigma as to how initial stuttering turns into a fully formed condition, or on the other hand, why many initial stutterers do not become permanent ones. They also enabled us to discover a basic similarity between initial stuttering, stuttering caused by embarrassment[119] and cluttering, on one hand, and types of aphasia on the other, with a much greater degree of clarity than had been possible up to then.

Due to lack of space I have to resist the temptation to further discuss this chapter here, which is so important for the understanding of many speech defects and especially of many types of aphasia. However, I cannot urge the reader strongly enough to pay attention to the literature in the field, since the emphasis on just one group of speech disturbances, namely aphasia, out of the large field of logopedics results in numerous difficulties that disappear when studying other areas as well. I would especially like to refer to Höpfner's *Stuttering as Associative Aphasia* and to my own *On the Present State of the Problem of Stuttering* which contains a detailed bibliography.

The following, in a broad outline, is the view of the Vienna School on the nature of stuttering.

It can arise from the most various conditions. A uniform type of development, however, is evident mostly in the so-called developmental stuttering, which occurs between the third and fifth years of life or in the beginning of schooling. In the first years it probably belongs to the physiological domain, since attacks of stuttering frequently occur among normally speaking children during the period of speech development. These can be explained by the fact that the child does not yet know the right form of expression and thus, in his urge to speak, keeps repeating one syllable until the right expression comes to his mind. It may also happen very frequently that children, induced by faulty pedagogy, talk a great deal without disposing of the required wealth of ideas. The pause during which nothing enters the children's mind is then being filled through repetition of the last syllable. In the initial phase of stuttering only the "clonic" phase of this condition, that is, the repetition of syllables, is present. An analogy to developmental stuttering is doubtless provided by the stuttering of adults when caused by embarrassment. For example, a man who made a serious mistake in a chess game wanted to justify himself and said: "But I have, I have, I have." He did not know what to say and thus started stuttering. Beginning stuttering therefore might be located in the cortical apparatus of word formation. As a result

119. See K. C. Rothe, "Über Verlegenheitssprachstörungen," *Zeitblatt für Psychoanalyse*, Vol. 3.

I would postulate the following: Beginning developmental stuttering frequently is the external consequence of a symptom of cortical deficiency. Gutzmann calls stuttering even in the earliest stage a cramp provoked by a disparity between will and capability, since he states (*Monatshefte für die gesamte Sprachheilkunde*, 1910):

> Kussmaul, too, emphasizes an innate, susceptible weakness of the apparatus for coordinating syllables as the underlying base of the disturbance... And yet it explains straight away why a stimulus of the will triggers a normal coordination sequence in a normal child, but causes a cramp in a child who has an innate susceptible weakness of the articulation apparatus.

Furthermore he states in a controversy with Laubi ("Nochmas die psychogenen Sprachstörungen," *Monatsschriften für die gesamte Sprachheilkunde,* 1912) that a writing cramp was likewise provoked by a disparity between will and capability, and that nothing could illustrate his view better than this analogy. However, there exists a big difference between stuttering and a writing cramp in that an attack of stuttering, even in case of the strongest visible muscle contractions, is never connected with pain.

Whereas beginning stuttering manifests itself in repetitions only and entirely without "cramp," this is no longer true in fully formed stuttering. Here the "tonic" element, or pressing in the speech organs, is thrown into relief. Then, the want of a thought or an expression is only rarely to be construed any longer as the cause of an attack of stuttering. The patients know very well what they want to say, but, nevertheless, get stuck in the middle of their speech. The stuttering of a patient may well be two consecutive pathological conditions separated from one another symptomatically as well as etiologically.

In case of fully developed stuttering the most outstanding symptom is the fear of sepaking, which is the reason for the entire remaining symptomatic picture. The child who in the period of initial stuttering stammers gaily and without any inhibitions is being made aware of his speech defect by his parents or playmates who often mock him; or he becomes conscious of it on his own due to a hypochondriac egocentric disposition. This fact might well be the connecting link to full-fledged stuttering, in addition to our speech organs being inclined toward habit formation in types of movement as well as toward a mechanism not unlike Pavlov's conditional reflexes (Fröschels & Pick, "Bewegung und Aufmerksamkeit," *Monatsschrift für Psychologie und Neurologie,* 1916). The primary reason may still very well be the incongruence between thinking and speaking, since to some extent repetition has already become a habit. The child now watching his language attempts avoiding the repetition of syllables and tries to overcome the attack by motor effort. He will "press," and thus the transition to tonic stuttering has been made. In case of stuttering due to embarrassment, an adult would not bother to replace the missing thoughts by way of motor effort. Therefore, stuttering almost never occurs in adults, with the exception of isolated cases of hysteria in aphasics and after heavy traumas.

Indeed, nothing has supported Kussmaul–Gutzmann's theory of stuttering as a condition of cramp caused by a susceptible weakness of the central articulation apparatus, more than the similar complex of symptoms also occurring in aphasia. Gutzmann delivered a paper on "Stottern als Herdsymptom" (Stuttering as a Herd Symptom)[120] which consolidated all cases, described up until that time, of stuttering due to anatomical lesions of the central nervous system. An attentive study of this paper shows clearly that the external symptoms are not sufficient to determine the central location of the illness. Furthermore, however, his paper shows that the cases described in this fashion suffered the repetition of syllables, at least in the beginning, in the same way as the cases of initial and embarrassment stuttering.[121]

How misleading it can be to speak of "aphasic stuttering" without more detailed analyses of symptoms, and why I have repeatedly suggested that we speak of stuttering with aphasia, or before or after aphasia, respectively, shall be demonstrated by some cases in my practice which have already been partially published elsewhere.

CASE 13: A 62-YEAR-OLD LAWYER

Some years ago I met a 62-year-old lawyer who offered the typical picture of amnesic aphasia. He had contracted syphilis 20 years earlier, suffered from aortic stenosis for some time, and began clonic stuttering 8 months before the meeting. The stuttering manifested itself first during a pleading in court and then became evident more and more frequently until it gradually became aphasia. This happened in such a way, however, that sometimes stuttering, sometimes the complete loss of a word took place for a certain length of time until finally aphasia completely dominated the picture. It may be assumed that

120. *Monatsschr. f. d. ges. Sprachheilk.*, 1908.
121. An almost classical proof for these two points is, among others, a new case by Liepmann and Pappenheim ("Über einen Fall von sogenannter Leitungsaphasie mit anatomischem Befund," *Zeitschrift für die gesamte Neurologie und Psychologie* (Vol. 27) which refers to stuttering by repetition with "strong twitching of the facial muscles." A postmortem examination showed the motor speech region as clear, and only one seat of disease in the temporal crown region.

the initially small aphasic disturbance manifested itself only in a delay in finding the word. But the patient, not used to this condition, and perhaps also in his eagerness to speak, repeated the last syllable or the last word respectively until he either caught himself doing it or until the desired word emerged. The patient died as a result of Lissauer paralysis.

The next case, No. 14, probably belongs in the same category.

CASE 14: A 19-YEAR-OLD INFANTRY SOLDIER

Infantry soldier Anton H., 19 years old, had received a bullet in his head at the height of the left temporal bone and had been brought to the reserve hospital in Ungvár on October 8, 1915 with a brain prolapse the size of an egg, where he received traditional treatment. On November 9 he was admitted to my section for soldiers with speech disturbances (Commanding Officer: Weiland, Director General of the Army Medical Services Department: Dr. Link). The examination showed the following: Skinny, pale man of medium height; pulse a rhythmical, steady, 92; heartbeat within normal limits; heart sounds pure; lungs normal. The right nasal labial fold was shallow, corner of the mouth hanging, no knitting of the brow possible, closure of eyes good. No deviation of the tongue, mouth, nose; ears were without abnormalities. No paralysis of the gum. Pupils were equally wide, and react promptly. At the level of the left temporal bone, a brain prolapse, the width of a finger and 5 centimeters long, stretched towards the front and the back in equal proportion, starting from the helix in an imaginary upward line. No Chvostek phenomenon. Sensitivity to touch of the entire body was much less on the right side than on the left. A weak reflex of the anterior abdominal wall could be induced only on the left side. Cremaster reflex on both sides; increased tendon reflexes of the upper right extremity; lively reflexes of the patellar tendons on both sides; no clonus of the foot. Positive right-side Babinski. Strength of the upper right extremity was somewhat diminished, with reduced mobility in the same place. At the time of admission, he had a case of practically total motor aphasia, which improved with exercise therapy. However, stuttering became evident. On December 5, for instance, he read the word *Edmund* as *Edmum Ed-m-m-m Edmund.*

Similar phenomena also occurred while he was answering questions or speaking spontaneously, which he did more and more frequently. Thus we were dealing with the type of stuttering usually designated as clonic. In our patient's case a fairly peculiar speech delay could be frequently noted—it consisted in his inability to pronounce some syllables in connection with the preceding one, or rather, in his exaggerated articulation of a sound, after intense reflection, before uttering the next one. On other occasions he would interrupt his speech altogether, and some time would be required, either with or without tentative articulation movements, before he was able to continue speaking correctly. Let us make only brief mention of the persisting paraphasia persevering and other aphasic phenomena, since we are concerned here only with symptoms characterized as stuttering. The last-mentioned type of speech delay in its outward manifestation corresponds to what is called tonic stuttering, and what we call "pressing."

CASE 15: INFANTRY SOLDIER

Things were much less clear in Case 15, where infantry soldier Israel K. exhibited a defect the size and depth of a chicken egg at the level of the parietal bone, spastic contraction of the left arm, and paresis of the left leg in addition to a stuttering type of speech-disturbance disorder. For instance, the patient pronounced one sentence as follows: *Ich ich ich bitte e e e Herr Doktor ich ich möchte Urlaub* (I I I ask uh uh uh the doctor I I like a furlough). Even so his speech was rather hurried, and while the impression sometimes predominated that he was stuttering because he lacked a word, other attacks of stuttering seemed to be triggered either in a purely dysarthric fashion or simply by habit. Let us quote here only that part of the total examination which relates to word amnesia. For this purpose the patient was shown models of objects, animals, and persons taken one at a time from Fröschel's so-called "aphasia treasure chest." The time which elapsed until he found the right word for it was measured by a stopwatch. He needed $11^2/_5$ seconds for the word *hatchet*, $3^4/_5$ seconds for *mirror*, and $15^2/_5$ seconds for *postcard*, although he found other expressions rather quickly. Thus even if this actually was a case of word amnesia, it did convey the impression that the patient also stuttered when a loss of words was not present. As mentioned before, various reasons for stuttering seemed to exist in his case.

It would be relevant here to incorporate Case 16, namely that of a child with paralysis of the right side resulting from scarlet fever. Here the stuttering seemed to be of a purely dysarthric and deeply subcortical nature.

CASE 16: A 7-YEAR-OLD GIRL

A 7-year-old girl suffered paralysis of the left side of her body during an attack of scarlet fever. There was no unconsciousness, nor loss of either speech

or understanding of speech. However, a small and rather odd speech disturbance occurred immediately. The child replied in orderly sentences but the
pronunciation of lingual consonants was slowed down and distinctly difficult.
This was true to a lesser degree for labials and palatals. The total picture was
that of tonic stuttering. I gained the impression that the child did not have the
right measure for the expenditure of energy that now, because of the paresis
of the speech muscles, was necessary for the formation of various sounds. She
was "overshooting the mark," and still using force after the correct sound
position had been achieved, a fact which caused a "pressing" in the articulation
zone for various sounds. Thus in the case of the *T,* for instance, the tip of the
tongue was pressed against the upper teeth. If she was made to pronounce the
sound singly and not within a word, it only took a longer time until the tip of
the tongue was brought against the teeth. Pressing against them, however, did
not take place. Seemingly this difference in behavior could be explained by the
fact that in the isolated sound the patient was able to devote her entire attention to the pronunciation, whereas while answering in words or sentences she
was too preoccupied with the process of thinking. Whenever she stuck out her
tongue, it deviated towards the left side. The existing picture of illness was
similar to that of pseudobulbar paralysis in children.

Our case strongly resembled the dysarthric stuttering case described
by Abadie. Its cause for developing was mainly located in the motor
speech paths, yet the influence of the thinking process was of crucial
importance, too. Thus again there exists an incongruence between
thinking and speech capability in which the motor action lags behind.
The voluntary effort plays a big part here, too.

To this group of stuttering belongs a case described by Pick in which a
softening of the cerebrum in vivo was assumed, whereas in reality several
seats with ensuing degeneration existed in the pyramids.

CASE 17: PATIENT WITH STUTTERING

Finally let us cite Case 17, in which a patient was left with stuttering as the
last symptom of a speech disorder caused by a bullet wound in the left temple.
The examination disclosed no delay in the naming of objects, actions, etc., no
difficulties in repeating, reading, and writing dictation. There was really no
aphasic symptom at all, but a rather lively stuttering. The very intelligent
patient indicated, however, that once in a while he still had difficulty, especially of a syntactical nature, in sentence structure. A careful examination of
his grammatical and syntactical capabilities likewise did not lead to any
pathological conclusions. It must be conceded, however, that very possibly

these speech processes took place more quickly and with less effort before his injury. We would be in the best position to decide that question if we or some other trained observer had known the patient during the period before he was wounded. In any case it is a fact that his lively stuttering was not in any right relationship to the severity of the aphasic symptoms, so that the author at least had to assume a combination of "nervous stuttering."

We may conclude our observations of stuttering in aphasics by saying that, first, stuttering may very well come about by way of cortical deficiency or loss, as in children; second, that more deeply situated stations in the speech path might be at fault; and, finally, that it may go hand in hand with aphasia as a neurotic symptom. Only after the most exacting examination can an exact diagnosis be established.

Chapter 21

THERAPY

*Conduction or Transcortical Aphasia
and Motor Aphasia (Broca)*

I do not intend to furnish here any additional description of the treatment of cases of aphasia. For so-called motor aphasics, treatment as a rule follows the optical–tactile method, which consists in showing the patient mouth position, so that he could feel air vibrations caused by the pronunciation of sounds at the mouth and nose of the doctor, and, if need be, himself put the organs of articulation into the correct position. In cases where a certain amount of progress has been made, meaningless syllables play an important role, an approach that we will now examine in closer detail.

For sensory aphasics, treatment consisting of hearing exercises, drills in remembering names, or again, artificial sound formation has to be considered. By the same token, in cases of alexia or agraphia respectively, reading and writing will naturally be practiced, in part by way of special methods, and the often existing apraxia must never be neglected. Medical measures of a general nature should come first in each case. Out of this whole huge treasure chest of remedies let us now specifically discuss the area of syllables without meaning.

We are fully aware that, in the practice of syllables without meaning, we have selected a path presenting greater difficulties, physiologically speaking at least, than that of practicing with words. According to Wundt (*Physiologie,* Vol. 3, p. 559.), experiments with normal people show that only as few as 6 to 7 unconnected words can be reproduced correctly after a one-time presentation. In case of sentences, however, between 15 and 18 individual words can be correctly repeated, signifying as many "as are able to coexist as a total concept in the general scope of consciousness under the same conditions." Yet the utilization of nonsense syllables presents manifold advantages. Above all, it is suitable for avoiding deception. If a patient is capable of repeating perhaps four or five syllables without meaning, he thereby demonstrates with certainty the ability to grasp and repeat sound patterns correctly. But in the process of having the patient repeat words, it may very well happen that the individual word is actually being acoustically perceived only in an incidental fashion. It may nevertheless call forth the old original correct memory image. If this then is put into words, the erroneous assumption that the patient correctly understood the spoken model is unavoidable. For instance, the patient in Case 12 repeats *Badewanne* ('bathtub') instead of *badewa* [no meaning]! The correct repetition of nonsense syllables, however, is a further test for the correct functioning of the circuit from the acoustic to the motor speech sphere, and of the latter itself. For we do have to assume that from the physiological point of view there exists a certain relationship between degree of stimulus strength and the reaction, in the sense that a certain stimulus, no matter how small, is able to trigger a reaction. If a person now repeats syllables without meaning, the loudness, the speed, and the distinctness of the spoken model are nevertheless a measure of the strength of the stimulus, whereas in the case of words, associative processes may also function as a stimulus. Although nonsense syllables may not entirely lack associative links, these will surely be present to a much smaller extent than in the case of words. If spoken words are the model, one is never certain which of the sum total of stimuli, especially by way of releasing association, has triggered the act of speaking. For that reason, different versions occur much more rarely and to a much lesser degree when repeating nonsense syllables instead of words. A patient who repeats *badelo* correctly, will also say *badelo* well most of the time, if he does not persevere. But it happens all too frequently that he can, for instance, repeat the word *Lippe* well, but *Pille* badly or not at all.

For the same reasons, the repetition of nonsense syllables is a more difficult achievement. Thus, in a certain sense, we may assume that the exercises we perform in order to accomplish this repetition amount to a higher degree of training because it is more difficult; so that we can count on having a good repetition of real words whenever repetition of nonsense syllables has been satisfactorily achieved. In certain types of aphasia that resemble Broca's aphemia—and whatever has been said up to now about nonsense syllables applies only to these types—this phenomenon is the forerunner of the ability to repeat over and over, and the latter is again the forerunner of spontaneous speech, so that the value of these exercises thereby becomes all the more positive.

Yet I do not believe by any means that only the purely articulatory process is being furthered through such exercises. If an aphasic is able to repeat nonsense sounds with assurance, by the same token he will probably be able from a certain point of view to do the same for words as well. It is true that in the case of real words the existing associations may intervene not only in a supportive manner as assumed in the foregoing, but may also have a disturbing effect. In many aphasics we can find an apparent lack of "predominant motivations" (Wundt) from the start. For instance, one patient may say *Ich bin gestern nach Hause Kutscher* instead of *nach Hause gefahren* ('I have coachman home yesterday' instead of 'I have gone home'). The correct functioning of thought and language consists, among other things, in a sort of equilibrium between the occurrence and acceptance of associations conducive to the desired thought–speech orientation; and in the elimination of any such associations which might interfere with the orientation. To achieve this state of equilibrium a correct functioning of all components of speech, including articulatory ones, is required. If a patient, for example, pronounces the sound *Sch* ('sh') as an *S*, he is more likely to slip into saying *Sattell* ('saddle') while wanting to pronounce *Schachtel* ('box') than somebody who is in complete mastery of *Sch* and *S*, all other conditions being equal. For patients with articulatory difficulties, inclined towards paraphrasing from the start, a precise learning of articulation will contribute to a decrease in the number of occasions for paraphasia.

However, cases of aphemia and its closely related forms likewise will enter a stage of paraphasia time and again after articulation has been learned. In cases of such severity it is probable that all possible components of speech have been affected, a fact which the advanced condition of muteness, existing before treatment began, simply covered up. Therefore, in these cases, too, only an articulation mechanism, conditioned as precisely as possible will be able to lessen the occurence of paraphasia. In my opinion, this result would not be achieved so well if one started with words from the very beginning; because even when starting therapy, associations of a purely intellectual and not articulatory nature would have a disturbing influence on the articulation process. This would apply all the more because with a sequence of thoughts not solidly established, a transition from these thought to words, and a corresponding difficulty in the execution of the words themselves, a state of affairs approaching confusion would result. It would probably consist of mutually conflicting central issues, and emotions that would render the central issues even more uncertain. Naturally, while taking into consideration the thought processes underlying the previous statements, we should not dwell on nonsense syllables any longer than necessary. Indeed we have cited cases excluding this type of treatment from the start (for instance, Case 6). In treatment, the advantages resulting from practicing words, and especially sentences, are being put into use as early as possible, although a great deal of effort is required to eliminate harmful elements, such as false associations, which can occur at the same time.

Two French authors, Froment and Monod, are opposed to the optical–tactile method in principle ("La réeducation des aphasiques moteurs," *Lyon Med.* 1914). Their objections may be summed up as follows:

1. Cases of motor aphasia are due either to defects in the mechanism for inducing sound–tone images, or they are genuine cases of "anarthria," (a term used in the literature to mean the obliteration of subconscious sound–movement images).

Cases of the latter type do not fit into the framework of the therapeutic method recommended by Froment and Monod.

2. That motor aphasia is caused by a disturbance of the mechanism for producing sound–tone images (L–K–M) should become evident from the following facts: (*a*) Whenever we are successful in producing the recalcitrant sound in the patient's mind through association of ideas or images and without having to demonstrate the articulation, we simultaneously eliminate the inability to repeat and to read out loud. [This line of reasoning opposes a theory, advanced by André Thomas and Roux, that the failure of the L–K–M process would also explain the lack of spontaneous speech.] (*b*) If we dictate a single sound to a non-agraphic motor aphasic, he will almost invariably write an incorrect one, although he will spell dictated words correctly. Presumably this is due to the fact that a sound devoid of meaning could be lumped together more easily with other equally meaningless sounds than with a word containing a definite meaning. In any event the influence of the L–K–M process on incorrect motor performances should be clearly made evident by the foregoing. (*c*) In such cases the pedagogic method works either by stimulating the sound image through the use of a continuous and clear speech model, or by way of using associations of ideas or images.

3. Successful achievements with the new method ought to prove the accuracy of their theoretical suppositions.

4. The pedagogical method might be dangerous in many cases.

In my monograph *Zur Behandlung der motorischen Aphasie*, I have already commented on these items in great detail. For this reason I will be brief here and also refer the reader to what has already been said in this study, especially with reference to items 1 and 2. There is only one thing I would like to stress once more: observation of some aphasics gives the distinct impression that internally they have something they want to say but cannot immediately pronounce it, because they first make groping articulatory movements, or reject or correct some of them, before they speak aloud. Here the L–K–M process seems to function, and only the motor execution appears to be defective. Item 3 contains a *circulus vitiosus* (vicious circle). The method consists of acoustic modeling of sounds, by means of a word–syllable–sound sequence. In this way, it may be possible for patients to isolate these sounds. The attempt to recreate missing expressions by means of thought association, such as through pictures and objects, may very well be effective in cases of a diseased motor speech system by reinforcing the triggering stimulus, either through very distinct acoustic modeling or through the use of association. Naturally a case of a damaged L–K–M process may also be helped by this method. Finally the optical–tactile method, on the one hand, is partically based on stimulus reinforcement; on the other hand, it does not allow us to draw any conclusion as to the existence of *one* possible type of motor aphasia. The reinforcement of stimuli consists, as far as is feasible, in directly demonstrating the necessary movements, and even performing them for the patient by putting his speech organs into the correct position and also by making use of his sense of touch. Here we must make a distinction between physiological and pathological phenomena. However, let us leave this point for the time being in order to continue our discussion of Froment–Monod. It is superfluous to state here the particular effect that the optical–tactile method might have had in each of the cases of motor aphasia which we have discussed. Item 4 is meant to indicate that using optical–tactile sense tools would harbor a danger that the patient might be led down a *nonphysiological* path. Occasionally, pathological conditions do indeed give us a reason to utilize non-physiological methods. Would anyone complain if a man who was amputated at mid-forearm level and who grasps objects with his stump could no longer call upon any physiological grasping mechanism of his own? Many aphasics lack a part of the internal physiological speech tracks, and therefore others must be enlisted in their aid. Froment–Monod's experience is derived from only a few light cases; however, I am familiar with a great number of very serious ones. In spite of this I have issued instructions to all practice therapists over a long period of time, and especially now that there is a war on, to refrain from using the optical–tactile method with all newly admitted patients, so that a more recent comparison can be made between the value of the acoustic–associative method and that of the method in use. Time and again in more severe cases we were compelled to go back to our method, after having administered as much as 6 weeks of frequent daily therapy exercises, because the acoustic method produced no improvement of any kind. Even in less severe cases, progress achieved through the optical–tactile method was achieved *substantially* faster.

One case that merits special mention here is that of a patient admitted to my hospital section with a case of brain prolapse and almost complete muteness (aphasia), but with good speech comprehension. Since the period of experimentation with the acoustic–associative method had already been terminated, the patient was to be instructed by the optical–tactile method. Although he always turned his ear toward the speaker and seemed to be very hostile to this method, it nevertheless led to very rapid and extremely favorable results. Today the patient, for all practical purposes, is cured.

Now the examination of this man to determine his type of sensory aphasia produced a result which could be interpreted as indicating that the patient is a strong acoustic type but was transformed by our method into a kinesthetic type in the domain of speech. Compare to this the statement made previously—that perhaps it is possible to find out, by establishing a sensory category in cases of so-called regression of a form , of aphasia—whether we are really dealing with a case of retrogression by . itself, or whether the patient did not relearn speech at least partially in an optical fashion and now uses an internal mechanism different from the one existing before his illness. In any case, the patient suffers no ill effects from it, for he speaks very well!

We were discussing the fact that the techniques of directly demonstrating speech movements and of letting the patient feel the vibrations of the air amounted to a stronger stimulus than simply letting him hear the sound. However, in this connection we must make a distinction between physiological and pathological conditions. Many singing teachers recommend detailed explanations, even demonstration of singing motions (respiration, position of mouth, condition of larynx,) whereas others condemn it outright. It is hardly possible here to establish general rules, especially since some otherwise healthy people show pathological symptoms as far as their voice is concerned. It is rather probable right from the start, that people with pathological cases require, partially at least, a different method of training than healthy people. Outside of that, however, along with other factors (such as, for instance, a case of hypochondria which cannot tolerate self-observation), we must definitely take the sensory type into consideration! This certainly does play a role in learning how to speak, in that some children observe the mouth of their mother more than do others. Therefore, something of a physiological nature will mean a natural increase of the stimulus to one person, whereas it will simply disturb and distract another. Under the pathological conditions of aphasia, however, it has been demonstrated, that in the overwhelming majority of cases the optical-tactile method represents a substantial stimulation increase when compared to the acoustic method.

The failure of the acoustic method and the constant success of the optical-tactile method—almost astonishing to anyone who has never seen it before—in cases of both aphasia and hearing muteness, was not the smallest factor in leading me to believe that there had to be a certain relationship between an acoustic stimulus and a motor reaction for the normal speech process, and that any disturbance within this relationship was liable to bring about the condition of motor aphasia or motor hearing muteness. Therefore, if a strong stimulus is required, either because the L-K-M process is not strong enough physiologically, or because the connecting network, or even the motor region itself, is not intact, then the optical-tactile method combined with an acoustic impression the importance of which is not to be underestimated, will provide that stimulus.

No examples need be quoted here, especially since numerous cases have already been discussed in detail elsewhere; one (Case 11) is included in this monograph.

In Chapter 12, mention was made of the three main types of disturbance liable to produce the picture symptomatic of so-called motor aphasia. One type, in which there is a lesion of the L-K-M process, has already been discussed in detail. Only at this point do I deem it proper to resume the discussion of the other two—the one arising from damage to the network connecting the temporal lobe with the motor region, and the other from a lesion of the motor sphere itself. We shall simply discuss the question whether it is possible to establish a differential diagnosis among the three types mentioned above, based on speech–performance itself *in vivo*. I assume that success, at least in individual cases, might be achieved in this respect by noting the type of behavior which the optical-tactile therapeutic method elicits. Since this method is indeed successful, it is quite evident that there have to be tracks connecting the optical and tactile centers with the motor sphere of speech. Indeed, connection between the latter and the optical and tactile centers have been proved. It probably can be assumed that a person whose motor speech area is intact will react to the optical-tactile method more rapidly than somebody in whom it has been affected by illness. However, a diagnosis based on this assumption must only be made after taking all clinical symptoms into consideration. A case of sensory aphasia, for instance, will not easily be improved by the optical-tactile method, for reasons stated in this monograph, and especially because of deficient blockage. At the present time it is difficult to decide the extent to which small deficiencies in the understanding of speech may be used toward a differential diagnosis between the expressive–auditive and the genuinely motor types of aphasia. For it is very likely, as I have already pointed out elsewhere, that a lesion of the motor speech region, in certain sensory types, could also result in a certain lessening of speech comprehension. This fact might be explained by a physiological observation which is occasionally made, that a foreign word is not successfully retained internally unless we ourselves have pronounced it. Furthermore, this line of reasoning is paralleled by my observation that persons suffering from so-called motor hearing muteness never possess really good understanding of speech.

Since an aphasic's individual sensory make-up might undoubtedly be of decisive importance in determining the manner in which he reacts to the optical–tactile therapeutic method, the diagnosis as to whether the symptomatic picture of motor aphasia is caused by the L–K–M process or in the motor sphere can only be made after sufficient progress in speech.

No matter how the reader may view this entire line of reasoning, it is a fact that various patients are being helped by the optical–tactile method in completely different fashion, although they might have proved equally uncooperative under the acoustic method. It is certainly worthwhile to speculate whether this fact is due only to the severity of the anatomical lesion, and not also to a different location.

I am unable to indicate how to succeed in clinically distinguishing a case of expressive–auditive aphasia from one in which there is an interrupted channel of communication between L–K–M and the motor speech region.

Finally a few lines should be devoted to the question of how the re-emergence of speech in cases of aphasia (mutism) can be explained. Here, too, I will be brief, and simply refer to my extensive article ("Über den zentralen Mechanismus der Sprache", *Dtsch. Zschr. f. Nervenheilk.*, 1916) for my views as well as to a bibliography on this subject. In this publication, I reject the notion that, in the case of individuals reeducated by means of the optical–tactile method, it was necessary to assume there had been a substitution of a part of the brain not previously involved in the act of speaking. Where there has been a lesion of the sound–tone image center, we shall have to expect that tracks leading to the motor speech region are permanently lost. If the patient now learns to speak by starting from vision and touch, one would be justified in assuming a better functional utilization of those motor speech parts of the brain at which the connections to the optical and the tactile center, respectively, terminate. It is already probable, at this point, that occasionally a part of the brain section intended for motor speech performance, of which the

Broca region surely is only a part,[122] may be utilized—in particular, presumably, the part at which the tracks connecting with the acoustic region terminate—a part which had little to do with speech from the physiological point of view in the case of the individual under discussion, and which was only slightly activated. This might be the case to a still greater degree if the motor speech region itself were affected by the lesion. In such a case, surviving parts no longer active to any great extent in speech activity, and which perhaps are serving other function, could be pressed into the service of speech.

This way of looking at the problem leads one to believe that the old "classical," narrowly restricted concept of localization is only a functional one, and attributes to certain parts of the brain the specific character of a function which under physiological conditions they do not serve at all, or only in a subordinate and secondary role. By doing this, however, the limitations of the old localization theory, to which I have referred at the beginning of the present book, are revealed.

122. Experiments by Franz (quoted in Durig, *Die Ermüdung*, Vienna,1916) showed that cats who, through excision of the frontal lobes, had lost skills acquired by training, reacquired them by renewed practice. However, when the still remaining *adjacent parts* of the frontal brain were removed, these newly acquired skills disappeared likewise.

SUBJECT INDEX